Teach®
Yourself

Motivate Yourself and Reach Your Goals

Frances Coombes

D1324939

For UK order enquiries: please contact Bookpoint Ltd, 130 Milton Park, Abingdon, Oxon OX14 4SB. Telephone: +44 (0) 1235 827720. Fax: +44 (0) 1235 400454. Lines are open 09.00–17.00, Monday to Saturday, with a 24-hour message answering service. Details about our titles and how to order are available at www.teachyourself.com

For USA order enquiries: please contact McGraw-Hill Customer Services, PO Box 545, Blacklick, OH 43004-0545, USA. Telephone: 1-800-722-4726. Fax: 1-614-755-5645.

For Canada order enquiries: please contact McGraw-Hill Ryerson Ltd, 300 Water St, Whitby, Ontario L1N 9B6, Canada. Telephone: 905 430 5000. Fax: 905 430 5020.

Long renowned as the authoritative source for self-guided learning – with more than 50 million copies sold worldwide – the **Teach Yourself** series includes over 500 titles in the fields of languages, crafts, hobbies, business, computing and education.

British Library Cataloguing in Publication Data: a catalogue record for this title is available from the British Library.

Library of Congress Catalog Card Number: on file.

First published in UK 2010 by Hodder Education, part of Hachette UK, 338 Euston Road, London NW1 3BH.

First published in US 2010 by The McGraw-Hill Companies, Inc.

This edition published 2010.

Previously published as Teach Yourself Self-motivation.

The **Teach Yourself** name is a registered trade mark of Hodder Headline.

Typeset by MPS Limited, a Macmillan Company.

Printed in Great Britain for Hodder Education, an Hachette UK Company, 338 Euston Road, London NW1 3BH, by CPI Cox & Wyman, Reading, Berkshire RG1 8EX.

The publisher has used its best endeavours to ensure that the URLs for external websites referred to in this book are correct and active at the time of going to press. However, the publisher and the author have no responsibility for the websites and can make no guarantee that a site will remain live or that the content will remain relevant, decent or appropriate.

Hachette UK's policy is to use papers that are natural, renewable and recyclable products and made from wood grown in sustainable forests. The logging and manufacturing processes are expected to conform to the environmental regulations of the country of origin.

Impression number	10 9 8 7 6 5 4 3 2 1
Year	2014 2013 2012 2011 2010

Front cover: Creative Crop/Digital Vision/Getty Images

Back cover: © Jakub Semeniuk/iStockphoto.com, © Royalty-Free/Corbis, © agencyby/iStockphoto.com, © Andy Cook/iStockphoto.com, © Christopher Ewing/iStockphoto.com, © zebicho – Fotolia.com, © Geoffrey Holman/iStockphoto.com, © Photodisc/Getty Images, © James C. Pruitt/iStockphoto.com, © Mohamed Saber – Fotolia.com

Contents

Meet the author   **ix**
Only got a minute?   **xii**
Only got five minutes?   **xvi**
Only got ten minutes?   **xxiv**
1 What is motivation?   **1**
   What is motivation?   1
   How motivated are you?   2
   Self-coaching questions for deeper awareness   8
   Preparing a well-formed outcome   10
   What would achieving your goal say about you?   12
   Apply the self-test questions and answers   15
   Success is doing – not wishing!   15
   What this book will do   18
2 Create the life you want   **21**
   We create the life we choose   21
   Recognize limiting beliefs   23
   How do you change beliefs?   25
   Act as if   29
   Celebrate your achievements   32
   Beliefs that build success   33
   Motivational skills wheel   33
   Create your blueprint for success   35
3 Motivation at work   **38**
   Matching motivation to the workplace   39
   Align your values with the work you do   41
   Values drive us and provide our motivation   41
   Bring your heart to work   42
   What do you value most in life?   44
   Motivation and peak performance   45
   Assumptions to adopt for peak performance   45
   Mental rehearsal trains the mind   47
   Take responsibility for making things happen   49
   You have the power to change your thinking   51

4 Create a compelling future **54**

Six habits that lead to success 55

How to use constructive feedback 57

Believe that what you want is possible 58

Visualize to create a compelling future 58

Anchor a positive state 59

Generate good ideas 60

What is your metaphor for life? 64

Imagine it, then do it 68

5 Incentives to produce good ideas **72**

Motivate others to generate good ideas 72

Incentive awards 74

What motivates staff to submit ideas? 75

Consult your ever-present experts 78

Generating good ideas – the creative process 81

Boost your creativity 82

Capturing good ideas – the strategy 86

Walt Disney's creativity strategy 86

Generate ideas and turn them into reality 88

6 Discover your life's purpose **91**

What would make your life more purposeful? 91

Purposeful people 93

The key to being on purpose 95

Whose purpose are you on? 99

Purpose comes from knowing 104

Finding out who you really are 105

Values at work 106

Find a purpose that makes your heart sing 112

7 Sharpen your thinking **115**

Learning new skills 115

We never fully develop all our talents 118

Gain leverage in relation to business goals 119

How effective are you at setting goals? 121

What are your criteria for success? 122

Strategic planning 125

Increase your pattern recognition skills 126

Develop flexible thinking skills 128

Chunk your thinking 129

8	**The power of setting goals**	**134**
	Means, motive and opportunity	136
	Don't kill your dreams	137
	Setting a career goal	138
	Align your goals so they flow in the same direction	140
	Define your goals	141
	Set your outcomes	142
	Tips for goal setting	146
	21 days to successful goal setting	148
9	**Step to the edge of your boundaries**	**152**
	Challenge habitual thinking	155
	How to confront negative beliefs	157
	Change your state	158
	Our feelings are the most important things	
	we possess	160
	Choose your patterns for success	161
	Thinking pitfalls to avoid	162
	Putting it all together	164
10	**Create circumstances for success**	**167**
	Chicken soup for the entrepreneur	167
	Walking on fire	169
	The core issues to deal with before walking on fire	171
	Club Entrepreneur for top performers	173
	Negotiation strategies in business	176
	Your senses give you immediate feedback	177
	Practise outcome thinking	178
11	**Recognize people's thinking styles**	**183**
	Types of thinking style	184
	Getting teams to work together effectively	184
	Do you recognize your thinking style?	186
	Thinking styles examined	187
	Share your people's view of the world	192
	How are people motivated to do things?	194
	Connect with your audience	194
	Manage your state of leadership	197
12	**Take control of how you think**	**199**
	For maximum impact notice listeners'	
	thinking styles	199

Checklist of thinking styles   202
Where do your decisions come from?   205
'Away' and 'towards' problem solving   206
Take control of how you think   207
Create a blueprint of your thinking habits   209
Changing beliefs   212
Changing unhelpful pictures changes motivation   214
To change a habit look at what holds it in place   215
13 Model success strategies   **217**
Noticing successful strategies   217
How do you score as a high achiever?   219
Modelling success at work – blueprinting technique   221
Start with simple observable skills that are easy
   to acquire   223
If a strategy can be described, it can be taught
   and learned   224
Easy skills to acquire   225
How modelling differs from textbook learning   229
What sort of skills would be most useful for you?   229
Choosing a skill to model   231
14 Pick a skill you want to acquire   **234**
Success strategies that work   234
Choose a skill   234
Modelling is a practical skill   235
Eliciting a strategy   237
What to look for when modelling a skill   239
Eye accessing cues   240
Coding a strategy   245
Getting the picture   248
Modelling skills in teaching and learning   249
15 Strengthen your completion drive   **253**
Where do you keep time in relation to
   goal setting?   253
Getting time on your side   254
How do you relate to time?   255
Be aware of the invisibles – beliefs, values and identity   261
Time in relation to goal setting   262
Procrastination: the art of keeping up with yesterday   267

Choose a better approach to time 268
Sense time moving 269
16 Listening and questioning skills **273**
Getting the right tone – listening skills 273
Why can't we listen? 276
How well do you listen? 277
How to listen 281
CRAFTY listening 283
Ask questions with a purpose 284
Challenging existing assumptions 287
Framework for listening and questioning: AEIOU 288
T-GROW coaching, a gentler approach
to questioning 290
17 Coaching your inner team **294**
Is your inner team really working for you? 294
Your inner team strengthens or weakens
self-confidence 295
How confident are you? 295
Examine your beliefs 296
Signs of low self-confidence 296
Sort out your inner team members 297
Get yourself a cheerleader 301
Logical levels give structure to thinking 304
Flashpoints 311
18 Tips for staying motivated **314**
Stay connected 314
Create a 'buddy' system 315
Have a mission statement and revisit it often 315
Decide to be happy 316
Have a mentor and be a mentor to someone 316
Stay in touch with yourself 316
Be fully present with people 317
Congratulate yourself 317
Things to do to help you feel grounded 318
19 Model success to master change **323**
Borrow other people's strategies 323
Collect strategies to improve your situation 325
Change your behaviour to enhance your results 327

Recipe for modelling a good decision-maker 328
Strategies people have modelled and why 334
Become aware of your behaviour patterns 335
A modelling challenge – how to ask for more money 339
20 Pulling it all together **342**
How committed are you to being successful? 342
Tools you will use for your future success 343
Hold your vision steadfastly in your mind 345
Align your beliefs and values 345
Your goals should be SMART 346
Follow your passions 347
Where are you now on the motivational skills wheel? 348
What is the next action you intend to take? 350
Gathering your resources 350
Your action plan for success 351
Taking it further **353**
Motivational trainers **353**
Helpful books **353**
Index **356**

Meet the author

I learned about NLP in the 1980s, when I was a freelance journalist writing features for the *London Evening Standard* about employment, motivational training, business and sales. I noticed that the main differences between highflyers who constantly achieved their goals and those who did not were that successful people acted more confidently, were motivated and had a plan. Many had coaches or mentors or were in the process of self-development.

Later I trained as an NLP Master Practitioner, first in business and then in education, and became fascinated with the NLP concept of modelling: the idea that we can model other people's success strategies easily and incorporate the learning into our own behaviour to achieve more successful results. I have collected over 300 excellent strategies for doing things well and, to test they work, have incorporated over 30 of them into my own behaviour with some interesting and far-reaching results.

Nowadays I am a freelance journalist, ghost write books, coach and teach 'NLP for Teaching and Learning' and 'New Developments in NLP' at the City Lit in London. At the Mary Ward Centre I teach 'NLP and Confidence Building' and 'Using NLP in the Workplace'. I am also an independent trainer, currently involved in modelling the latest 'New Developments in NLP', aspects of Professor Richard Gray's Brooklyn Program, a course for people working with substance abuse, in which 30 per cent of users have tested drug free on random urine analysis after one year.

From observing hundreds of course participants I realize that often people are only five or six skills away from achieving the big successes they want in life. There are few, if any, books

written on how to model strategies, so I have included a
section on this in this book.

I hope you find this book inspirational and highly practical.
It is written for people seeking to build their confidence and
motivation and get the string of successes they want from life.

www.francescoombes.com   francescoombes@yahoo.com

Only got a minute?

Get motivated and reach your goals

Getting the things we want in life should not be left to chance. We need to choose our desires carefully, then take deliberate actions that propel us towards our goals.

We become smarter when we work with tools that increase our potential and widen the range of possibilities around what we can achieve. For instance, using a computer lets us do lots of things we could not otherwise do alone, and in a fraction of the time. Are we smarter? Yes and no. Yes, we are smarter when using a computer, however, we are no smarter when we are simply working alone.

Gather tools to reach your goals

We may search for solutions in more powerful computers, yet fail to develop the mental software between our own ears. There are simple strategies we can use to 'power up' our thinking skills. Coaches, agony aunts, the military and governments use feedback strategies to forecast how they can make goal setting and reaching outcomes better next time around. Here is a tool to help you capture information from past experiences and carry the learning into new ventures.

With any action you take, notice what happens:

Think back to a previous situation when things went extremely well.

▸ Did you plan how you would achieve your outcome beforehand?
▸ Did what you expected to happen actually happen?

Noticing what happens provides the necessary feedback about the extent to which you are on target.

- ▶ How far were you off target?
- ▶ What actions could you have taken to put things right?

When taking actions to achieve new goals, **Test**, **Operate**, **Test** and **Exit**.

TEST: to see whether you are getting nearer to your goal, and if not,

OPERATE: take actions – do what you think will bring you nearer to your goal.

You may have to **TEST** and **OPERATE** many times before you eventually reach your target, then **EXIT**, taking the results of your learning with you, so you can reposition your next attempt.

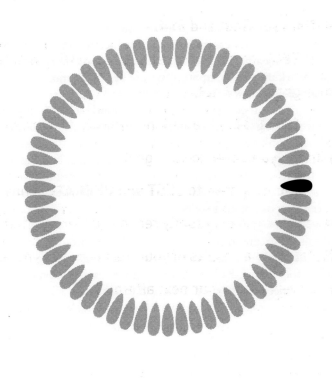

5 Only got five minutes?

Get motivated and reach your goals

Computers expand our knowledge and make information easily accessible to us. They can help us clarify objectives and reach our goals. The danger is that as we depend more upon them, we are not just working with computers, we are becoming more like them. We manage our diary time on screen in chunks. Conversations that once spanned sentences are completed in sound bites. We spend less time thinking, and produce forms with handy tick boxes so that others don't have to waste time thinking either. The result is that many people are becoming more left-brained, limiting themselves to analytical and process type thinking, similar to the software they use, and shutting down on their full potential to use a wider range of thinking styles.

Yet if businesses are to stay ahead of the competition they need creative ideas, the sort that can only be generated by people who think for themselves. Failing to question what seems obvious frees us from the need to make changes, and then change (like that happening in our economy and workforce sectors) will be forced upon us.

Developing mental muscle

With practice you can increase your thinking skills and develop the mental software you have between your own ears. You can build and accumulate thinking strategies in order to 'power up' your brain.

Begin by questioning the familiar. What are some of the messages you receive every day, ones that you don't seek to question, that may limit your search for solutions? It might be:

▶ 'They are in charge; they must know what they're doing.'
▶ 'I'm only a 'cleaner/clerk/sales assistant/nurse/teacher… my word does not count.'
▶ 'It is the economy; this is how it is done. I have no control over the outcomes.'

Now start clearing mental roadblocks. Take one of your commonly held beliefs and question it. Ask yourself, 'Is what I am saying about my commonly held belief a Truth, a Possible Truth, or a Limiting Assumption?'

Truth?	Possible Truth?	Limiting Assumption?

This question may seem deceptively simple but it forms the basis for a very powerful way of uncovering our own and other peoples' limiting beliefs and stumbling blocks.

Recognizing limiting beliefs

If you watch public enquiries on television, you may notice that the committees are seeking to answer enormous questions using this same deceptively simple form of questioning, one frame at a time. For instance, questions such as:

▶ How did the banking crisis come about? Who was responsible? Could we have foreseen it?
▶ What were the steps that lead us to the Iraq war? Who questioned decisions? How can we prevent a similar situation from happening again?

At each stage the inquirer seeks to establish whether the answer the person being questioned gives is a Truth, a Possible Truth or a Limiting Assumption?

It is vital to establish at what point our thoughts deviate from truth or fact, possible truth or fact, to one of limiting assumption, because once we convince ourselves that a limiting assumption is a truth, we search for information to substantiate our belief and exclude all else. This occurrence can be seen in appeal cases where the wrong person has been imprisoned. On re-examination it often turns out that once a likely suspect has been apprehended, the information gatherers shut down on all other possibilities. Once our thinking becomes derailed, we search only for patterns that match our assumptions – and we find them. We can sometimes believe so strongly that our assumptions are 'truth' that even when we are shown evidence to the contrary, we may still argue passionately for our limiting beliefs.

There is a saying, 'A familiar sight provokes no attention.' Examine some of the everyday messages that you accept as truths. Start to question your own limiting assumptions by listing the phrases you use each time you include the word 'should' in a sentence. List your six most commonly held 'should' phrases to start with, for example: 'I *should* know all the answers', 'I *should* have got it right', 'I *should* have seen this coming'.

When you have six 'I *should* …' phrases on your list, ask yourself, is this belief you hold a Truth? A Possible Truth? Or is it a Limiting Assumption? Either way you will learn from the experience.

PRECISION QUESTIONS

Challenge each of your limiting beliefs further with the following precision questions. For example, to the limiting belief, '*I should be more productive*' ask:

▶ How do you know that you can't … *be more productive?*
▶ What would happen if you could … *be more productive?*

▶ What are you assuming that is stopping you from achieving that goal ... *being more productive?*

Now stop and listen for the answers.

Asking precision questions lets you shine a light on unhelpful thinking and encourages more helpful beliefs to emerge.

Software for the brain strategies

'Most people are only five or six skills away from achieving the successes they want in life,' said Robert Kiyosaki, author of the multi-million pound New York best seller, *Rich Dad, Poor Dad*. Which six strategies could you acquire to generate powerful leverage in the areas you seek to excel in? It may be:

▶ Better communication skills at work, or to build rapport with others.
▶ To get your message across to customers, negotiate or listen with greater insight and clarity.
▶ To discover how another person weighs up a situation in order to make a decision.
▶ To anchor a confident state when you may not feel that way.

Below are strategies for anchoring a positive state and discovering how individuals make decisions.

What is an anchor?

An anchor is any stimulus that changes your state. It can involve any kind of sensory input – **visual, auditory, feelings, smell** or **taste.** Your state is created by your sensory experience, your memories and thoughts. Pavlov's dogs salivated when bells rang because he had conditioned them to think ringing bells meant they were about to get food.

Everyday examples of anchors are:

Smelling a perfume and immediately thinking of a particular person; **hearing** a song that brings back memories, or makes you want to dance; **seeing** an old adversary and immediately feeling apprehensive.

What does an anchor do?

Anchors fire associations or memories, and can put you into 'feeling good' or 'feeling bad' states.

Anchoring a positive state:

We can all anchor negative states at will. Someone only has to say, 'remember that awful day when that terrible thing happened …' and people do the rest with self-hypnosis. Their eyes will drop and glaze over as they imagine the event, their energy will drain, shoulders sag and they will sigh in a sorrowful way.

If we can anchor negative states at will, we can also anchor positive states with practice. One of Elvis Presley's roadies who watched him perform each night said: 'When Elvis left the dressing room he was an ordinary person.' Between the dressing room and the stage he underwent a transformation. 'His stature and confidence appeared to grow as he came nearer to the crowd and by the time he stepped onto the stage he had become Elvis Presley.' What he is describing is the act of state management – and we can all do it – provided we practise enough.

How to anchor a confident feeling

▶ Think of a time when you did something exceptional and felt really confident and good. Go back in time and relive that experience: step into your body, **see what you see, feel what you feel, hear what you hear.**

- At the peak of that experience, anchor the feeling of excitement and joy with a small pat on your leg, or a gesture you can easily replicate.
- Practise recalling and running your good feeling often, so that you can access it at will.

Recall your positive anchor when under pressure or if you want to motivate yourself to reach a goal.

Notice how people make decisions

One of the most useful skills you can develop is that of noticing how people make their decisions. It may be the steps leading to them buying a new product, changing their job, electing a new prime minister or choosing a restaurant meal. If you can identify people's thinking and behaviour patterns in advance, you can determine or influence how they make their choices in the future.

You can use this questioning for any actions people take. It may be how they decided to change a job, buy a new car or computer. Or you might want to know how people choose a restaurant meal, and use the information you gather to attract more customers to your restaurant for a meal?

How people make choices

Talk to at least six people and ask them how they chose their last restaurant meal and record their answers.

THE PROCESS: Ask them what is the first sensation they are aware of as they start to think of food and make their choice.	What was their process of choosing? Get them to take you through the steps up to the point they made their decision.

(Contd)

NOTICE SENSORY LANGUAGE: Did they get a **feeling** first that told them they were hungry? Did they **see** the food in their mind's eye? Did they **talk** to themselves and run through each dish in turn, **imagining tasting** it? Build up a whole sensory sequence for how they made their choice.	**Was their language mainly: visual** (describing what they were seeing); **auditory** (describing what they were saying to themselves); **kinaesthetic** (giving a sense of how they were feeling about the experience)?
IDENTIFY THE TRIGGER: Where did their trigger begin? Was it with a feeling/a smell/a taste/a picture/something they said to themselves before taking the action?	**What was their trigger point:** how did they flip from indecision to having made up their mind.

How might this information be useful?

▶ People tend to run patterns of behaviours in similar situations. If you know how they behave in one situation, you can predict how they are likely to behave in a similar situation in the future. To attract **visual** diners, show bright pictures of what the food will look like. To appeal to **auditory** diners have menus that give sensuous and appetizing descriptions of the meals. To attract the **touchy feelies** have lighting and décor that creates a warm and inviting atmosphere.

▶ If you want to attract **visual**, **auditory** and **kinesthetic** diners then ensure your restaurant meets the criteria for all sensory preferences.

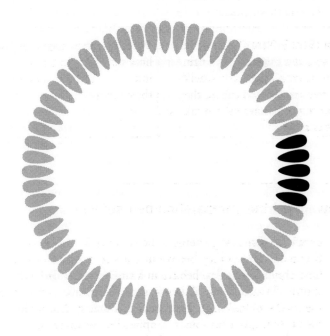

10 Only got ten minutes?

Strategies to help you reach your goals

Many of the people we hail as genius are simply clever people who have developed strategies for doing things incredibly well. Human beings have limited brainpower, there is only so much we can remember and learn. But we have abilities to invent tools, devices and strategies that expand our capabilities.

Tony Buzan devised the idea of mind maps, a colourful visual form of note-taking that lets people capture and explore aspects of their thinking that might otherwise escape if they use conventional linear note-taking. The maps contain a central idea or image and themes are explored by following branches that radiate from it.

The technique is a simple artefact that expands the range of things that people can do. Mapping is useful for brainstorming for new ideas and topics can then be explored by following the branches that connect to a central theme.

Another technique was developed by Walt Disney, hailed as a genius for his breathtaking Disney film cartoons such as *Fantasia*, *Bambi*, and *Sleeping Beauty*. Disney used strategies to take his teams through creative processes, such as developing storylines, to make sure dialogue and animation fitted perfectly.

Disney's 'Dreamer', 'Realist' and 'Critic' strategy can be used by anyone to improve the quality of ideas they generate, articles they write, books they structure, and concepts or products they are planning to launch.

Use Walt Disney's creativity strategy

THE DREAMER STAGE

When you are brainstorming for new ideas, act as if you are the most knowledgeable person in the world. Disney had different rooms for different types of thinking, and during the Dreamer stage, designed to convey a starburst of ideas, no one was allowed to criticize anyone's input.

THE REALIST STAGE

At this stage people work out what is possible – the theme, form and structure – and flesh out the outline. This is the practical stage from which the first draft emerges.

THE CRITIC STAGE

When the Realist stage is finished the inner Critic steps in. At this point you become the most critical person in the world and look to find the flaws in your creation.

I use this technique for feature writing and brainstorm at the kitchen table. There is a whiteboard on the wall so I can capture good ideas. For the Realist stage I move on to the computer and input, structure and comb through my work to get it into shape.

At the final Critic stage I stand at the polished kitchen worktop and read my copy aloud as if I am another more critical person. At this stage, I can hear my 'inner' editor commenting and telling me what changes to make. Then it's back to the computer to hone the feature and send it off.

Creative copying: the NLP modelling strategies

The NLP modelling strategies are simply a fantastic way of acquiring other people's successful thinking and doing patterns when they are performing at their best.

WHAT IS MODELLING?

Modelling is the NLP process of finding out how other people do things incredibly well. Once something can be described it can be taught and learnt. We observe, question and listen in order to find out how people do something particularly well, whether accomplishing a task, performing a skill, being in a certain state or living life excellently.

HOW DO YOU APPLY MODELLING SKILLS?

▶ **Negotiations:** if two parties disagree, modelling allows you to put yourself in each person's shoes and to see the world as they do. Often you will gain valuable insights into the person's thinking and beliefs.
▶ **Better communications:** you might want to understand colleagues better in order to get your message across more effectively.
▶ **In the workplace:** you might want to listen with greater insight to people's points of view before asking someone to change their behaviour.
▶ **Counselling, disciplining or giving bad news:** you may want to match a person's body language, sensory language and breathing pace to build rapport with that person.
▶ **Teaching or learning:** modelling can help you acquire skills to work out why someone can't do something, so that you can then give them a better strategy.

A good starter point for developing better communication skills is to become expert at seeing the world from different people's viewpoints. Learning to use the different perceptual positions also works out cheaper than paying for focus groups, surveys, data capture and analyst skills to tell you what is good and bad about the way you relate with your customers. Developing more flexible thinking skills will give you greater insight and understanding of what is going on for the people you are communicating, or failing to communicate, with.

Using perceptual positions

Think of a situation between you and another person where you would like to gain more clarity into what is going on. You might be having problems relating well to each other, and you want to move past this situation to something more agreeable.

IN FIRST PERCEPTUAL POSITION (PERSON A)

Relax in a comfortable place and imagine you are having a conversation with the person you are experiencing the difficulties with. Tell the person out loud your side of things and how you perceive the situation to be ... and then wait patiently for the answers to emerge. Have you gained any new insight at this point?

IN SECOND PERCEPTUAL POSITION (PERSON B)

Next, imagine you are that person, lets call her Sarah, having a similar conversation with you. Shift your position to another chair so that you can focus back on the place where you were sitting and imagine and talk to yourself that is sitting there.

You are Sarah (Person B) explaining her side of the situation to you (Person A), lets call you George. While you are being Sarah, and speaking her thoughts out loud, explain the situation from Sarah's point of view. What is happening for her? How does she feel about the situation? What are her thoughts about you? What could be done to make things better for her? What new insight have you gained?

IN THIRD PERCEPTUAL POSITION (PERSON C)

Take the information you have gathered with you and move on to another chair, or spot, where you become Person C, let's call him Carl. He is a neutral observer. He is looking on from a distance, has no axe to grind, and is simply a wise and impartial observer.

Carl is just watching the interaction between the two of you. What does he think is going on? Have Carl talk out loud about how he views the situation. Does he have any advice to give to Sarah? What advice would he give to you? Is there any way that the situation might be made better? Have you gained any new insight from Carl at this point?

What points have you learned about the situation that you were unclear about before? Do you have greater understanding? How might you take the information you have gained from each person's insights and use it to make the situation better?

This exercise might be seen as an intuitive one of modelling how others are thinking and feeling, and it is. We instinctively know a lot more about situations and what is going on with other people than we realize, and we lose a lot of valuable insights when we shut down on our inner knowing.

Trust in sixth senses

Have you ever had a gut feeling about something but chosen not to trust your judgment? Intuition can be crucial to our success in work. Intuition can be developed and has a place in team decision-making processes in work. It is not a substitute for analytic thinking, but it can be complementary, providing leaps of imagination, gut feelings or flashes of insight into strategies and timing of actions.

Marketing manager Erica Spence decided to hone her intuitive thinking after a product launch disaster. She says, 'I discovered afterwards that several people had felt uneasy about the product. None of us had spoken up, because it belonged to a successful range of products, and there was no logical reason to think it would bomb so badly.' Spence now believes that to make team decisions without encouraging people to put forward their gut reactions is to ignore a vast amount of non-analytic information that can make the difference between success and failure.

PRACTISE GETTING INTUITIVE

▶ When faced with new situations, pay close attention to where in your body your initial feelings come from. Keep a feelings journal and begin to recognize the difference between: a gut reaction in the pit of your stomach, or feeling the hairs on the back of your neck standing on end. Record the type of events that follow these feelings.
▶ If you experience strong visual pictures with emotions attached to them, take time and ask yourself what your mind is telling you with this flash of insight. Notice associated tastes, whether they are pleasant or bitter, and heightened smells that may signal victory or defeat.
▶ Set yourself little intuitive tasks, such as guessing who is ringing you, before you pick up the phone.
▶ Before making any decision, ask yourself, 'How do I really feel about this?'

Innovation and developing new strategies

It is a good idea to combine and build your strategies upon each other in the way you would cement bricks when making a wall. Once you have gathered a few well-chosen tools and techniques you can begin to generate your own unique strategies. For instance, by combining concepts developed by Charles Faulkner, an internationally recognized NLP trainer and modeller, and a mapping tool acquired from Tony Buzan, famed for his mind-mapping techniques, I have mind mapped 37 distinct solution-finding patterns of thinking which experts use when problem solving. I have mapped them so that I can apply any of them to different situations and events. I call the process, 'consulting my mentors'.

Bringing several experts' different thinking styles to bear on a problem situation generates lots of ideas and solutions that I would never have thought of alone. Over time I have blended five of my experts' habitual thinking patterns and devised a thinking through strategy, called a 'push through'. If I feel blocked, need an extra push to find my motivation, or want to work out how to tackle a new project I can simply apply a 'push through'.

New developments using NLP techniques

Modelling lets you take the skills you learn in one situation and apply them to other areas. As an NLP trainer I am about to run sessions based on modelling Richard Gray's Brooklyn Program, an exciting new concept using NLP techniques, a new development in which a staggering 30 per cent of substance abusers tested drug-free on urine analysis after one year.

BROOKLYN DRUG ADDICTION PROGRAM

The Brooklyn Program operated as an in-house substance abuse treatment program for the Federal Probation office in Brooklyn, New York, between 1997 and 2004. During this time it treated offenders with little personal direction who had drug addiction and substance misuse disorders.

The program is unique because it is non-confrontational and non-directive. Instead of addressing the problem behaviours, the program at first helps participants to learn new skills.

Richard Gray Phd., Assistant Professor at the School of Criminal Justice, Fairleigh Dickinson University, says, 'The work does not immediately focus on the problem, instead it emphasizes that participants can learn to enhance their memory, feel better emotionally, gain control over their emotions, choose how and when they want to feel differently and then to design a meaningful future. It is important that the skills be valued for themselves, not as drug treatment.'

There is a behavioural success criteria for each stage of the program so that participants performance can be gauged. Once they have achieved a feel-good factor they learn coping strategy interventions they can use to curb their own behaviour. Clients are taught NLP skills that focus on giving them more choices on how to behave in stressful situations. Richard Gray adds: 'Clients are not directed to use these skills with drugs or problem behaviours. They are encouraged rather to learn the skills and to discover how and where they will work best for them.'

Intervention was based on awakening in clients a personal identity, giving them practical new skills they could use immediately and asking them to imagine a more highly-valued future. At times of cravings or feelings of being locked into a cycle of repetitive behaviour, clients had options and other behaviours should they choose to use them.

Many of the basic techniques used in the Brooklyn Program were taken from NLP, a set of therapy tools and strategies developed in the mid-1970s by Richard Bandler and John Grinder who modelled the behaviours of therapists such as Milton Erickson, Virginia Satir and Fritz Perls, renowned for their abilities to modify unwanted or un-useful behaviours in clients.

ANCHORING STATES

Offenders were taught to 'anchor' resourceful states. Most people can remember bad things that happened and replay them on demand. And with practice they can also learn to access good memories to use as a recourse to build confidence and self-esteem.

Richard Gray says, 'Clients were taught to take memories of real experiences of focused attention: making a good decision, discovering the moment of behavioural consolidation – like when learning to ride a bike, an experience of fun, and an experience of personal competence and to enhance each of these experiences of personal competence to ecstatic levels. Then they were taught to connect each enhanced state to a distinctive conditioned stimulus so that each would become an internal resource state that clients could access instantly and at will.'

Participants were encouraged to practise their anchoring of good states into multiple situations so that they could be generalized and used in other areas of life. Richard Gray says, 'One of the most striking outcomes in the course of the program was the near universal and spontaneous use that people made of anchors for anger management.'

People realized they had a reliable means to control their emotions, and they began to use anchors to create choice about how they were feeling in the moment. One offender who had violated paroles for bank robbery because of his cocaine habit said that he had turned-up where he usually bought his drugs and felt agitated and confused and did not know what to do. Richard Gray says, 'Importantly, he left and went home without buying drugs, and apart from one lapse, he has never taken drugs again.' Clients did not have to behave instinctively, because they had choices and additional resources which were not available to them before.

Offenders used NLP well-formed outcomes so they could set future goals and evaluate them in terms of their impact on their current life and the lives of the people around them.

Participants reported an increase in self-esteem and positive feelings, and a high proportion, 30 per cent of those who completed the program and had random urine analysis testing, were still drug-free after one year.

(Article extract courtesy of *Positive Health* magazine, 'Mind Body Link', Copyright Frances Coombes)

Use creative copying to generate new ideas

Each of the techniques we have looked at becomes more powerful when you build upon them and combine them with other strategies. Whenever you come across a new strategy think about how you might redesign or adapt it, and use it for your own purpose. Explore how this idea might enable you to link into even more exciting possibilities, concepts and applications.

You can gain leverage by knowing at every stage which strategies you want, who has got them and how the tools will take you towards your goals. Whenever you see someone who has a really clever way of doing something, ask them, 'How do you do that?' Then listen, really listen for the answer.

Plan well-formed outcomes

The key to maximizing all of your inner resources is to:

▶ know what you want
▶ take actions to make things happen
▶ plan your success in advance using visualization, reflection and well-formed outcomes
▶ be flexible in your behaviour – if what you are doing is not working, then do something else!

1

What is motivation?

In this chapter you will learn:
- *your motivation is a state of mind*
- *what motivates you*
- *why you may need to change your habits*
- *how to set a well-formed outcome*

What is motivation?

> 'Whatever you do, or dream you can, begin it. Boldness
> has genius and power and magic in it.'
>
> Goethe 1747–1832

Motivation is a state of mind, an attitude, a way of thinking, being
and doing that can reap rewards beyond your wildest dreams.
Just as preparing for a team sport or getting ready for a first date
requires you to think tactically and become aware of how other
players may engage, becoming highly motivated requires that you
develop new skills and a new sense of awareness that wasn't
necessary in your less ambitious state.

You were highly motivated as a toddler when, with a little bit of
encouragement, you taught yourself to walk, talk, discover the
world and enjoy doing new things. Imagine how determined you
were to urge your small body to repeatedly cling on to surfaces
in your efforts to stand. You may have suffered knocks and shed

tears of frustration. But your sense of curiosity was aroused and the only way you could find out what was happening beyond your boundaries was to walk. You didn't give up, you battled through false starts, tears and tottering and kept trying – and then, one day it happened. You walked.

Insight

Write your goals down. Nothing exists until it is written down. Until your goals are written, all you have is ideas. An idea is only a notion – unless an action happens. So write it down.

How motivated are you?

'Success is not the result of spontaneous combustion. You must set yourself on fire.'

Reggie Leach

Some people are lucky enough to discover a purpose and passion in life that grips them: it may be music, a hobby, sport, helping other people, collecting money, religion, politics. Others have to work at first finding their motivation and then channelling it into achieving bigger goals in life. The good news is that we can all become more purposeful in our actions, provided we are prepared to discover how our own motivation works. Even better, as you discover how you tick so you develop greater insight into how other people tick and how to motivate them.

Insight

Our own internal working styles drive us to achieve our desires. At one end of the scale they may motivate us to achieve, at the other extreme they can become habits that ruin our lives. So identify how your 'internal drivers' work. (See Chapter 11, Recognize people's thinking styles.)

WHERE ARE YOU ON THE MOTIVATION SCALE?

I read about a man who spent all his time lying on a sofa watching television. He had lost the most basic motivational drives that keep people alive. After four years of inactivity his mind and body gave up and he died.

Most of us are motivated to take actions to get the things we want in life. At a basic level these are food, shelter, clothes, warmth, then friends, self-esteem and kinship, a feeling of belonging. If all these needs are met then some of us seek self-actualization, the chance to grow and become motivated to find and achieve a meaningful life purpose (Figure 1.1).

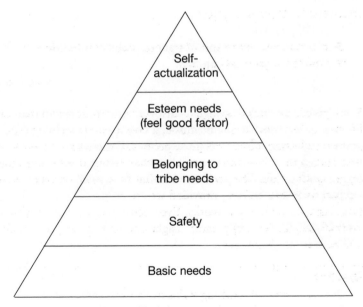

Figure 1.1 Abraham Maslow's Hierarchy of Needs.

If our lower needs are met, we may wonder about what is our purpose in life? How do we achieve the things that we feel passionate about and are meaningful to our lives?

Insight

Ask yourself the Big Question: what do you really want?

Thought provoker

The same intelligence that created the universe also created you. Have you discovered yet what your purpose in life is? Are you only here to breathe in and out? What are you, or could you be, doing with the innate intelligence and inner knowing you possess?

Knowing who you are and discovering what you really want is the key to taking actions that will propel you towards greater successes.

Thought provoker

▶ *What are the things that you are naturally drawn to?*
▶ *What are the changes you will need to make to get the life you want?*

People often say they know what they want and may spend their time engaged in displacement activities, only to find after they have swapped their job, partner or location that they have carried with them their feelings of discontent. They have changed what seemed obvious in their lives but have not identified the main changes that will make the difference to them.

Thought provoker

What, if any, legacies would you like to leave behind? If you could leave behind three things to say that you have lived your life well, what would they be? If you were serious about achieving only one of those aims, what would be the next step you would take today to make that dream a reality? Write it down.

When you know what you want in life, and can recognize the environment, behaviour, lack of skills or resources, or limiting beliefs that may be holding you back you can begin to solve problems that might be preventing you from achieving your full success potential. One way to do this is to ask yourself lots of questions out loud. Human beings have evolved by solving puzzles; they are problem seeking missiles, designed to home-in and find answers once a question has been voiced.

Thought provoker

How motivated are you to achieve the things that are really important to you in life? Do you identify with any of the methods below that people employ to achieve their aims in life? On a motivation scale of 1–10, where do you fit? Write your answer in column 2.

Wish list You wish you had achieved your goal, but nothing happens and you wonder why.	
Want it You want your outcome and you start out to achieve it, but when things don't go your way you give up frustrated.	
Want it, sometimes get it, often don't When you do give up it is because you realize halfway through that the price is too high.	
Want it, envision and plan your route You achieve your goal, celebrate, move on to a new target and expect to get that too.	

There are no shortcuts to achieving self-fulfilment. Discovering your purpose is an ongoing process, one that requires self-questioning, reflection, and a readiness to take the risks and actions necessary to achieve the things you want in life.

Thought provoker

We make our decisions a choice at a time. A common pitfall for people who go with the flow instead of planning ahead, is that they end up doing what is convenient, rather than what is the right thing for them to do.

Think back to the last few decisions you made. How did you make them?

Unplanned decisions
▶ Doing what is convenient
▶ Avoiding conflict
▶ Doing what others wanted

Planned decisions
▶ Doing what fitted your overall plan
▶ Taking calculated risks
▶ Honouring commitments you had made

Reflect on your actions
Each time you make a decision, ask yourself whether you are doing whatever is the most convenient thing to do at that time, or are you choosing to honour your commitments about how you want to shape your life?

Being motivated is the nearest thing to magic you can achieve because it develops a 'can do' attitude, which is the most critical accessory to success in any endeavour. Anyone who is totally motivated and achieving his or her goals on a regular basis may find it hard to understand the person who settles for dawdling through life and accepting whatever fate, or the result of their inaction, chooses to deal them. So let's start thinking about changes you want to make.

WHAT DO YOU WANT?

To imagine your goals in terms of outcome thinking you will need to imagine stepping forwards into the future having already achieved them. The thinking you generate by visualizing a successful outcome is motivation towards achieving something that you really want. And by thinking of it in terms of having already achieved it, you will have gathered a lot of sensory information about obstacles in the way, resources needed, possible leads or blocks to what needs to happen to achieve the outcome.

> ### Insight
>
> A well-formed outcome is your personal map towards your goal. It is a framework used to help you define clear and achievable results. If you start out with your own unique map of how to proceed at any point along your route, you will wildly increase your chances of success.

You would be amazed at how many people do not know what they want. Statistics show that less than 7 per cent of the population thinks strategically, and this includes having the ability to set and plan compelling goals. Frequently people answer the question of 'what do you want?' by telling you all the things they do not want. While knowing what you don't want can be useful information, being able to state your goals in a positive way is absolutely essential if you hope to achieve any of them.

USE POSITIVE OUTCOME THINKING

If you notice that you are framing what you want in a problem-centred way, such as:

▶ *I don't want to work here*
▶ *I don't want to be unfit*
▶ *I don't want to be stressed-out*

you can change your thinking to solution-focused outcomes by asking a follow-on question:

▶ *What do I really want instead of that?*

Keep asking the question until all the negative things you do not want are replaced with positive outcomes.

So an outcome of 'I don't want to be stressed-out', can be reframed by asking the question 'What do I really want instead of that?'

Your brain will then give you a list of criteria of all the things that are necessary for you to feel relaxed.

Self-coaching questions for deeper awareness

Once you know what you want, the next step is to know what evidence you will require to let you know you have been successful.

People are often clear about what their goal is, but unclear about what achieving that goal would do for them or allow them to do. To find your motivation for doing anything, you need to carry out some inner questioning about why you want these things. For example, you may say, 'I want a new house'. The questions to ask are, 'What would "doing that"/"having that"/"being that" do for me?' and 'Why is that important to me?'

Self coaching questions:

Q What would having a new house **do for you?**
A It would give me my own space.
Q And what would having your own space **do for you?**
A It would give me a feeling of freedom
Q And why is a feeling of freedom **important** to you?

What will learning to question yourself about your deeper reasons for wanting things give you? It will give you a greater understanding of what motivates you, your beliefs and the qualities you value. When you know what you want in life and your reasons for wanting these things, you are more likely to achieve them.

APPLY THE QUESTION STRATEGY

Take what you have learned from the above form of questioning and apply it to your own goals.

Q What would having ... do for you?
A It would ...
Q And what would having ... do for you?
A It would ...
Q And why is ... important to you?

Then ask another question to clarify why you want your goals.

Q What would your goal give you that you wouldn't otherwise have?

WHAT WOULD YOUR GOAL GIVE YOU THAT YOU WOULDN'T OTHERWISE HAVE?

This is a brilliant question for exploring your deeper emotions and values, the ones that fuel your dreams and desires. It is important that you know exactly what your desires are, if you hope to fulfill them.

You may say, 'I want a gleaming new Porsche'. The questions to ask to start eliciting your desires are:

Q What would having a gleaming new Porsche give you that you would not otherwise have?
A Power: people would look at me and say 'Wow'.
Q And what would people looking at your car and saying 'Wow' give you that you would not otherwise have?
A I would feel powerful, alive and love every moment.

When you set a goal, it is important to clarify exactly what you want. It is equally important to know what achieving your goal will give you that you don't have now. It is also vital to know what evidence of success you will need to see to convince yourself that you have achieved your aim.

APPLY THE QUESTION STRATEGY

How will you know you have got your goal? When you have a goal, for example 'I want to be rich', the questions to ask to ascertain how you will know when you have achieved your goal are:

Q How will you know you are rich?
A Because I won't have to work.
Q And what will you see, hear and feel when you've got what you want?
A I will see myself sitting in a lovely apartment by the beach. I will feel free and easy and contented as I hear my family playing in the pool.

You can continue the questions above by asking: 'And what else will let you know...?', 'What else will you see, hear and feel?' The more vividly a goal is imagined, the more the unconscious mind will strive to achieve it.

WHAT ARE YOU LIKE WHEN YOU ARE AT YOUR BEST?

This is a good question, one to ask yourself over and over again. Acquire as many memories as you can of what you look, feel and sound like when you are doing any task at your best. Your first answer to the question might be: 'It feels like magic when I am performing at my best.' However, it is important for you to articulate all these thoughts and feelings into plain words that describe your state 'magic'. Think of key words, such as: 'focused', 'calm', 'relaxed'. If you know these words relate to how you are feeling when you are performing at your best you can use them in the future to help you access that 'magic' state at will.

Preparing a well-formed outcome

By modelling the steps that most successful people follow when setting their outcomes, you will increase your chances of achieving your goals. Besides asking the questions above, 'What do I want?'

and 'What will I see, hear and feel to let me know I have achieved my goal?', other questions to consider are:

▶ *Where do I want my outcome (at home/at work)?*
▶ *How will me achieving my outcome affect my workmates, my family, my friends?*

Think about the impact of you initiating this new goal and how you would deal with any difficulties that might arise. What are the costs and benefits of achieving the goal? What will you gain from achieving your aim? What do you get from what you are doing at present? Is there anything you might lose by achieving your outcome?

HOW MUCH CONTROL DO YOU HAVE OVER YOUR OUTCOME?

You will probably never have complete control over any situation where other people or finances or market changes are involved, but the more influence you can have over the outcome, the more likely you are to be able to achieve it.

WHAT RESOURCES DO YOU BRING TO THE UNDERTAKING?

▶ *Skills?*
▶ *Knowledge?*
▶ *Information?*
▶ *Time?*
▶ *Money?*
▶ *Connections?*

Do you have any or all of the resources you need, or know how to get them? For instance, you may not have the money, or all of the knowledge, but do you know someone who does? Could you barter with them for their input if it helps to increase your chances of success?

▶ *What is a realistic timeframe to set for your goal?*
▶ *What will you do about anything that may get in the way?*

What would achieving your goal say about you?

- ▶ *If you achieve your goal, what else will you get?*
- ▶ *What is this goal a step towards?*
- ▶ *What is the next step in achieving your goal?*
- ▶ *Do you still want your goal?*

By framing your goals in a well-formed outcome you give yourself the greatest chance of achieving them. The process also helps you to clarify whether or not you really want the outcome before you set out on the undertaking. By thinking the situation through you will have saved yourself time, possibly money, and effort, which you can use to focus on the things you really burn to achieve.

Well-formed conditions are:

1. **Your goal should be stated positively:** *for example, I want to do something; I want to work my way around the world.*
2. **Your goal should be sensory specific:** *you need to be able to describe it in enough detail to say what you will see, hear, feel, taste and touch.*
3. **Know how much control you have over your outcome:** *is it something that can be initiated and controlled by you or do you need resources and collaboration from other people?*
4. **What will the process actually involve?** *Your goal needs to be SMART, that is: Specific, Measurable, Achievable, Realistic and within a Timeframe.*

Plan your well-formed outcome

P = POSITIVE	What do you want? (Stated in positive language)
A = ACHIEVEMENT	How will you know that you have it? What do you see, feel and hear? How will someone else know that you have achieved your goal?

C = CONTEXT	When do you want your goal?
	When do you not want it?
	With whom do you want it?
	Where do you want it?
E = ECOLOGY	What would happen if you achieved your goal?
	If you achieve what you want would you lose anything? (A relationship, a positive benefit?)
	What would achieving this goal say about you?
R = RESOURCES	Can you initiate and maintain this goal?

Having worked through a well-formed outcome, you may find you no longer want your goal. This is really good news, as it helps you to weed out half-hearted 'wishes' and 'wants' that masquerade as goals. It is better to know at the beginning than halfway through an undertaking that you do not want it enough to stick with the commitment when the going gets tough; this stops you diluting your efforts on undertakings that are really important to you.

Undertake a well-formed outcome on every new goal that you set and it will substantially increase your chances of success. Use the 'well-formedness' conditions:

▶ *when planning a career move or making life changes*
▶ *as a check, when you want to do something new*
▶ *when you are not getting the results you want – it may be a sign that one of the conditions is not being met.*

WHAT WOULD YOU DO IF YOU KNEW YOU COULD NOT FAIL?

Many people fail to achieve their dreams because they are held back by fear of failure. One way they close the door to success on their dreams is to refuse to allow themselves to even dream about what might be possible for them to achieve.

Happiness doesn't come from playing a role but from bringing your inner self to your work. Make happiness a way of travelling, not just a destination. A major source of stress is postponement of happiness. Make the process as important as the results.

Apply the self-test questions and answers

If you're starting out on the path of self-discovery here are some questions to ask yourself. Spend 20 minutes listing your answers and don't censor yourself – just write down everything.

▶ *What are the things that I enjoy doing?*
▶ *What am I good at?*
▶ *What seriously do I want out of life?*
▶ *What things could I do to achieve it?*
▶ *What is the next step I could take right now?*
▶ *What price would I have to pay to achieve it?*
▶ *What is the worst thing that could happen if things went wrong?*
▶ *Am I willing to pay the price?*
▶ *If I did know the answer to this question, what would it be?*

> ### *Thought provokers*
> In this chapter you have learned some powerful self-coaching questions.
>
> ▶ *Which, if any, of the questions and new learning will you carry into your next undertaking, or use in your daily life?*
> ▶ *Choose the three most powerful questions and commit to asking them to yourself every day for a week. Keep a diary and write down your answers.*

Have you learned anything new about yourself from performing this exercise? Is there a mind seed, a kernel of an idea, anything you can take away and use towards creating the life you want?

Success is doing – not wishing!

A lot of people make their changes when the pain of staying where they are becomes greater than the fear of moving on and stepping into an uncertain future.

Below are some of the reasons people gave for why they decided to make big changes in their lives.

Vic Taylor, a further education teacher, was 49 when he was made redundant. He now runs MyNewt Enterprises a one-man, environmental roadshow for children; his parties are booked months in advance. He says: 'I created this job because I needed the money. I felt I was too old for anyone to want to employ me, so I sat down and planned my future. I enjoy it so much I wish I'd done it earlier.'

Pierre White, restaurateur, put his ambition down to watching his talented but cautious father's behaviour. 'He was ambitious but could not bring himself to take a risk or dare, and had to live his life knowing he had never reached his potential,' says Pierre. 'His failure was an important lesson for me.'

Illness forced Tom Cook, who worked on television projects in Australia, America and Britain, to change career at 49. Tom explains: 'I came down with hepatitis in Singapore and was incapacitated for over a year. During my recovery I would lie in bed and say, "How am I going to get out of TV?" And suddenly the penny dropped – I already was out. I could barely go to the loo.' Tom started painting and found he had a flair for it and sold some paintings. He looked round for a way to support himself, using art rather than relying on his experience in television. Tom is now an artist and creativity workshop facilitator for Alternatives in London. He says: 'The words of a 12th-century poet, Rumi, gave me a lot of motivation. Rumi said: "The same intelligence that created the galaxies and the universe also created me." It is so simple, and technically inarguable. Suddenly I realized how powerful we all are. It's just that some of us don't know it yet.'

No matter what your circumstances are, you have the power to change your thinking and doing habits. You can choose to bring more of your creative energies into the things you do or make happen. You can choose the directions you take in life, and the projects you undertake, which are an expression of who you are.

'Winning is a habit. Unfortunately, so is losing.'

Vince Lombardi, Football League Coach

WHAT IS THE MOST IMPORTANT THING I CAN DO?

One of the most powerful questions anyone who wants to start achieving can ask themselves each day is, 'What are the most important things I can do today to take me nearer to my goals?' Then, and this is important, **they follow through with actions.** Initially it might be:

▶ *a telephone call to find out more about something*
▶ *looking for books or ideas about someone who's done similar things*
▶ *a plan of action*
▶ *sorting out your skills and abilities*
▶ *attending seminars and workshops*
▶ *finding and talking to people who share your dreams*
▶ *looking for the next step to take that leads towards your goals.*

An idea is only a notion – unless an action follows.

WHAT THINGS DO YOU REGRET NOT HAVING DONE?

A magazine survey of people in their eighties, which asked the question 'If you had your life over again, what would you do differently?', reveals that the majority of people said:

▶ *I would focus more on my values and larger goals and not be driven by day-to-day decisions.*
▶ *I would have more courage in taking risks in my career and relationships.*
▶ *I would leave a legacy, do more things for other people.*

What would you do differently?

What this book will do

This book will help you to identify patterns of thinking and behaviours you may be repeating that could be holding you back from achieving the successes you want in life. It will enable you to move from just thinking about the things you would like to achieve to actually doing more of them.

You will learn how to develop the habit of:

▶ *visualizing your goals*
▶ *committing to the goals that are worth achieving*

- *planning your approach to goal setting*
- *most importantly, taking the action necessary to achieve the outcome you desire.*

The book offers tools and techniques for motivation and will help you gain insights into what makes you tick. When you know how your motivation works you can more accurately assess a situation and your likelihood of successfully completing a task. You can train yourself to achieve more without making energy-draining false starts towards goals which you drop halfway through when the going gets tough, because now you will have learned how to focus on what is important to you, and to plan and assess a situation from the start.

Insight

How do you know if you really want your goal?

Imagine an outcome you really desire. What are you 'seeing' and saying to yourself? Describe the emotions you feel. Now imagine not pursuing your goal. The feeling you have now is the difference you will feel between pursuing your goal or shutting down on that desire. Do you still want your goal?

THINGS TO REMEMBER

▶ *You can increase your motivation by changing the way you think.*

▶ *Reflection and self-knowledge will help you to find your motivation.*

▶ *Change your habits and you increase your chances of success.*

▶ *Learning to set well-formed outcomes will put you ahead of 94 per cent of the population who do not think strategically.*

2

Create the life you want

In this chapter you will learn:
- *to recognize beliefs that undermine*
- *to formulate questions that change beliefs*
- *to create your blueprint for success*

'**None of us can change our yesterdays, but we can all change our tomorrows.**'

Colin Powell

We create the life we choose

We create the life we choose, one choice at a time. You may not have decided, 'I want to move to London, meet someone special, get married, split-up and then become unemployed', but if that is where you are at present, you got there through the choices you made: weekly, daily, a moment at a time.

Insight

If what you are doing isn't working, do something different. Act as if you already have the outcome you want. See yourself in the situation and know what the next thing you intend to do is.

Holding negative beliefs about ourselves, our capabilities, the people around us, or how things are in the world can limit our abilities to achieve the successes we dream of attaining in life.

What's more, the limiting beliefs we hold about ourselves may not even be our own; many will have been given to us by the people who influenced us in childhood.

BELIEFS THAT UNDERMINE

Do you know people who hold beliefs about themselves or their abilities that undermine them? What type of things do you hear them say about themselves that reinforce their beliefs? Have they chosen partners or friends who reinforce these ideas for them?

Have you challenged any of the beliefs that you have been carrying with you for a long time? Beliefs that may get in the way of our achievements could include:

- *I'm stupid/scatterbrained/incompetent/not clever enough.*
- *People like me don't run successful businesses/achieve success.*
- *I don't deserve it.*
- *I'm too old/too young/unqualified/I don't know how to do it.*

'If you believe you can, or if you believe you can't – you are probably right.'

Henry Ford

Insight

Work out the key things that are really important to you. Then focus on the few methods that will give you the outcome you want. Who around you is already successful in this area? Observe their strategies and try them out to see if they will work for you. (See Chapter 13, Model success strategies.)

Recognize limiting beliefs

Listed below are some of the commonest beliefs that limit people in their chances of success. Tick any with which you identify, and add any of your beliefs that may have been holding you back from achieving success.

Afraid of failure. I will not strive for what I want because I am not sure whether I will get it.	
Others can get it, but not me. I believe that I don't deserve the things I want in life. I am dependent on what others give me.	
I am too old/young, not pretty enough, not clever enough. My physicalities prevent me from getting the things I want in life.	
I must serve other people's needs before my own. I cannot satisfy my own needs and care for other people at the same time.	
I must not boast about my successes. It will make other people feel bad. I do not want people to envy me.	
I must not take risks. I may lose what I already have.	

(Contd)

I run away when things get tough. I do not have the staying power to see difficult situations through.	
I cannot make my decisions without other people's approval. This can translate to: I could have succeeded but nobody who I look to for approval thought I was good enough.	
I have to do everything myself. I cannot ask other people to help me.	
I must be perfect in everything I do. This can result in procrastination, or finishing the task when it is too late and nobody wants the results any more.	

Write down your limiting beliefs in a list so you can look at ways to challenge them, one by one, and change them to beliefs that will support your aims.

RECOGNIZING SELF-LIMITING TALK

Now here's a limiting belief: 'I can't change'. Another one is: 'It's always been done like this', which implies that something cannot be changed because it's always been the same. Changing your thoughts, behaviour and beliefs one at a time and in small ways is often all that is needed to begin to change your limiting beliefs and to start steering your life in a direction that brings success.

Your beliefs are not carved in stone, you are constantly changing them throughout your life, based on the incoming information you receive. Can you recall the first time someone told you that Santa Claus wasn't real? What did you do? Most children carry on believing until overwhelming evidence triggers disbelief. Child star Shirley Temple said she stopped believing in Santa Claus when she was taken to a department store to meet him and he asked her for her autograph. What other major beliefs have you changed over time?

How do you change beliefs?

How do untidy children, who turn into untidy adolescents, and then tidy adults (well most of them) make that transition? They change their beliefs around tidiness.

An untidy person who wants to tidy up their mess but holds the belief 'I don't know how to tidy up,' or 'Someone else will do it,' will find their progress to becoming tidy will be inhibited. Often simply changing their thinking to be more enabling, such as: 'I am not the sort of person who leaves my mess around for other people to clear up,' or 'I take responsibility for my actions and take control of my environment,' will be the catalyst that launches them into becoming a tidy person.

Insight

To change limiting beliefs, recognize that whatever you think most about is what you get, whether you want it or not. So spend some time considering how you might change your thinking and beliefs to ones that support your dreams.

Initially you might not recognize the actions that lead to 'tidy' – but you have started a chain of thinking events and your brain looks around for comparisons.

People hold beliefs about all sorts of things: Santa Claus, tidiness, religion, work, politics and their own capabilities. Once these beliefs are established, we may never challenge them again, unless there is overwhelming evidence to do so.

Tackle limiting beliefs one phrase at a time, as you hear them. Beliefs that go unchallenged grow roots and become entrenched and harder to dig out.

Afraid of failure

'I will not strive for what I want because I am not sure whether I will get it.'

Many people are held back from achieving their true potential by a fear of failing. Often the fear may be so great that they close the door on all of their dreams. A question that opens up that door is: 'What would you do if you knew you could not fail, if you were successful at everything you tried?' This will often flip people over the threshold of their limitation so they can glimpse new possibilities about how things might be. A powerful alternative is to ask: 'What would you do if you knew it was alright to fail?'

Others can get it, but not me
'I believe that I don't deserve the things I want in life. I am dependent on what others give me.'

Limiting beliefs are like hidden icebergs, 90 per cent of what is going on is below the surface of what people are saying. To raise the belief to the surface, the question to ask is: 'Why is it like that?'

The explanation given might be: 'Because I don't have enough time/money/help.'

To uncover more limitations a good question to ask is: 'How do you know that is true?' Once more of the belief is revealed, you can ask: 'How does you not having X cause Y?'

The explanation will reveal more hidden limitations. Often if you can cite an example of someone else who has achieved what they want with similar restrictions it will be enough to start them thinking about how they might be able to make the change.

I am too old/young, not pretty enough, not clever enough
'My physicalities or abilities prevent me from getting the things I want in life.'

For example:

Sue:	I want to be an actress, but I can't because I am too old.
Question:	How do you know you are too old?

Sue:	Because I do; all the actresses you see on television are young.
Question:	All of the actresses you see on television are young, every single one?
Sue:	Well no, not all of them, but most of them. I just get a feeling that producers want young, sexy actresses.
Question:	Everyone, every single producer, wants young, sexy actresses?
Sue:	Well no, not every single producer, there are parts that call for older people.
Question:	So there are parts that call for older actresses?
Sue:	Well yes, a few …
Question:	Have you seen any …?

People often impose rules on themselves and then act as though the rule is really true. Example: 'People like me don't go to university.' A question that cuts through their judgmental thinking is: 'According to whom? Who says that people like you don't go to university?'

Again, if you can cite one instance where someone in their circumstances did what they claim to be unable to do, it is often enough to re-ignite their thinking processes around how they might overcome their limiting thoughts enough to take action and achieve the things they want. Do not allow your brain to make negative statements about you without challenging it to support the facts.

I must serve other people's needs before my own
'I cannot satisfy my own needs and care for other people at the same time.'

When people imagine a situation to be true in all circumstances they use words like, 'always' and 'never' and may generalize a situation that is particular to them as if it applies to everyone. Example: 'I could never leave my family alone to go to tap dancing classes; I must always be there when they come home.'

To break the generalization you can repeat the words they use as a question: 'You could never leave your family alone, never? Never ever? Not in any circumstances? Not even if you had a baby sitter? Not even if you were having another baby and had to go to hospital?'

Letting people see that there are circumstances in which they may break, or might have already broken, their generalized belief of how a situation should be, may be enough to open up their thinking. There is the possibility that there may be situations where it is okay to change their beliefs in order to satisfy their desires.

I must not take risks
'I may lose what I already have.'

Often when people are afraid of taking risks it is because they are prone to imagining all the terrible things that could go wrong. Asking them to imagine what things would be like if all went beautifully and according to plan can open up new possibilities in their thinking.

Chronic negative thinkers may argue that they could not even imagine themselves taking a risk, let alone actually doing it. To catch them off-guard ask: 'How would it be if you could imagine taking the action?'

In order to answer this question the listener has to imagine doing the task, and will respond with some kind of answer, like: 'Well it might be okay.' At this point ask them to describe the image in more detail.

Get them to tell you how they would do the task, and once you are sure they know what to do, ask: 'And what would doing/getting/being what you want do for you?'

Often this is new territory for people who have never strayed beyond their thinking boundaries, so allow for lots of hesitations, silences and false starts.

I run away when things get tough
'I do not have the staying power to see difficult situations through.'

Ensure you have good rapport with the person to whom you ask this question: 'So you run away when things get tough? Why is that bad for you?' The answer might be: 'People I look up to might be angry with me.'

Ask the question again: 'And why would that be bad for you?' The answer might be: 'I would feel upset because I have let them down.'

Keep asking: 'And why would that be bad for you?' Be prepared to help the person accept the feelings they have uncovered in order to move on and deal with the problem.

I must be perfect in everything I do

This can result in procrastination. The person finishes the task when it is too late and nobody wants the results any more.

Everyone has values which are important to them. Asking them, 'What is important to you about being perfect in everything you do?' will give you an idea of the person's values. An example may be: 'It's important that I do good work, it's just that I don't seem to be able to get it done on time.'

The question to unstick the person could be: 'How would you like to be able to get it done?'

The procrastinator will tell you how to do things on time and list what needs to be changed in order to get things done on time. Feed the information back to them and ask how it would be if they used this process for getting things done on time.

Act as if

Presuppositions are beliefs individuals hold about themselves or others, or how they think situations are in the world. We presuppose that these beliefs are true and act as if they are.

PRACTISE CHANGING 'I CAN'T' TO 'I CAN'

Action

Think of an action that you once believed you couldn't do, but can do now, say riding a bike, roller-skating, swimming, giving a talk or chairing a meeting. How did you feel before you performed the feat? Did you think you would ever do it? What happened to change your thinking from 'I can't do that' to 'I can do that!'?

Think of something you cannot presently do but would like to do. Ask yourself some questions about the actions you need to be able to do in order to achieve it. People often think in absolutes such as 'I can't do that ...' So let's take something that you currently believe you could not do and play with some new questioning strategies to loosen up the language.

Present belief	New question
I can't do that ...	What would happen if you could?
I can't do that yet	What will happen when you can?

Changing your language and moving from 'I can't do that' (an absolute) to 'I can't do that yet', (which presupposes that you can see a time in the future when you can), offers a glimmer of hope. Having freed-up the questions a little, imagine in detail that you have performed the action and answer this question: 'What did I do differently, or what was different about me, that enabled me to do it?'

Insight

Worrying about things that may happen drains mental energy and makes us less effective at dealing with problems. If you are worrying a lot, then either act and don't worry, or decide not to act and don't worry. Constantly worrying and doing nothing is not useful.

The human brain processes both fact and imagined events as real. That is why you can imagine something sad, make an association and start crying, even though you have not experienced the event. In this case your brain may have imagined you were riding a bike, even though you do not yet know how to. You have asked it a question about how you did that and, even though the experience was not real, it will give you the answer you require with all the steps you took and how, and at what point your feelings and beliefs changed in order to perform the task. For someone else who does the same task the process might be different.

Try asking yourself some more questions about your capabilities. You might believe: 'I can't give a presentation in front of people.'

Present belief	New question
It's too difficult.	What would have to happen for it to be easier?

If you relax and listen your brain will tell you what you need in order to make the action seem easier.

It's easier now but ...	And what else would you need to make it even easier than that?

Celebrate your achievements

Have you ever performed a task incredibly well, so well you thought it was achieved by magic? It may have been in school performing a sport, persuading a group of work colleagues to agree to your plan, being heard in difficult circumstances, making a sale to a particularly difficult customer or asking someone for a date. Perhaps you imagined beforehand that you were already in the situation seeing events as they unfolded, hearing the sounds of surprise, excitement, or enjoyment from the others involved, seeing their faces become more animated, and feeling the sort of feelings that you experienced in the actual situation.

> ### *Thought provoker*
> When the event occurred:
>
> ▶ *did it feel as if you were playing your part with ease?*
> ▶ *had you mentally prepared for the event and rehearsed it in your mind?*
> ▶ *were you purposeful in your thoughts, beliefs and behaviour?*
> ▶ *were the people with whom you were interacting aware of this?*

Our behaviour stems from our beliefs. In the above example, you believed in yourself and that you would do whatever you set out to do. The vision of your success is stored in your imagination and body, and you can imagine the event by playing it back in your mind. You may see the event in colour, like watching a movie, and recall each frame in sequence. In your body you may feel the same feelings you felt in synchronicity with the events you saw.

Here is an interesting question to put to yourself: 'If I take all my past memories and images of success, and the bright pictures and strong emotional feelings that are tied up with them, and carry these types of beliefs about my capabilities into the future, – what sort of feats might I be able to achieve if I knew I simply could not fail?'

Beliefs that build success

- *What do you believe to be your most important belief that would lead you to outstanding success?*
- *List three limiting beliefs that have held you back from success up until now?*
- *If you were going to take the first step in challenging one of these limiting beliefs what would it be?*
- *What limiting beliefs do you want to remove now, so that you can move towards your next success?*
- *If you could take one positive belief into the future with you, what would that belief be?*

Getting rid of just one of your limiting thoughts about your capabilities will let you dispose of excess mental baggage and will help you focus on the things you really want in life. As your confidence builds and you are recognized as a motivated person, you will become more attractive to others both financially and emotionally, because people are attracted to confident people with positive energy.

WHAT YOU CAN DO

By building your level of motivation you can make a difference to what you can achieve in the world. Once you successfully obtain the results you want from life every day, your sense of fulfilment and satisfaction will increase and your confidence to reach higher goals will grow.

Acting as if you are already what you want to become, and knowing that you can become that person, is the way to remove self-doubt and enter your real magic kingdom.

Motivational skills wheel

Below are some of the main skills that successful people either have or work hard towards achieving.

1 **Motivating yourself to do things.**
2 **Visualizing.** *Imagining the future and what you want. What does better look like? Harnessing the power of emotions.*
3 **Feeling purposeful.** *Can you remember how you felt in a particular situation and describe how you felt? Do you know how to align your beliefs and values to your purpose?*
4 **Goal setting.** *Do you know how to create well-formed goals?*
5 **Getting rid of procrastination.** *Do you know how to motivate yourself into action?*
6 **Communication skills.** *How good are you at interpersonal skills and understanding how to motivate other people?*
7 **Challenging limiting beliefs.** *How good are you at challenging limiting beliefs that may be holding you back?*
8 **Taking risks to move on.** *Do you have a strategy? Are you prepared to take risks to move closer to your goals?*
9 **Modelling.** *What have you learned from observing successful people's behaviour and its practical applications?*
10 **Time management.** *How good are you at working within time frames and putting things together?*

In Figure 2.1 imagine each spoke of the wheel represents a skill or ability at which motivated people are accomplished. How do you rate your level of competency under each of the headings on a scale of 1 to 10? (Number 1 is at the centre of the wheel and 10 is at the outer rim.) Now draw a dot on each of the spokes to represent your competency level in each of the ten skills. This is only a thumbnail sketch for your own benefit, so don't think too deeply, quickly draw your dots wherever you think they should be. The result should resemble a star with uneven points.

If you have high scores on all skills but there are at least three areas which you feel need improvement, say Visualization, Communication, Modelling and Taking risks, then perhaps it's time to extend your boundaries in a controlled way.

What have you learned about yourself and your particular strengths and weaknesses from doing this overview exercise of

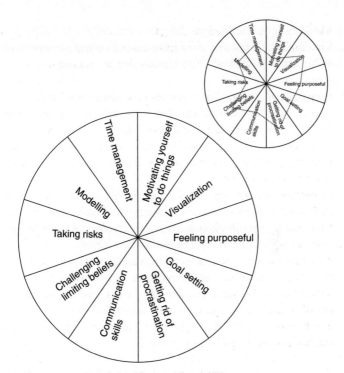

Figure 2.1 The motivational skills wheel: building your skills and abilities.

the ingredients that go towards making your recipe for a highly motivated you?

Insight

Apply the 80/20 principle to your 'blueprint for success'. Often small amounts of energy applied in particular areas give leverage and generate massive returns that lead to the great achievements in our lives.

Create your blueprint for success

You are now armed with your personal assessment of your skills and abilities. Remember, these are only the beliefs you hold about your competencies and may not be wholly accurate. If you're in a negative frame of mind you may have scored yourself lower than you would on a day when you're feeling happy or confident – but it doesn't really matter. Like a visitor who uses a route map to travel on the subway, you now have an overview of the areas you wish to utilize in order to become a successful achiever in the shortest possible time. You can either choose to work on the areas that seem to need most improvement first or read through this book and then decide what to do. It is up to you.

The experience should be enjoyable, so the 'Action' exercises contained in this book are short, but designed to challenge and move you quickly to the next step of your journey and towards your goals. By the time you fill in the motivational skills wheel again, towards the end of the book (see Chapter 20), you will find that your confidence will have grown in several, or maybe in all areas. That is really what motivation is about – having the confidence to act on your dreams.

THINGS TO REMEMBER

▶ *Recognize limiting beliefs that may hold you back from success.*

▶ *Practise questions that challenge limiting beliefs.*

▶ *Use the motivational skills wheel to recognize and build your talents and skills.*

▶ *Develop a lifelong learning habit and constantly update your skills.*

3

Motivation at work

In this chapter you will learn:
- *about matching motivation in the workplace*
- *how values drive us and provide our motivation*
- *to identify what is important to you, using values*

'If you follow what you love, you will be amazed at how often it leads to a job.'

Barbara Sher

Employers increasingly ask for self-starters and self-motivated staff. But how many people can consistently say they understand what motivates them? You may have the qualification for the job, but do you have the right personality? How do you ensure that you display the right degree of enthusiasm, distance or motivation at interviews?

The level of enthusiasm you display about a job should be tempered by what you know about the culture of the organization you want to work for. If you are not an emotional chameleon, how do you ensure you display the appropriate degree of enthusiasm, focus or energy required for the job. The answer is to first know what motivates you, so you can make the right choice of work. Then find out about the emotional culture of the workplace you hope to join.

Insight

If you want to succeed, then do the best you can, wherever you are, and with whatever you have got. Keep your mind open and be alert, not only to take opportunities, but also to make them.

Matching motivation to the workplace

In some industries bosses know that customers like friendly service from staff. So they pick job applicants who best display these emotions, and then capitalize by selling their employees' friendliness as part of the service they provide.

Firms weed out potentially unfriendly staff prior to interview by asking for people who can display suitable emotions. The words 'enthusiastic', 'cheerful', or 'bubbly' in an advert indicate you are going to have to act with enthusiasm at interview. Applicants unable to display suitable emotions for 'have a nice day' organizations will be discouraged from applying by the wording in the advert.

If you can't fake enthusiasm, then consider joining a more muted establishment. Doctors, undertakers and lawyers' practices work to a 'have a neutral day' script. These groups favour the method-acting approach whereby the right words are expressed, but without emotion.

There is a third script, the 'have a rotten day', favoured in areas such as debt collecting where a little table thumping can be a useful attribute. At interviews employers are looking for staff who display signs of irritation. Once in the job, however, employees may be disciplined if they become aggressive, because the trick is to 'act' the emotion, not actually be it.

If the company is large you can find out what the culture is like by visiting other branches. Notice how staff treat you: are they cheerful or sullen?

▶ *Read a job advert and highlight all the desirable adjectives required of applicants. Spend some time acting out each of the attributes listed, such as 'caring', 'enthusiastic', 'positive'. Then construct a little anecdote about each attribute so that you have a ready example of how you are an 'enthusiastic team-player' or a 'cheerful all rounder'.*

▶ *Some jobs, such as court work, demand you distance yourself from clients. At interview pause before answering the question and move your body slightly backwards into your chair to show you are distancing yourself, and reflecting on what's been said. This will indicate that you are unlikely to act impulsively if chosen for the job.*

▶ *If the advert says applicants should be energetic, remember it's hard to fake energy if you haven't got it. Once employed you will have to continue being energetic and smiley, or be labelled a fake.*

▶ *At interview you may be asked how your energy transformed itself into tangible outcomes in your previous jobs, so list six projects you initiated and condense each of them into a couple of sentences.*

Notice in your current environment how colleagues display their emotions. Are you in a 'have a nice day' or a 'have a neutral day' culture? Do the scripts switch depending on whether workmates are talking to clients, colleagues or the boss? If so, then the way staff relate to the boss will give the truest indicator of how things really are. Do you fit in well and are you happy to manage your emotions and relate to clients and colleagues in the way the company requires? If so, you will probably enjoy working in a work culture which requires similar emotions.

If being nice to people at work is an effort and your fake smile keeps wavering, then are you suffering from the strain of holding two inconsistent beliefs, your own and the company's. If you cannot reconcile the two then you are likely to feel angry, emotionally drained, unmotivated, or not see the work you do as being of value, which can lead to minor illnesses or burnout. It may be time to start looking for a job in an environment whose emotional culture fits your personality and values and in which you would feel motivated.

[Motivation at Work, courtesy of *London Evening Standard*,
'Just the Job' © Frances Coombes]

Align your values with the work you do

Insight

The secret of living a meaningful life is to know who you are, and what your values are. Combine this with knowing where you are going in life and have a written blueprint for how you will get there.

Values are the principles which drive our behaviour, they give meaning to our lives. When we engage in what we do with our values then we engage in projects with our hearts and minds.

Our beliefs and values define who we are and what we do. They can be described as the personal rules that we choose to live by. How acquainted are you with your values? Could you list your ten most important values in order of priority?

Values drive us and provide our motivation

We all have unique value systems, although it is likely that your friends and family will share values similar to your own. Once you move outside your close family circle, to your workplace, you will meet people whose values may differ from your own.

Some values are referred to as core values. These are the values that are relevant to the majority of areas of your life. For example, if you have a deeply held religious conviction, this is likely to be a core value in your life. Your core values will affect what you say, what you think and the actions you take. Three people may be asked to take on an identical challenging new job and each one may view the same situation differently, because their personal values inform them differently. The first person might see the situation as a chance to explore new opportunities, the second as a chance to use their creativity, the third person (who values security) may see only all the pitfalls and risks involved.

Values are what make us the way we are, they drive us and provide motivation for how we live our lives. When we know what our values are and are aware of the behaviour that springs from holding those values, we are in a position to set clearer goals and make decisions about what's important to us and what we want in life. Values are the key to living a motivated, successful and rewarding life.

['When did you last check your values?' courtesy of *Positive Health* magazine, [PH] Issue 128, Oct 2006, www.positivehealth.com © Frances Coombes]

Bring your heart to work

IDENTIFY WHAT'S IMPORTANT TO YOU, USING VALUES

Start thinking about the things you value most. Use this list to prompt you and add your own values to it.

achievement	fun	justice	security
adventure	growth	kindness	self-discipline
beauty	happiness	knowledge	self-esteem
charity	health	leadership	service
community	honesty	love	spirituality
creativity	honour	peace	strength
dignity	humility	power	supportiveness
ethics	independence	pride	surrender
family	individuality	reason	trust
freedom	integrity	respect	truth
friendship	intimacy	risk	wisdom

Pick ten values which are most important to you. Beside each one write the reason why this quality is important to you. You might write:

Creativity *Creativity is important to me because ... it lets me express myself.*

Freedom *Freedom is important to me because ... I want the freedom to decide what I do.*

List your values and the reason why they are important to you. If you cannot decide about a particular value, ask yourself the question 'What is important to me about ... in this context (say, *freedom*) in the context of ... (*my career, sport, relationships, life purpose*)?'

▶ *Make a list of the things that are important to you about each value, and then ask the question again: 'What is important to me about ...?' Often when you think you have exhausted the answers new answers appear.*

▶ *Think of a time when you were really motivated, when you were thinking or doing something involving this value. What was it about that situation that motivated you? Add the answers to your list. These are your values.*

▶ *Rank your list of values in order of priority from 1 to 10 and ask of each value, 'Why is that important to me?'. The purpose is to get a sense of whether your motivation and attention for each value is directed to getting more of what you want (towards your goal), or to get away from what you do not want (away from discomfort).*

'Away from' ⟵⟶ 'towards goal'

▶ *If you cannot decide whether you rate one quality over another, write the individual words on pieces of paper and put them face upwards on the palms of each hand. Look at the words on each piece of paper in turn and balance them as if you were using weighing scales until an outright winner emerges.*

▶ *Repeat the procedure with all the pieces of paper until you have your values rated in order of priority.*

What do you value most in life?

There is a scene at the beginning of the film *City of Angels* where a little girl lies ill in a hospital bed. Moments later we see her walking slowly down the corridor holding the hand of an angel. The angel turns to her and asks, 'What was the best bit for you, what did you really enjoy about being alive?'

Action

When did you last think about what means most to you in your life? What are the things that you would fight for, and strive to attain?

Ask yourself these questions:

▶ *What do I really value about my life?*
▶ *What do I really value about the work I do?*
▶ *What do I really value about my relationships?*

Write your answers down so that you can go back, reflect on them, and update them. Motivation is strongest when you move towards what gives you energy, and away from what depletes your energy.

Reflect on each area of your life regularly, and ask:

▶ *What can I do today that excites me and gives me energy?*
▶ *What can I do today that aligns with my beliefs and values?*
▶ *What can I do today that fuels my passions and takes me in the direction of my purpose in life?*

Once you know what your values are the next thing to find out is what actions associated with those values would make you feel you were achieving your life purpose.

Motivation and peak performance

Motivation and peak performance come from knowing what you want to achieve in life. Many of us move through life with a few goals and objectives but without a real sense of purpose. Our goals are often more about what we don't want rather than moving towards the things we do want. We might say we want a better job, partner, or home, but our main wish is to get away from our current situation.

Assumptions to adopt for peak performance

Positive assumption	Reason
If what you are doing is not working, do something else.	If you do what you have always done, you will get what you have always got.
There is no failure, only feedback. What really matters is that you learn from the results.	Whatever occurs, you can use the feedback to change your future behaviour and improve your results.
People have all the resources they need to make changes that will make a difference to their performance.	You already know the answer. There is always something you can do to make a difference and the answer is usually an inner resource.

(Contd)

Positive assumption	Reason
We all have different versions and viewpoints about how we view reality. To build rapport with someone, join them in their world.	We filter information about the world through our senses and each person focuses on different aspects and creates different models of reality.
You cannot change another person, you can only change yourself.	Changing your behaviour will change other people's responses to you.
Visualizing and thinking about the changes you want to make is the first step to making improvements in your life.	Changes start off as thoughts, they are structured and communicated in pictures and words and become actions.

HOW WE REDUCE HAPPINESS

A popular belief is that we must have 'things' to make us happy. When contemplating future goals many people imagine that their goal must happen before they can start to really live. We put conditions on our happiness because we believe that getting the things we want is dependent on other people and events which are outside our control.

HOW WE DEFER OUR HAPPINESS

We begin the cycle of deferred happiness by thinking 'I will be happy when ...'.

- ▶ *I will be happy when I meet the right person.*
- ▶ *I will be happy when I get the job I want.*
- ▶ *I will be happy when I get the right car, television, house.*
- ▶ *I will be happy when I am immensely rich and successful.*

Make up your mind to be happy today, and then use your energy and motivation to work towards this point.

OUR ACTIONS STEM FROM THE MENTAL PICTURES WE RUN

The images we repeatedly run in our mind's eye, and the words we constantly repeat to ourselves create our mental maps of the world.

If we have a scarcity mentality then we dwell on images of what is lacking in our lives. We invest our mental energy into what we don't have and our experience of life is 'I don't have enough … (love/money/time/energy)', because our mind is caught up in what is missing.

People who see positive images in their mind will look for and expect good things to happen and notice and remark on it when it does. Their mind is caught up with what is positive and abundant in their lives.

Our actions come from the pictures we run in our minds most often. Many people believe they do not have control over what images they see, or the thoughts that they think, and thus they are not in control of their lives. But we can change our perceptions of the world by changing the way we choose to view it, and once we do this we can begin to create our future circumstances.

Mental rehearsal trains the mind

Mental rehearsal prepares you for events and trains your unconscious mind to perform tasks in a predetermined way. Most physical tasks, such as breathing, walking, driving a car, are carried out unconsciously, once the initial preparation work of learning has been done. By mentally rehearsing future successful outcomes you are communicating with your mind through pictures, inner dialogue, feelings, tastes and smells, and building up patterns about how events will play out.

STRENGTHEN YOUR MENTAL SUCCESS PATTERNS

When we hear a few bars of familiar music and we want to jump up and dance we have anchored a behavioural response to a sensory stimulus. The Russian scientist Pavlov was able to demonstrate the same effect with dogs. He trained them to associate the dinner bell with food, and when he rang it without giving food the dogs would salivate in expectation.

We anchor memories throughout our lives. An anchor is any stimulus that changes your state. It can be evoked through any of the senses, a smell, a sight, hearing a snatch of music, that creates an association in your senses and give you a familiar feeling. You may imagine a baby sleeping, its smile, its smell and warmth, and feel protective and loving. A smell of a particular soap or perfume may evoke strong memories of people or places you have known and loved. An anchor is a stimulus that leads to a response.

ANCHOR A GOOD FEELING

To anchor a feeling, say of confidence, think back to a past experience when you did something really well. You felt confident, and motivated and powerful, the way you would like to feel in the future.

USING ANCHORS

You can use anchors to put yourself in a good state before an interview, presentation or exam, in fact any situation where you need to feel confident and good about yourself. By thinking of a time when you were at your best, it will make you feel more confident and ready to handle the next challenge you meet. Think about what makes you feel successful and in a really confident state.

How to use an anchor

▶ *Think of a time when you felt really confident.*
▶ *Now close your eyes and relive that experience. What were you seeing, hearing, feeling?*
▶ *What were you saying to yourself? What did you notice?*

Take responsibility for making things happen

With peak performance comes taking responsibility for making things happen. It involves living your life by creating your future stance rather than drifting through life and reacting to situations that happen to you. People who have high levels of personal mastery continually expand their ability to create the results in life they want to achieve.

TAKE A COURSE IN PERSONAL MASTERY

Reflect upon how much of what you do is based on randomness? How much of what you do is done on purpose? How often do you hear yourself say 'the opportunity came up so I took it'?

▶ *Do you set objectives in isolation that are unconnected to any other goals?*
▶ *Do you set objectives that are based on living your purpose?*
▶ *Are all of your goals in alignment and are they moving towards your purpose?*

Clarify your purpose

The following questions will help you to clarify your
definition of purpose. Write two or three sentences in
answer to each question.

▶ *What things are you good at, things that energize you?*
▶ *What type of life do you want to lead?*
▶ *What type of work creates positive energy in you?*
▶ *Do you use the skills you are most passionate about in
your work?*

Does what you are doing fit?

Many people are capable of doing much more than their
work demands, but they stagnate where they are because
they are afraid to challenge themselves to live their life
more purposefully.

▶ *What risks are you prepared to take to achieve the things
you want?*
▶ *How will what you do affect people around you?*
▶ *Do you have active goals that relate to your purpose?*

Most goals involve taking some actions, so it is good to have a plan of
where you want to be and how you intend to get there. Some people
like to plan each part of the process, others prefer the intuitive
approach, getting clear about the goal and then trusting their
impulses to get them there. It helps if you always know what your
next step towards achieving your goal will be.

To improve your chances of being successful at whatever you do, go back to the motivational wheel you drew in Chapter 2 and think about what you need to change to improve the segments where scores are below 6 or 7. Whatever skills you need to develop, plan a process that will get you there.

You have the power to change your thinking

You have the power to change your thinking at will. You can change your thoughts now in order to achieve the feelings you want to have when you have achieved your goal. The idea is to bring those feelings from the future forwards so you are feeling them right now, before you have achieved your success.

Do everything in your power to bring these feelings closer to you now. If you want to own a gleaming red Ferrari then go to a showroom and ask to have a test drive. Feel the upholstery against your body, smell the newness of the car, caress the steering wheel and enjoy the sensations as your fingers tingle with excitement. Harness the emotions you experience that come with handling this expensive car.

FEEL GOOD, BEFORE YOU ACHIEVE YOUR OUTCOME

Think about a particular goal you want to achieve. It might be 'I want to become the best person that anyone could choose to hire in my particular area of expertise'.

Now imagine that you already are that person: feel it, see it, hear it.

▶ *What are the extra qualities you, as your successful future self, possess that may not have been present before?*

▶ *What extra skills have you acquired, and why?*
▶ *Write down three main new beliefs you are holding about your future self and your abilities that make you feel happy and assured of your future success.*

Start with a simple statement, for example:

'Clients/jobs/partners/breaks in life (whatever it is for you) are easy to come by because I have these beliefs or qualities ...'

Tell yourself that it is true, and then listen to your inner voice and gather evidence to support your belief. For example, 'I know that I am a fabulous therapist, the best that anyone could possibly have because ...'. Then listen and gather information from your subconscious about the sort of behaviour, capabilities and beliefs that you would need to support what you have said.

FEEL GOOD NOW

Tell yourself: 'I want to feel good now, and this is how I am changing my thinking in order to do so.' Select the new beliefs to hold about your fabulous self and repeat them to yourself each day. For example:

▶ *I feel happier because all tasks are easy and they don't take long to do now that I have developed easy strategies for doing them.*
▶ *I trust my subconscious to be working for me.*
▶ *I know that new work/clients/jobs are easy to come by.*

You will be amazed at how this exercise helps your confidence grow. Make up your mind to be happy now, see what you will see, hear what you will hear, luxuriate in the experience of feeling the feelings you will have when you have already achieved the outcomes you want. The more easily you can experience and visualize the things you want the more easy it is to attract these experiences into your life.

THINGS TO REMEMBER

▶ *Match your motivation to your work.*

▶ *Align your values to the work you do.*

▶ *Values are what drive you, give you passion, and provide your motivation in life.*

▶ *Use values as your motivational drivers to achieve motivation and peak performance.*

▶ *Mental rehearsal trains the mind.*

▶ *Take responsibility for making things happen.*

4

Create a compelling future

In this chapter you will learn:
- **success has a structure**
- **the metaphors of success**
- **about imagination and getting good ideas**

> 'Imagination is the beginning of creation. You imagine what you desire; you will what you imagine; and at last you create what you will.'
>
> George Bernard Shaw

'Dream it – then do it!' This may sound simplistic, but that is exactly how we determine our level of achievement. We imagine vividly the things we want to achieve and then take the actions that propel us towards our goals.

Your level of motivation is the key to success in every area of your life. The more frequently you see yourself achieving the things you aim for, the more likely you are to achieve them and to picture yourself as a winner.

Insight

Your success depends upon:

- ▸ *the things you choose to focus on in life*
- ▸ *the meaning or interpretation you put upon the information you receive*
- ▸ *the action you take as a result of processing that information.*

Six habits that lead to success

This is a model of the principles for success, taken from neuro-linguistic programming (NLP), studies of human achievement and the behaviour that goes with attainment.

1 **Start with the end in mind.** *Always know your outcome before you start any project. If you can define your outcome appropriately, and know all the necessary steps to achieving it, you are more likely to reach your goal.*
2 **Use your eyes and senses.** *We take in information about the world through our senses: what we see, hear, feel, taste and touch. Sharpen your sensory acuity to notice small subtle changes, so you sense what is going on more acutely.*
3 **If what you are doing is not working – try something else.** *Take notice of the feedback you receive through your senses so that you get a fuller picture and feedback of what is going on. Be flexible and prepared to change your behaviour and do whatever is necessary to achieve a successful outcome.*
4 **Build and maintain rapport with yourself and others.** *Notice what is going on within you, how you feel about the things you want to achieve, what fires you up, or dampens you down. Build rapport with others and sense the changes in them. Create a relationship of trust and co-operation.*
5 **Operate from a state of excellence.** *By heightening your sensory awareness, planning your outcome, building rapport, and being prepared to change your behaviour to get what you want, you are operating from a totally resourceful state. Boost your confidence by starting with small objectives that you can easily achieve and build up to bigger goals gradually. Do things that will empower you so that you become familiar with picturing yourself as a winner.*

6 Take action. *Without action there are no results. An idea is only a notion, unless an action happens.*

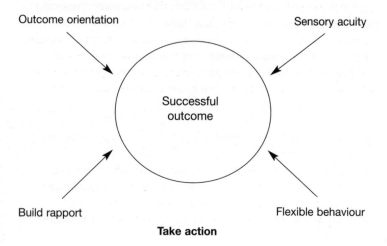

Figure 4.1 Six habits that lead to success.

Summary

▸ Start with the end in mind. Always know what you want.
▸ Build good relationships with people and yourself.
▸ Be flexible and generate lots of different types of behaviours until you get the responses you want.
▸ Notice when you get the responses you want.

If you adopt this behaviour you will achieve the things you want.

How to use constructive feedback

Using these operating principles of NLP will give you constant feedback on your behaviour, and whether what you are doing is achieving the results you want. Take note of all feedback you receive and ask yourself how you can improve your performance and avoid any unwanted happenings next time. Isolate the behaviour or actions you took that did not serve your purpose, and plan what might work better in the same circumstances.

Case study – Joan Cross

Joan Cross, a freelance feature writer, wanted to break into a new newspaper market. She put up ideas to her target editor on the phone and then listened to the response. Using the operating principles for success she:

▶ **started with her aim in mind.** *She went in with the intention of selling her ideas, had an outline of the feature, the slant and the names of people she intended to interview.*
▶ **built a good relationship with the editor,** *by being alert, attentive and sticking to the point.*
▶ **was flexible and generated lots of different ideas.** *Editors live in an ideas vacuum, so she always had at least three different feature ideas ready, and if one idea did not find favour, then she had another one ready for editorial consideration. She was ready to change the article to take account of the editor's ideas for how a feature should look, and to change interviewees depending on the editor's choices.*
▶ **noticed when she achieved the responses she wanted.** *Over a couple of phone calls she began to recognize how the editor preferred to be approached. She achieved several commissions by: noticing that the editor liked her to comment on or praise some aspect of the newspaper*

(Contd)

section's content; stating when she would get back in touch with the editor; stating who she would use for case studies. In order to remember, Joan wrote down the criteria for achieving good results and consulted it before making each phone call.

Believe that what you want is possible

Define exactly what works for you and do more of it. Keep a record of the behaviour that serves you well and use it as a template for future success.

Notice small details in your own and other people's behaviour. It is not enough for someone to say 'I know I can do that'; always ask, 'How do you know you can do that? What are you seeing, feeling, saying to yourself that lets you know you can do it?' Build up a sense of the events and sequences people need to imagine, feel and hear in order to know whether they can or cannot do something. If you know exactly how someone else does something excellently that you would like to do, you can take that knowledge and model their behaviour so you get the same results.

Insight

The greatest gift you can give yourself is to allow yourself to dream. The actress Whoopi Goldberg had no screen role models to copy when, as a child, she imagined herself a movie actress. From an early age she visualized herself being a successful movie star. She stayed constant to her dream and became a movie star.

Visualize to create a compelling future

Visualization is the act of creating compelling and vivid pictures in your mind. When we constantly visualize achieving our goals:

- *we focus on our outcome and our brain becomes attuned to notice available resources*
- *we attract others to us, who bring the opportunities and resources we need to achieve our goals*
- *we enhance our performance.*

We dream about the things we want to achieve and then take the necessary actions that propel us towards our goals. The more frequently you see yourself achieving your goals the more likely you are to achieve them and to see yourself as a winner.

Being successful at reaching your goals is the biggest and most important gift you can give yourself. By increasing your imaginative abilities to build strong visual images of whatever you want to achieve, you are more likely to get it.

Anchor a positive state

Most people can associate with different states and feelings at will. All it takes to trigger their mental movie is to say to them, 'remember when … we went to the party/stayed out all night/got lost on the way to cousin Delia's wedding?' and they will do the rest themselves.

Notice how people's eyes will fix on a spot where they see the events happening? It is as if they are in a trance. Their shoulders will crumple, their breathing slows down as they relive the emotions they felt that first time. You can choose a ritual like this for you, linked to success. Use it as a trigger to recall a time when you felt truly alive and powerful, when everything you did seemed like magic.

- *Think of a personal moment of success that you have experienced and vividly run through the events several times in your mind.*
- *Associate with those feelings and notice what you see. Are there events happening which bring those pictures near? Notice what you feel; are you excited, buzzing, on a high?*

What does it feel like for you? What can you hear going on around you? Are people talking or listening?

▶ *When you feel at the height of your experience freeze-frame a mental snapshot of what is going on.*

▶ *Use a signal, such as pressing your middle finger and thumb together as a trigger to anchor that feeling at its height of intensity, so that you can recall the picture at will whenever you want to, and get the good feeling when you touch your fingers together.*

In the future, by repeating the finger pressing action, you will be able to summon up your successful state, picture and feelings at any time you want to feel powerful, successful and in control.

Successful people, regardless of their areas of achievement, have patterns of motivation and behaviour which they display in order to reach their aim.

▶ *They decide what they want to accomplish.*

▶ *They focus on its attainment, and visualize the possession, recognition and acclaim they will receive, and how they will feel when they have realized their dream.*

▶ *They believe that the outcome they want to achieve is possible.*

▶ *They take the actions necessary to reach their goal.*

Generate good ideas

Insight

Educators and employers tend to ignore that people do a great deal of learning outside the educational system. This prevents employers and society from harnessing the creative ideas which employees could contribute to business and social life.

Good ideas don't just come to a few gifted people: they are free to anyone who is prepared to put their minds to work and imagine how they will create their dreams. They will calculate their odds of winning at whatever they want to achieve and the type of skills and talents that they will require to reach their goal, and who they will need to help them on their way. The bigger the dream the more likely it is that they will need to inspire other people to help them reach their target.

BUILD A SHARED DREAM

Successful people in many fields use imaging. Effective leaders in industry, sport, politics and anywhere where team effort is required seek to influence their teams by their actions and words. To motivate others successfully they need to have energy and a good image of themselves as winners, and to convey the excitement and challenge of what they are doing to engage their workforce, the foot soldiers responsible for making success happen.

Motivators often define their aims by using a shared vision or metaphor of what it looks or feels like while they are engaging in the activity that makes them successful. This shorthand description of how their leader sees success enables team members to recognize instantly what it feels like when they are acting effectively in pursuit of team goals.

Here is part of an interview with a successful businessman talking about his company. Notice that as he talks he also shares his visions of how he sees success.

Case study – inspirational voice

38-year-old Neil Gandhi, vice president of sales at Attenda, a web design company currently spearheading its way into Europe, has had a phenomenal success in selling. When I asked him why he was successful in business he spread his hands high in the air in front of him and said 'I believe it's all out there – you've just got to go out there and get it.'
(Contd)

At 21, Gandhi recognized the potential for busines-to-business mail order computer systems and set up his first company, Elite Computer Systems. By the age of 24, he had sold the company and moved to Wordperfect in a channel marketing role. Neil says, 'Wordperfect wanted someone with energy and the ability to make a deal and I had that. I was responsible for £20 million revenues when I arrived and turnover was about £40 million when I left. The market was growing massively at the time, demand for Wordperfect was huge. Selling in a market that's going up is like riding a wave.'

'The channel marketing role was all about having masses of energy and it worked perfectly for me. I created a pull-through effect, ensuring that our products were always in customers' thoughts. I spent each day on one of the huge sales floors with 200 telesales agents, motivating the sales force to sell our products.'

[Courtesy of MPMG Ltd, *Sales Director* magazine, © Frances Coombes]

Notice how Neil sees success as something 'out there' – as if he can reach up and pluck it from the air. He uses a sporting metaphor to describe the way he feels success: it's like 'riding a wave'. Motivating 200 people on a sales floor is nothing like surfing waves, but he is giving us an insight into how he feels when he is doing something successfully. People tend to use descriptive language like this when they are describing events that are magical or heightened experiences for them.

What you see repeatedly in your mind's eye is what you tend to achieve. If you see yourself as successful then you become it. However, imaging is not a substitute for action but a supplement to it. You can visualize yourself being a pop star or world-class athlete, yet unless you also take the follow-through actions towards it, nothing is going to happen.

LOOK FOR THE METAPHORS IN LANGUAGE

Metaphors are words and stories that people use to describe the way things are, and how they view the world. To know how people view a situation and organize their lives listen to the metaphors they attach to what they are describing. Metaphors contain the structure of how we view our obstacles and desires.

Thought provoker

Look for the metaphors, the descriptive words, that people use to see how they view situations because this will tell you what their inner world looks like:

▶ 'It's a piece of cake' – they think something is easy to do.
▶ 'It's a minefield' – they see the situation as dangerous and believe that unexpected difficulties are likely to arise.
▶ 'With a good wind behind us' – provided there are no unexpected happenings they feel they are likely to achieve their aims.
▶ 'I feel blocked' or, 'hemmed in' – they feel there are almost physical objects standing in the way of what they want to do.
▶ 'I feel on top of the world' – they feel really great, as if they are standing on top of the situation.
▶ 'I can't get around it/over it/under it/through it' – these descriptions all illustrate that they feel there to be a block or barrier between where they are now and whatever they want to achieve.

METAPHORS OF SUCCESS

If you want a snapshot of how a person sees the world, listen for the little personal metaphors they include when they describe an action, an event or the world as being like something else. This tells you what things feel like to them. We've seen how one person thinks who is motivated and successful in his career. Let's turn the spotlight on you and look at the images you convey to yourself and other people about how you view your world. Do this quickly – it should take only a few seconds.

Action

Forrest Gump, in the film of that name (1994), said his mother always said that 'Life is like a box of chocolates, you never know what you are going to get next ...'. What is your shorthand metaphor for life? Quickly and without thinking finish the sentence with the first words that leap into your mind: 'Life is like ...' Don't cheat, it must be the first, not the second or third idea that comes into your mind.

If you said life is like a 'battlefield' then we might assume that you see continual conflict in your life. People give all sorts of descriptions for this, some see their world as being 'orchestrated by a conductor', 'one long holiday', 'a nightmare', 'like a roller coaster' or 'full of wonder'. These people could all be sharing the same office but still have completely different ways of interpreting the incoming information they receive from their surroundings, based on how their individual models of the world work.

What is your metaphor for life?

Write your description in the shapes below.

In the shape below write your metaphor/description that encapsulates how you feel your life is right now.

A nightmare/An adventure
(What sort of adventure?)

A journey/A game
(What sort of game?)

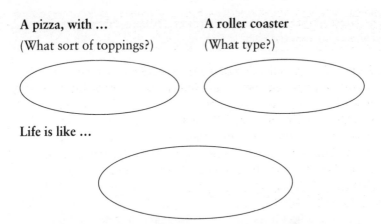

A pizza, with ...
(What sort of toppings?)

A roller coaster
(What type?)

Life is like ...

Now write your description of how you would like your life to be.

Life is like a ... with lots of ... and ....

What are the main things you want in your life?

List three actions you could do today if you really wanted to make your new metaphor/description a reality.

1

2

3

Have you come any closer to recognizing the recipe for exactly how you would like your life to be?

We experience life through five senses: what we see, hear, smell, feel and taste. Each of us perceives the world and reality differently, according to how we absorb information, organize it, and filter it in ways that are meaningful to us. We all use self-talk and imagery to describe what we think is happening around us. We look for and filter what we want to see and minimize what we do not want to see.

Have you noticed how if you've bought a particular make of car you suddenly start to see lots of the same type of car, or if you've just had a baby you start to notice babies? There are not suddenly more cars or babies, but your brain is now searching for them.

The effect of this type of information filtering is that you get more of what you expect to get.

To free up your thinking and find unexpected and better solutions, change the type of words you use to describe a situation.

The following are phrases and words people commonly use. Read the column that describes difficulties and, if you use any of these words, work out how you could employ the word in the desired state column (i.e. 'solution' instead of 'problem') when you construct a sentence.

To describe difficulties	To describe a desired state
problem	solution
blocked	freed-up
gone into torpor	fast moving
confused	focused
I'm feeling down	I'm high
barrier	breakthrough

Thought provoker

If you woke up tomorrow and decided to change your metaphor for life to just the way you wanted it to be, what would you change it to? Think quickly, don't censor. Simply write it down and say it out loud – change it until you hear it and know it suits you: 'I would like my life to be like ...'.

Can you see how changing your metaphor for life from an image of a 'battlefield' to one of 'a place with unlimited opportunities', or 'full of friendly faces' could change how you view the world, connect to other people and how you make decisions in it?

TRY ON OTHER PEOPLE'S METAPHORS FOR SUCCESS

Listen for the descriptions that people give for when they are performing at their best. Collect a list of the expressions that please you.

Write some descriptions of what you are like when you are at your personal best, for example:

▸ *When I'm doing what I'm good at, it's as easy as slicing butter with a hot knife.*
▸ *I make things happen by taking actions.*
▸ *If someone else can do it so can I.*
▸ *To win more, I'm prepared to fail more.*

This next exercise is to construct a strong visual image and imagine how success looks and feels, and what it sounds like to you.

CREATING GOOD IDEAS

Before you can make your visions a reality, you have to create some good ideas that align with the sorts of things that others want and which are currently in demand. We create our ideas by thinking about what often seem like problems and imagining how we might resolve them. Solutions usually come after people have done the necessary preparation and have gathered information around the subject.

If history is correct, then evolution does not seem to have changed our thinking processes or the way we achieve our creative breakthroughs. First we have a problem to solve and we worry about it and think of all the possible permutations for solving it that we can. Then when our mind is idling, we make the imaginative leaps that lead to a solution.

▸ *In the third century BC, Archimedes had his 'eureka' moment while getting into the bath. The King of Syracuse, Hiero, asked him to find out if the newly commissioned royal crown was made of pure gold or had been substituted with a less valuable metal. As he relaxed and stepped into his bath, Archimedes noticed that his bodyweight displaced an exact amount of water and the idea struck him that a solid gold crown would have an exact weight as well. Archimedes was* so thrilled by his discovery that he became the world's first documented streaker when he took to the streets shouting 'eureka'.

▶ On a warm afternoon in 1667, Sir Isaac Newton was sitting under the shade of some apple trees. He had just eaten, had a few drinks and was feeling in a 'contemplative mood', when an apple fell to the ground and the notion of gravity struck him.

▶ Kekule hit on his molecular architecture in 1858 as he relaxed and dozed in front of the fire. He dreamed of snakes made out of long rows of atoms. Suddenly one snake seized hold of its own tail and Kekule woke up with the beginning of the theory of the benzene ring.

In a study, 200 scientists were asked if a solution to a problem they were thinking about had ever just popped into their heads – nearly 85 per cent said 'yes'. It usually happened when they were away from the problem.

When it comes to really brilliant ideas, it seems that purely rational thinking can lead only so far. When you have collected and sifted all the relevant information, there comes a point when you deliberately need to distance yourself from the problem, switch off and wait for the imaginative leap. The imaginative leap is not just finding the solution to a problem; with it comes an unshakeable belief that something that could not be done before can now be done.

Imagine it, then do it

Believing that something can be done sets the wheels in motion to find a way to achieve it. Until Roger Bannister ran the four-minute mile in 1954 nobody believed a human being could possibly run so fast; it was believed to be medically unsafe. In the same year that Bannister achieved his dream, 30 other athletes broke the four-minute mile record – simply because they now had evidence and believed that it could be done. Our beliefs, which are not necessarily reality, determine what we can and cannot do.

Do you have dreams that you would like to achieve that you presently think are impossible? Why not allow yourself some time to dream about them? Is it worth spending ten minutes to examine whether some of the things you secretly desire might just be achievable? After all, you have nothing to lose.

Action

Think of something special you would really like to achieve, but feel you can't. Write it down. Suspend judgement of yourself and your capabilities and spend ten minutes of completely uncensored fun just listing all the reasons why you know that you are the person to do this thing.

Changing beliefs from can't to can

Can't ----------------X----------------X--------------- Can
                              Belief

▶ *If you have a skill even remotely linked to what you want to do, maybe one that could be developed, write it down.*

▶ *If you are in a unique position to have knowledge about this thing, say because it's in your workplace, write it down.*

▶ *If you believe that you could achieve your aim if only you believed more strongly, write it down.*

▶ *If you know what would have to happen to convince yourself you could do it – write it down.*

▶ *If you know people who could help you, it doesn't matter whether you think they would or not, write it down.*

▶ *If you know some or all of the steps you would have to take to achieve your goal, write them down.*

Has your thinking changed about reaching that goal? Do you feel in any way that your outcome might be closer and more possible now? Sometimes people who do this exercise come up with an idea completely different from the one they originally thought of.

THINGS TO REMEMBER

▶ *Follow the six habits that lead to success.*

▶ *Use constructive feedback to improve your performance.*

▶ *Discover your metaphor for life – and if necessary, change it.*

▶ *The secret is in imagining – dream it, then do it.*

Incentives to produce good ideas

In this chapter you will learn:
- *how to understand the creative process*
- *about brainstorming*
- *about the creative process*
- *how to boost your creativity*

> **'You can dream, design and build the most wonderful place in the world, but it requires people to make that dream a reality.'**
>
> Walt Disney

Motivate others to generate good ideas

Insight

What worked yesterday for businesses, and brought in customers, sales and a comfortable lifestyle, may not work today. Companies are waking up to the fact that buildings and stocks may no longer be their biggest assets to their economic wealth – instead it will be the creative thinking capacity of their people.

Ideas are ephemeral – like butterflies, they flit through our minds, and if we do not have a net standing by to catch them then they fly away. Andrew Wood is an ideas catcher, who shows companies how to net employees' good ideas. He has spotted the potential revenue companies forego when they lose out on workers' innovative ways of thinking.

Wood was a founder member and past chairman of the United Kingdom Association of Suggestion Schemes, a British ideas' management and employee-recognition initiative. In its heyday, member companies made savings in excess of £300 million a year, by harnessing the bright ideas of staff and using them in the workplace. He now splits his time between the UK and the United States advising, setting up and running idea-management schemes around the world.

Wood says: 'German employers are keen to recognize their employees' innovative ideas. About 600 of the largest companies, such as Mercedes, Porsche, Volkswagon and BMW, run schemes. Ideas are sent to headquarters and are scrutinized by a centralized team of managers who receive ongoing training on trends and evaluation methods. German staff prefer payment for their ideas, so recognition is heavily geared towards financial awards.

'European companies give prizes of 15 to 25 per cent of first-year savings made from an implemented idea, whereas in North America and the UK, cash awards tend to be 10 per cent.'

IDEAS THAT TAKE OFF

Case study

The highly successful British Airways Brainwaves scheme staff awards are based on financial savings, or the impact of ideas on customer care or employee awareness. In one year the scheme received 800 staff ideas, implemented 12 per cent, and made savings of £5.5 million. An idea from cargo agent Geoffrey Hall, which reduced manual handling of cargo at Gatwick, netted him a certificate and an award of £10,000, based on annual savings of £175,000.

Andrew Wood says: 'British bosses use the North American approach of tiered schemes, where departmental managers pick up little ideas that make everyday things better, and implement them straight away. Potentially big ideas will be routed to the main organization or research and development team.

'American employers favour non-monetary motivators, such as staff-recognition awards with lots of hand clapping and razzmatazz – which doesn't work with British staff.'

British bosses opt for giving workers lunch, theatre tickets or tickets for sporting activities, plus financial awards.

In the Middle East, workers get only two weeks' holiday, and many prefer an award of several days' leave, so they can extend visits to relatives.

Wood advises: 'The award has to be something that workers want, otherwise they won't participate and employers lose out on potentially big ideas.'

Incentive awards

Case study

Julian Richer's hi-fi chain Richer Sounds is the most prolific company in the UK for creative staff suggestions. Each employee averages 20 ideas a year, and 60 per cent are used. Small motivational awards, up to £25, can be made and suggestions implemented immediately. Ideas such as: 'We should install door bells at wheelchair height for disabled customers', may not save money, but contribute to customer service.

Andrew Wood comments: 'The most critical success factor in any scheme, is having top management support. The chief executive turning up to shake the winner's hand is not enough.' In one finance business's scheme run by Wood, managers' performance is linked to how many ideas they get from their staff, and implement. Wood says: 'They get far more suggestions than most organizations do, per employee, and the implementation rate is high. Staff get points that build to different sorts of awards. At the end of the year, they can spend £700 at Christmas because they've amassed the points on, say, 60 suggestions.'

What motivates staff to submit ideas?

Siemens, the giant Munich-based electronics company, surveyed its staff to find out what motivated them to submit ideas. The results were:

- *'It's an opportunity to improve or help implement something.' (29 per cent)*
- *'To ensure my own workplace security.' (24 per cent)*
- *'To get an award.' (15 per cent)*
- *'For someone to pay attention to my idea.' (13 per cent)*
- *'To implement an idea without my supervisor's agreement.' (9 per cent)*
- *'To receive recognition.' (4 per cent)*
- *'To participate in special lotteries and raffles,' and 'additional awards for team suggestions.' (2 per cent)*
- *'Responding to the encouragement of my supervisor.' (1 per cent)*

[Courtesy of *London Evening Standard*, 'Just the Job',
© Frances Coombes]

'There is really nothing elusive or mysterious about creativity. Anyone who can talk is able to write. Anyone who can see is able to visualize. And anyone who can think is able to have ideas.'

Stephen Baker

IDEAS COME FROM ASSOCIATION AND COMBINATION

Most of the ideas we get are not new, they come from associating different aspects of products, inventions and ideas produced by other people and putting them together in a way that is novel. Often the environment in which people work can be a hotbed for creative, inventive and imaginative ideas because people on the shopfloor can see exactly what the problems are.

▶ *Shirley Langridge, a Post Office counters section worker, was concerned that queues were building up because short-sighted pensioners were forgetting their glasses. She came up with the simple but effective idea of introducing magnifying sheets in post offices attached to counters so that short-sighted people could see to fill in forms.*

▶ *Two Royal Air Force electricians, Martin Childs and Steve McBride, found a way to save the RAF £500,000 a year in time spent sucking out fuel from aircraft during routine maintenance. They found a way to reverse the aircraft's refuelling capability to suck out fuel by disconnecting only one wire in the aircraft's complex electrical system. Now the once lengthy fuel-draining procedure for Tornado fighter bombers can be completed in minutes.*

▶ *Philip Barnes-Warden, a uniform services' support manager with the Metropolitan Police suggested recycling old police uniforms. The idea was taken onboard and now a recycling company provides a textile skip; clothes are sent to developing countries or recycled into padding for the motor industry. In addition to the annual savings of £12,000 on skip hire, the Met receives £65 per tonne from a recycling company for the clothing collected – which generates £6,500 a year.*

▶ *Detective Constable Steve Hobson, a community safety officer for Greater Manchester Police, came up with an idea for a safety video for people with learning difficulties, which has gone on sale throughout Australia, New Zealand and the South Pacific countries. He says: 'I get a real buzz out of coming up with ideas and seeing them actually come to fruition.' He has also come up with an idea for another video called Forceful Ideas which gives students advice on how to stay safe in the city. It tells them how to use products such as personal alarms which can be stretched across the back of a bedroom door and which automatically sound if an intruder breaks the seal by opening the door.*

'Never underestimate the value of luck, but remember that luck comes to those searching for something.'

Stanley Marcus

DO SOMETHING DIFFERENT

Case study – Jurgen Wolff

Script writer Jurgen Wolff wanted his scripts to be accepted. At a time when other writers who were looking for work attended writers' events and met other writers, he thought of the maxim 'Birds of a feather flock together'. If he wanted his scripts to be accepted he knew that, rather than networking with other writers who were also seeking commissions, he needed to associate with producers who were searching for scripts.

He joined producers' associations and has since written scripts for American sit-coms and a film called *The Real Howard Spitz*. Wolff produces a free monthly internet bulletin called Brainwaves that gives insight into how he and other people have used simple yet effective ways of creative thinking to achieve their desired outcomes.

Wolff says: 'Be persistent and don't let rejections get you down. It is not the number of times you get rejected that matters, it is the number of times you get accepted.'

Consult your ever-present experts

Take note of clever people's thinking strategies. Jurgen Wolff's strategy for tackling a new situation, or working out how someone else has produced theirs, is to notice what works for that person and break it down into:

- ▶ *problem*
- ▶ *strategy used to get a solution*
- ▶ *final outcome of using the strategy*
- ▶ *lessons learned from going through the strategy*
- ▶ *questions to ask yourself when looking for a solution*
- ▶ *tips for getting past the barrier.*

Wolff believes that one of the most neglected techniques for achieving the things you want is to ask for them. He says: 'The worst thing that will happen is that people will say "no".'

GENERATING IDEAS TO SOLVE PROBLEMS

Stimulate new ideas and fresh creative insights:

- ▶ *Talk to people and see what they suggest. Often you will not be the only person with this problem.*
- ▶ *Describe the problem in another way.*
- ▶ *Decide what is the most important and real issue by constantly asking, 'why is that so?'*
- ▶ *Listen to experts: what would they do?*

Thought provoker

Imagine you have a team of experts, at least four, and put the problem to each person to see what they say. You could have, for example:

- ▶ *Mr Spock, from the Star Ship Enterprise, who has come from another planet*
- ▶ *Lieutenant Colombo, a police detective*

It is a good creative idea to keep a store of other people's thinking habits, and use a variety of them for problem solving to see which work best. Something that will help you to do this is the spider diagram. This helps you to pool ideas and generate lots of thoughts on a topic.

SPIDER DIAGRAMS

Spider diagrams (Figure 5.1) mirror the way the brain works, making use of linking and associations of ideas, and grouping them together for ease of use. Ideas are easier to recall because they are displayed visually on one sheet of paper. Different aspects of a subject can be colour co-ordinated for easy reference.

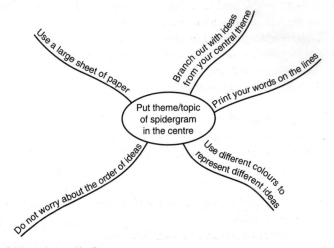

Figure 5.1 How to draw a spider diagram.

The advantages of this method over listing ideas is that each tentacle of the diagram can be extended and built upon, so new ideas fit in easily. Links between similar ideas are easier to see. Having a one-page spider diagram can give you a 'big picture' overview of a whole situation, something which is less likely to happen if you are writing lists.

Use spider diagrams to:

▶ *gain insights into situations or problems*
▶ *generate new ideas*
▶ *compile books, reports, essays*
▶ *structure courses, talks, presentations*
▶ *take notes at meetings.*

FRAMING YOUR IDEAS

To make sure that great ideas don't slip through the net, you need a framework that you can use to organize your ideas so that you can present them to interested parties. Start by brainstorming and asking yourself the following questions.

Solution generating technique

Write three sentences detailing:

1 *what the problem is*
2 *how the problem has arisen*
3 *what is your desired outcome?*

Use these sentences as headings to flesh more detail under each. Then ask yourself questions such as:

▶ *Is a solution necessary?*
▶ *What will happen if things stay the same?*
▶ *What will solve the problem for me?*
▶ *How will my suggestion resolve the problem?*

Draw diagrams or pictures that will help others to understand your idea more clearly.

Estimate what the saving will be in time or money if the idea is implemented.

Generating good ideas – the creative process

The greatest minds in history have acknowledged the importance of imagination. Einstein said: 'Imagination is more important than knowledge.' Shakespeare wrote: 'Imagination makes man the paragon of animals.' Disraeli said: 'Imagination governs the world.'

There are at least five stages to being imaginative with ideas, although some people have many more.

1   *You see the problem, need, aim or goal – you want to achieve something and you think about what you would like to do.*
2   *You investigate all the possibilities you can for developing the idea. You look at what went before, what might work, and you imagine combinations of ideas to see what you can come up with.*
3   *This is the incubation period where you put your subconscious to work. You may be doing something totally unrelated and relaxing like playing with the suds in the washing-up bowl, when suddenly stage 4 – the 'eureka' moment – happens and you run out into the streets wearing your rubber gloves.*
4   *Illumination – the moment when suddenly you are struck by the answer. Often it's so simple you wonder why you didn't think of it before.*
5   *You put on your logical head again and seek verification of your hunches and insights. Using the brainstorming method for workplace ideas shown earlier in this chapter can help with this.*

There are also three distinctive types of thinking involved in generating an idea that you know will be implemented. These are:

1 **Uninhibited brainstorming to generate ideas.** *At this stage it is best to consider yourself to be the most knowledgeable person in the world and just keep brainstorming for ideas.*
2 **Logical procedural thinking to assess how things will work.** *At this stage you are testing the idea by looking for any obvious problems or oversights.*
3 **Critical thinking to get an overview.** *At this stage you think of the sort of things that could happen to stop your idea being a winner.*

Brainstorming is probably the most enjoyable part of idea generation. When you are brainstorming to come up with ideas it is important that you don't limit yourself in any way by being critical, or negative about the ideas you think up.

If you feel your brain could do with a workout to become more imaginative at making connections between unrelated objects then try the following exercise. Each morning for a month practise building your ability to force relationships on unrelated objects and I can guarantee that you will become even better at thinking-up bright ideas.

Boost your creativity

On the opposite page is a creativity boosting exercise. Once you can achieve high scores for uses with single associations move on to combining two and then three unassociated objects, and finding all sorts of zany uses for them. Then when your brain is really buzzing, start working on a solution to your own particular challenge.

Following the exercise there are a couple of simple but elegant examples of the type of solutions individuals can generate when using combining exercises to work on real problems.

Creativity boosting exercise

Spend 10 minutes a day increasing your ability to think creatively about the different ways in which everyday objects can be used. Aim to think of at least 30 ideas to do with each object, for example, a brick, a bin lid, a wheel, a paper bag, a dinner plate. Work under timed conditions and put some effort into it. Pick a different object each day and aim for a score of 30 or more. For example:

Day 1 – thirty things to do with a ladies' stocking

A ladies' stocking can be used: (1) to wear; (2) to tie up string beans; (3) to stuff cushions; (4) as a splint support; (5) as a water filter; (6) to catch tadpoles; (7) as a container for marbles; (8) as a cosh; (9) as a mask to rob a bank; (10) to keep hair in place.

Now you've got the picture – it's your turn. Pick an object and brainstorm as many different uses for it as possible.

Scoring Less than 10: unimaginative; 10–15: you're getting better; 15–19: good; 20–24: congratulations, you're really motoring; more than 25: you're a genius.

Creativity boosting example 1

British Telecom's Hereford Communications Centre was having problems because rabbits were continually tunnelling under perimeter fences and setting off intruder alarms.

(Contd)

Ingredients:

1 *Perimeter fence*
2 *Rabbits*
3 *Solution?*

Pause here to think how you might solve the problem before moving to the solution.

Solution

Ian Collins, an employee at BT, came up with a simple but clever idea which solved the problem. He suggested burying ceramic pipes under fences to allow the rabbits to get in and out without compromising security. The idea worked.

Creativity boosting example 2

The vision of the Prison Service's security cameras was becoming obscured by insects and spiders, who found the camera housing ideal for nesting and spinning webs. Because surveillance cameras were located up high, it was time consuming for the staff to find ladders before wiping clean camera lenses.

Ingredients:

1 *Camera equipment*
2 *Insects/spiders*
3 *Solution?*

Pause here to think how you might solve the problem before moving to the solution.

START IMAGINING YOUR OWN SOLUTIONS

Imagine the current problem to which you want a solution has already been solved. So what would the answer be? Ask yourself what would I have needed to do to achieve this? What type of tools, skills or people would I need to have access to? Draw a picture, an abstract will suffice, of what the solution might look like, as sometimes this will be enough information to send your imagination into new-ideas mode.

AN IDEA IS ONLY A NOTION – UNLESS AN ACTION FOLLOWS

Once you begin flexing your mental muscles and generating lots of ideas, follow up immediately with actions so you become used to achieving your goals on a regular basis. Start with small tasks first and work your way up to the biggies. Each small success will reinforce your belief in yourself as a winner.

If you have a brilliant idea about changing or finding a solution to a problem at work, how would you capture it and turn it into reality? Andrew Wood advises: 'To make sure that great ideas do not slip through the net, you need a framework to get your ideas into a shape so that you can present them to interested parties.' Start by brainstorming and asking yourself the questions in the following section.

Capturing good ideas – the strategy

Write three sentences:

1 *Detail what the problem is.*
2 *How has it arisen?*
3 *What is your desired outcome?*

Use these sentences as headings to flesh out more detail under each. Then ask yourself questions such as:

- ▶ *Is a solution necessary?*
- ▶ *What will happen if things stay the same?*
- ▶ *What will solve the problem for me?*
- ▶ *How will my suggestion resolve the problem?*

Draw diagrams or pictures that will help others to understand your idea more clearly. Estimate what the saving will be in time or money if the idea is implemented.

Walt Disney's creativity strategy

Walt Disney, whose animated films charmed generations of children, would separate out the roles of 'dreamer', 'realist' and 'critic' when generating creative ideas, so that each aspect could be focused on and explored separately. At the 'dreamer' stage he would brainstorm ideas without inhibition; he would then switch to the 'realist', a more practical role, to work out the framework and details of how things would be done. Finally, he would become the 'critic' as he checked and looked for inconsistencies in his work.

You can use the Disney strategy:

- ▶ *alone or when you want to generate creativity within a team*
- ▶ *when you have an idea and are in conflict between the practicalities of implementing it and the dream*

▶ *when you want to test several ideas to see how they might be realized.*

If you are working in a group you could ask people to take on the different roles and view ideas from 'dreamer', 'realist' and 'critic' viewpoints. Ask the dreamer to tell you about the possibilities of an idea. Then ask the realist to imagine what would be involved in turning the idea into reality. Finally, ask the critic to evaluate the strengths and weaknesses of the idea.

THE REALIST

Ask questions such as:

▶ *What would have to happen in practical terms for this idea to become a reality?*
▶ *Is this the only way?*
▶ *Is this the best way?*
▶ *Is it what I want?*
▶ *What is important to me about going with this particular idea rather than one of the others?*
▶ *What would this idea give me that the others do not?*

THE CRITIC

Test the idea by asking:

▶ **What assumptions are being made?** *Have you taken anything for granted, or left anything out? Have you used an isolated incident to generalize and come to a sweeping conclusion?*
▶ **What evidence do I have to support my assumption?** *Are you dealing with facts or opinions? If what you have is an opinion, can you trust the source? If it's a fact, is this always true?*

Could there be any other explanations? If this is true, what else follows?

▶ **Can I think of a good illustration of my idea?** *Does your example fit in with anything else that is familiar? Can you give an example?*
▶ **What opinion or conclusions can I draw about taking action on this idea?** *Are your conclusions justified?*
▶ **What are the unique points about this idea?** *Write down the key points and new points. Which of the points is it essential to know, and which of the points are just padding?*

Generate ideas and turn them into reality

You need thinking time to achieve creative thought and action. Begin by listing your ideas and block off large amounts of time to concentrate on them.

Create a sense of urgency about whatever you want to achieve. Some people tend to procrastinate at the ideas stage; give them a month to come up with an idea and it will take a month, give them a day and they will hatch it in a day. Generate the necessary pressure by giving yourself challenging but reasonable deadlines for objectives and stick to them.

Choose projects that fire you with enthusiasm, rather than those that drain your energy. Enthusiasm plays a major part in helping people to generate creative ideas. If you are fired up you will be able to imagine, structure, build and turn your ideas into reality more quickly. So make sure you have an ample supply of the excitement factor. People rarely succeed at things that do not excite them.

GIVE YOURSELF AN INCENTIVE

> ### *Thought provoker*
> Give yourself an incentive, a compelling reason for generating new ideas. What is in it for you – money, status, a new and better career? Write down the rewards you feel you will reap from making the effort to generate new ideas. Use a well-formed outcome exercise which will give you a 'big picture' view of the wider range of rewards and spin-offs you are likely to reap with success.

THINGS TO REMEMBER

▶ *Learn what motivates staff to submit good ideas.*

▶ *Use incentives to harness your own and other people's creative ideas.*

▶ *Consult your ever-present experts for advice.*

▶ *For generating ideas use the Walt Disney strategy, of approaching ideas from three viewpoints.*

▶ *Use a framework for capturing, structuring and presenting good ideas.*

▶ *Give everyone an incentive to generate ideas.*

6

Discover your life's purpose

In this chapter you will learn:
- *to recognize what would make your life more purposeful*
- *how following your passion will lead towards your purpose*
- *how you could make a difference*
- *how to align your beliefs and values so they flow towards your goals*

> **'If you die without finding a purpose, you leave the world nothing but a mass of waste product.'**
>
> Marsilio Finino, fifteenth-century Italian philosopher

What would make your life more purposeful?

Insight

If you are reading this book, then at some level you have decided that you are not on earth just 'to be', to languish in a corner and just breathe in and out. You are here with a purpose, to plan ahead, to take actions and to be a force in the world that makes things happen.

Why is it that some people who possess what seem to be only average abilities achieve outstanding successes in life, while others with amazing talents achieve little? The answer is that being on purpose is what counts – if you have a belief in a long-term purpose that you really care about and burn to make it happen then all your thoughts, actions, achievements and goals will flow together towards realizing your dreams.

People who have good self-esteem usually have a sense of purpose. Their sense of purpose connects with who they think they are and what is important to them. They link their beliefs and behaviours to their identity and then take the actions that propel them towards their desires.

What do you feel passionate about? Could you change the way you do things to make your life more purposeful? Have you thought about ways in which you could make a difference?

Your key to success is to build a strong purpose that you care about with a passion strong enough to take you through the difficult times. The joys of being on purpose are immeasurable. When you are purposeful and constantly motivated towards your target your senses are heightened and you feel truly alive. Purposeful people feed off the energy surges from remembered past successes to create bigger, bolder and more inspiring challenges to master. Confident they will succeed, they radiate an energy that is charismatic to others who are drawn to their cocktail of vibrancy and action like moths towards a flame.

Passion is an indicator of what you value; it is what draws you, holds your attention, keeps you thinking late at night. It is the one thing you would do if you had all the money and resources that you needed – what would you be drawn to then? What work would you do for nothing?

'The essential conditions of everything you do must be choice, love, passion.'

Nadia Boulanger

What do you feel passionate about?

Before deciding to make meaningful changes in your
life you first have to identify what is important to you and
whether it aligns with your values. Ask yourself:

▶ *What is really important to me in my life?*
▶ *What is really important to me in my work?*
▶ *What is really important to me in my relationships?*
▶ *What would I fight for?*
▶ *Where can I start to make changes?*

Purposeful people

Case study – Slimming with Pete

Anyone who's met Pete Cohen is immediately struck by his
sense of purpose. Over the past 15 years this best-selling
author, *GMTV* and *This Morning* resident Life Coach, has
helped thousands of people to lose weight, get fit and feel
great about themselves.

'Do you like chocolate?' he asks the audience. 'I luurve
choc-o-late,' he whispers seductively. 'In fact I luurve
it so much that I like putting it all over my body. You wanna
see some more?' He opens up his waistcoat to reveal
even more confectionary stapled to the inside of his clothes.
Pete jokes, 'I like to choose where I put my chocolate; I
might put it around my stomach, or I could move it to my
butt.' With the audience transfixed he delivers the killer
punchline: 'Of course, you don't have any choice where

(Contd)

you put your chocolate – when it's on the inside of your body.'

And so begins a workshop in which a staggering 68 per cent of participants not only lose pounds but have maintained their weight loss after one year, compared with 5 per cent for other programmes.

Watching Pete perform, you might think that life has always been easy for him – but you'd be wrong. He was marked out from an early age as a lower-achiever. His teachers said he would never amount to anything and he left school at 16 with no qualifications. Later in life he was diagnosed as being severely dyslexic.

Pete went on to get a good education and has worked as a sports psychologist and coach to some of the most famous athletes in the UK; he is now a professional motivator. He set up his own business, started his revolutionary slimming programme and has become a television personality who motivates millions of viewers on the *Inch Loss Island* programme to lose weight, conquer their phobias and increase their confidence. He says: 'I don't take myself to seriously, I'm approachable – and that means I can help people make changes. The secret is to make it easy for them.'

He achieved his aims by turning his teachers' negative predictions about him into a motivational tool that spurred him towards his dreams. He worked hard and now has an impressive list of qualifications in almost every aspect of sports and fitness training as well as coachng and remedial work.

His second motivation was self-belief. He says: 'I knew what I wanted so I spent plenty of time visualizing my success. I always knew exactly what it would look like and feel like. I knew that however long it took I would eventually succeed if I kept myself focused on the outcome I wanted. If you lose sight of your goal, it's easy to lose heart when times are tough.'

'This is the true joy of life, the being used for a purpose recognized by yourself as a mighty one ... being a force of nature instead of a feverish, selfish little clod of ailments and grievances complaining that the world will not devote itself to making you happy.'

George Bernard Shaw

The key to being on purpose

- ▶ *The key to being on purpose is in finding what you want to do.*
- ▶ *Working out how by achieving your purpose you can serve others.*
- ▶ *Looking for a way you can combine the two to make money doing what you love.*

Purpose brings energy, purpose brings focus, purpose brings new ways of thinking and feeling, and looking for ways to achieve your aims in life. Purpose comes from self-knowledge. So here are some idea-sparking questions for you to answer. Think about what your writing reveals in terms of your personal aptitudes and passions.

Action

Leave half a page under each heading to catch your ideas after asking the following questions:

▶ **What are you naturally good at? What do you perform with ease?**

Are you a good communicator, a natural athlete, do people say that you're a clown, or can you pick up on a situation quickly and effortlessly? Are you intuitive, or a born organizer, good in a crisis, sympathetic, or a persuasive speaker? The abilities and talents at which you excel are often indicators of where your life purpose lies – especially if you enjoy doing those things.

▶ **Have you achieved any successes in relation to the areas associated with your talents?**

What things do you consider to be your greatest successes? It may be as simple as lending a sympathetic ear to someone in distress, or something you did that other people remarked has improved things. You might have an aptitude for making sensible decisions, or have won recognition for boosting company sales. Write down:

1 *How did it benefit others?*
2 *How did it make you feel?*

▶ **Is there a cause that you feel passionate about?**

Is there something that holds your attention because you care deeply about it? Could your life purpose be based around it? Write your answers down because somewhere in there is the key to finding your purposeful direction in life.

Some people may say that their purpose in life is to make huge amounts of money, but money is only an exchange mechanism, a lifeless pile of paper to be exchanged for the feelings associated with having the things you desire.

When you dig deep you find that a lot of what people want from wealth is changes in the way that they 'feel'. Aristotle Onassis, the Greek shipping billionaire, when asked why he still worked so hard when he was fabulously rich said: 'Because I never want to experience poverty again'. He was rich beyond most people's dreams and yet the feeling that spurred him on to greater effort was the fear he felt at the thought of losing all his wealth and being poor again.

IMAGINATION IS THE KEY TO ACHIEVING YOUR DREAMS

Action

Imagine a future when you have already achieved your purpose; what feelings do you want to experience? Do you want a feeling of 'freedom', 'being loved', 'recognition', 'security', or other kinds of feelings? Do your feelings come mostly from having accumulated vast sums of money or are they tied in more closely to your personal achievements?

Case study – Leo Angart's vision workshops

Leo Angart's purpose is to let the world know that poor eyesight and wearing glasses is not an inevitable result of the ageing process. He corrected his own eyesight using energy exercises that he came across in a book,

(Contd)

and later he discovered the eye exercises pioneered by William Bates. By bringing in his own expertise in the field of hypnosis and healing he has come up with a recipe for improving eyesight the natural way. He claims to have 20/20 vision and has not worn glasses for six years.

He believes that children are often wrongly prescribed glasses and, once labelled as having poor eyesight, those children end up wearing spectacles for life. Leo says: 'Children's eyesight is constantly changing according to the tasks they are performing and their levels of health, nutrition and tiredness. Myopia is not a natural state. People from cultures with no written tradition don't suffer from short-sightedness. Yet when their children attend Western-style schools they stare at books and blackboards and develop myopia. Putting them in glasses is like putting a broken arm in plaster and then expecting that arm to get stronger – it doesn't, it gets weaker.'

Leo devised his vision workshops and now teaches children in Hong Kong how to relax and exercise their eyes. His Magic Eyes workshops are going strong in Mexico, Austria and Manila and his teaching methods are expanding into Moscow, Dubai and Brazil. He is shooting a video in the US which will be released in different languages, and there is talk of introducing this type of training into the US army.

Leo is only one of many motivated people who wake up knowing what they have to do each day and the steps they need to take towards achieving their goals in life. They know that the magic formula for personal success is to find a need that they care deeply about, then devise ways to satisfy it.

▶ *Have a purpose.*
▶ *Find out how, by achieving your purpose, you can serve others.*
▶ *Devise a way to spread the knowledge.*

By focusing on their vision, motivated people create a model in their minds of what success looks like, then their imagination kicks into action to create compelling ideas that propel them towards their goals. This doesn't mean they won't fail at times but their happiness does not depend on external circumstances, their purpose is strong enough to carry them through the difficult times.

'Life is either a daring adventure, or nothing.'

Helen Keller (born blind, deaf and mute)

Case study

A solicitor had worked his way up the ladder to become a senior partner in his firm, yet he didn't feel either happy or successful. He had a wonderful home and family whom he adored and a good lifestyle – yet on most days he said he felt his achievements were empty and that he wanted to do something else. He, like many people, had worked really hard towards a purpose that was not his own but one his parents had chosen for him.

Whose purpose are you on?

▶ *Whose purpose are you on?*
▶ *Is it time to change what you are doing?*
▶ *Did you choose the life you are living now? Or did someone else choose it for you?*
▶ *Or, did you fail to make a choice and just happened to end up where you are now by default?*

Self-knowledge lets you understand more about how you think in relation to the world. It is the key to discovering your identity and the types of things you are drawn to. It comes not just from being aware of what is happening around you and in the wider world, it also comes from exploring you own inner space. To 'be on your own purpose' your mind and body must know what you want, so that you can develop new types of behaviours that support your goals.

You will need to develop a level of sensory awareness that most people do not have if you are to hold a strong image of success in your mind, and see possibilities in situations that others can't see. The ability to see fine details undetected by the casual onlooker is how forensic detectives solve the crime; it is also a tool you can use to see new possibilities in everyday situations.

You already possess tools for noticing very fine details – these are **sight, hearing, touch, taste** and **smell**, so let's start to fine-tune your sensory acuity.

IMAGING YOUR FUTURE

Visioning

Imagine yourself ten years from now having done something that you really burn to achieve. It could be in relation to building your own business, promotion in work, a better home or social ife. Build up your picture by imagining it to be a movie using only your sense of sight. When you've played it and noticed what you see, then play the movie again and notice how it looks when you include sound and feelings to create a more intense image.

▶ **Vision:** *First, see your great event happening. Play your mental movie of success with you in the starring role. What happens when you make the colours bigger, bolder, brighter and bring the screen closer to you? Do you feel more excited and involved?*

- ▶ **Sound:** *Play your movie again, and this time listen intently to hear if there are any sounds in your movie. Is someone talking? Are there crowd scenes with people mumbling, traffic noises, distant birds, hums or whirrs or complete silence?* (Not everyone hears sounds.)
- ▶ **Feeling:** *When you play your movie the third time, concentrate on what sort of feelings you get. Then notice what happens to the intensity of your feelings when you bring the picture closer to you and make it brighter, or move the picture further away from you and fade the colours to black and white. Bring the picture back again and make it big, bold and bright. Note where you hold particular types of feelings, say fear, excitement, or curiosity, in your body.* (Start to recognize the feelings that come with particular events, and where you hold them in your body because often feelings come before knowing the actual success is certain. Hence the saying – 'I can feel it in my water'.)
- ▶ **Taste:** *Are there any tastes associated with your movie. Sometimes when emotions are heightened there are tastes associated with them. People will often remark that someone has 'tasted success'.*
- ▶ **Smell:** *If your movie is in an outside setting can you smell anything associated with it – grass, tarmac, early morning breeze, the sea?*

All our impressions of the world come from our senses of seeing, hearing, feeling, smelling and tasting – the jury is still out on whether we have a sixth sense called intuition. When a person talks, many of their descriptive words will be in their most dominant sensory system. So someone who is predominantly visual might say 'I see what you mean' or 'I get the picture', whereas someone who is auditory might reply, 'I hear what you're saying' or 'that rings a bell'. Someone who relies on gut feelings might say, 'I feel we should do this' rather than 'I think we should do this'.

Knowing people's dominant sensory systems allows you to know more about how they take in information from the world outside and the sort of things they are likely to notice. You can build rapport with them by switching your language to their style, 'visual' or 'auditory', so you can begin to understand a bit more about how they see the world. Listening to yourself and others and the language used will also give you greater insight into the level at which a person is thinking.

RECOGNIZE PEOPLE'S THINKING STYLES AND NOTICE WHAT THEY DO

If you intend to build your purpose by fulfilling other people's needs, trying on their sensory systems will become essential to you when you are creating new ideas for products, training programmes or concepts in which you hope to interest them.

Modelling other people's behaviour and noticing the things they do is an immensely helpful tool in creating high expectations of yourself, especially when you need to develop new skills and maintain them. Once you are clear on the outcome you want to achieve, and you have found somebody who already has the skill, you can model them to find out their strategy.

Americans Richard Bandler and John Grinder are famed for the formative work they have done on modelling human excellence. They studied therapists who were judged to be particularly good at treating patients, to discover exactly what they did.

A good starting point for finding out more is the book *Frogs into Princes* by Bandler and Grinder (Eden Grove Editions, 1990). Their work, which became known as neurolinguistic programming (NLP) showed that people who possessed particular skills and types of behaviour used strategies to achieve them. The authors found that often, when people are extremely accomplished at a task, their skills are so intuitive that they are unaware of exactly what they do to achieve their good results. Modelling is the process used to get this information from them so that you can take it and make it your own.

What Bandler and Grinder noticed was that people use strategies for everything they do, from tying their shoelace to driving a car or addressing an audience. Interestingly, it was found that people who did not do things well also ran strategies for the things they could not do.

All human behaviour, including yours, is based on strategies, which are reproducible. By understanding how your own and other people's strategies work, you can learn to reproduce the ones you want at will. If you want to excel at something, you can model someone else's behaviour in order quickly to enhance the skills you need to achieve your goals.

Below is an example of how a teacher who understands other people's strategies for doing things well has modelled a spelling strategy from people who spell excellently and then taught the strategy to adults and children who can't spell.

Case study – Cricket Kemp

Cricket Kemp, Training Consultant and Educational Advisor of NLP North East and Learning Exellence, runs magical spelling days for children, teachers and adult non-spellers. In one session she teaches them a spelling strategy used by excellent spellers.

Cricket's passion is to make a difference to the lives of children and adults, who may have been labelled stupid in the past, by teaching them a spelling strategy that works for them.

Cricket says, 'I started to experiment to discover how you could teach the spelling strategy to people who didn't naturally hold it or who had difficulty learning to spell, by changing them to using a visual process.

'This has resulted in an elaboration of a Robert Dilts strategy which he pioneered in Californian schools, and in many new strategies for teaching spelling. Most children who learn the strategy increase their reading age by an average of 13 months within 3 months – a result which is off the scale for reading improvement schemes.'

Cricket Kemp says: 'When you notice people's patterns for doing something well the pattern can be evaluated, tested, taught and learned. This is really useful because it allows us to accumulate information and pass it on.'

By observing what good spellers do when they are spelling and what people who can't spell are doing when they attempt to spell, Cricket noticed that good spellers almost always use a visual spelling strategy; they imagine seeing the word in their mind's eye, to learn new words. People who couldn't spell or who were poor spellers attempted to learn to spell using auditory methods – saying the word out loud and then repeating it in their heads.

In Cricket's case success and purpose do not necessarily translate to making money: 'It is also about what brings meaning into people's lives.' She sells her 'magic' spelling strategy books at a price which is just enough to cover the cost of printing, and is happy spreading the word by teaching the spelling strategy at workshops around the country.

Purpose comes from knowing

Purpose comes from knowing that the things you do align with your beliefs and values.

Values are things which are important to you. You may value good manners, good service, punctuality or people telling you the truth. And mostly, you can see whether these values are being upheld.

Beliefs are different from values. You can believe things that are not actually true. You can believe that your house is safe, until it's flooded or the ceiling falls in. You can believe that you have a happy relationship until your partner tells you he or she is leaving you. At this point you start to re-examine your beliefs about how safe your house is or how good your relationship was.

Whole groups of people or nations can share the same beliefs. The American nation believed it was invincible until terrorists flew an aircraft into the side of the World Trade Center. At times like this, when a disaster happens, people have the painful task of re-examining what they had believed to be true – in order to know what they now believe.

Finding out who you really are

Beliefs, values and purpose are our drivers, they are the things that motivate us and make us who we are. If you don't know what drives you, you cannot motivate yourself to be more effective or press your own triggers to get the results you want from life.

What makes you get out of bed and into your place of work in the morning? Is it pain or pleasure? Are you an action person designed to hit the tarmac running? Do you have a mission in mind? Does greeting another workday bring a smile to your face, or a knot in your stomach that tells you you're stressed out, unappreciated or working for a lousy boss? If you're unhappy, your health suffers. Unhappy people make themselves inefficient, sick, absent and eventually leave their jobs.

In a recent survey of employers, 80 per cent said that their workers suffer stress. Heart attacks are most likely to happen on a Monday morning, either on the way to or on arrival at work.

There are thousands of groups of people keenly interested in finding out what makes you tick. They may be: manufacturers who want to sell you their products, newspapers, magazines, fashion designers, television sports channels or internet providers. Governments want to persuade you that what they are doing is the right thing and influence your voting habits, and many employers use psychometric testing to find out what motivates potential staff.

Companies whose competitive edge rests with its workers need a committed workforce. But as organizations downsize, merge and have fewer permanent staff – they can no longer bank on the loyalty of remaining staff, many of whom don't feel secure in their jobs. So what can companies offer, besides money, to attract people who are committed to the work they do?

Values at work

> **Insight**
>
> Can an organization that goes through change, say from public to private status, still hold the same stated values that were pinned up on their premise walls at the start? Employers and staff need to re-examine their values regularly and new mission statements and values need to be defined.

According to Wendy Sullivan of Discovery Works, an independent workforce trainer, 'companies must offer meaningful work in relation to people's lives and values'. She says: 'Often, managers read about values and think they're a good thing to have. So they'll stick them on the walls and think, "We now have a values-led company". Except it doesn't work – people need to have an emotional connection to, and an understanding of, company values. All staff need to be given the opportunity to question, challenge, influence and get involved with company values, so they can develop a deep shared understanding of them.'

'Values, once installed in the workplace, provide the basis for true staff empowerment. If the staff know the values the company is based on, and are aware of the behaviour that springs from holding those values, they are then in a position to make clearer work decisions for themselves.'

Organizations that are not values-led are obliged to have a lot of rules and manuals that give all the 'dos' and 'don'ts' in a bitty, procedural way and may also need lots of layers of management to direct staff.

Wendy Sullivan continues: 'From the company's viewpoint it's good news because you don't need huge numbers of procedures in place, or masses of management. To make the most of a values-led company, staff should be given the tools that enable them to understand how their own and the company's values might connect in a way that brings meaning to their life through work. And that's going to help the person feel that they are leading a rewarding life.'

Nevertheless, what happens if, when you get in touch with your own values, they are not compatible with your organization's values? Wendy Sullivan says: 'Some staff may stay put and go through the motions of doing the job. Others may decide to change a couple of values that no longer serve them well and so become more aligned with company values. Some employees may decide to move on – which is an advantage to everyone concerned. It's not useful to the company to have somebody who has totally different values, hanging around and not buying into things. And it's not useful for the individual either, because it's unlikely they are getting any job satisfaction.'

['Values at work', courtesy of *London Evening Standard*, 'Just the Job'

© Frances Coombes]

WHAT IS WORK LIKE FOR YOU?

Everyone can find a metaphor for how they would like to think about work. For example, work is 'like a roller-coaster'. This might mean that some bits are safe and boring and others are fast and out of control. Or work can be 'like gardening' where you are nurturing seedlings and growing plants to be in harmony with each other. Work can be 'like a war' where you need weapons and skilled fighters beside you to vanquish enemies.

When you ask people to think of a metaphor for how they would like to feel about work, that metaphor will contain their values.

What is important to you about the work you do?

BEING ON PURPOSE

Nick Williams, motivational speaker, and author of *Unconditional Success* published by Bantum Press says: 'People often change their jobs for one of two reasons – desperation or inspiration. Often it takes a bit of both to get them to shift. They're motivated to get away from what they don't enjoy, say overwork or unrewarding jobs. But when you say: "What do you want to do then?" they don't know.'

'Before deciding to make meaningful changes in your life you first have to identify what is important to you. You may not consciously ask yourself "what is really important to me in my life, work, relationships – what would I fight for? Where can I start to make changes?"'

BRING YOUR VALUES TO WORK

Start thinking about the things that are important to you and choose a context. You might choose 'What are my values in life, or in love, but here we will choose in work. Choose six things that you value most about your work. If nothing springs to mind choose from the list below and add any more you can think of.

routine	advancement	high earnings	helping others
responsibility	change	harmony	recognition
comradeship	targets	location	growth
appreciation	innovation	truth	fame
confidence	risk taking	respect	loyalty
loyalty	control	fun	precision
freedom	independence	working solo	teamwork
using initiative	creativity	learning	status
initiative	entrepreneurship	motivating	variety
delegation	friendly	socializing	progression
			route

Choose six of these values and beside each one write the reason why it is important to you. It might be:

Creativity is important to me because … it lets me express myself.
Freedom is important to me because … I want to decide what I do.

When you have listed your values you can begin to number them in level of importance. If you can't decide whether you rate one thing over another write the words on pieces of paper and put them face upwards on the palms of each hand and look at them and try 'weighing' them to indicate which one has greater value to you.

As soon as you start thinking about values, your brain starts processing the information and so the order of some of the things that are important may change. Or you may find in a few weeks that you have a completely new order to your list of values.

Wendy Sullivan of Discovery Works has an interesting metaphor for the work she has created. She is responsible for generating her own work and says: 'Work – it's like a conveyor belt going past with all these packages wrapped up as presents. And I have to tear the wrappings off as quickly as possible to see what's inside and make sure that nothing gets away.'

It is difficult to set future goals without having a base line of how things are now to compare it with. So before asking yourself the next question it is important for you to have your metaphor in place for 'how work is now'.

Metaphors or stories are part of our lives and who we are, we learn lessons from them and are enriched and challenged by them, and sometimes, as a result of hearing other people's stories, we change our own.

Thought provoker

If your work was just the way you wanted it to be and you were doing all the things you wanted to do, what would that be like?

Describe it in one sentence and take five to ten minutes to refine your sentence so it is just right for you.

Your metaphor for what you would like work to be like, once deciphered may have boiled down to any number of conclusions, such as:

- *I want to work in a successful team and be recognized.*
- *I want to work alone and be recognized.*
- *I want to have more control over my working life.*
- *I want to work less and earn more.*
- *I want to do something that makes a difference to me and the people around me.*
- *I want to give my employers more value for their money.*
- *I want to feel secure and the money from my job gives me that.*
- *I want more enjoyment from my work as well as earning money.*

If by this point you know your purpose in work that's fine. If you don't know, then the exercise below will help to clarify your purpose.

Action

If you have a friend who can ask you these questions, that's great. If not, you will have to ask yourself. Take your boiled-down metaphor, write it at the top of a sheet of paper and then ask yourself some questions. Each question is formulated by taking a couple of the descriptive words used in your previous sentence and feeding it back. For example:

> **'I want to work in a successful team and be recognized.'**
>
> **Question:** 'And what would that do for you?'
> **Answer:** 'It would make me feel good about myself and give me an adrenalin surge and give me recognition.'
> **Question:** 'And what would feeling good about yourself say about you?'
> **Answer:** 'It would say I am good at what I do, and am working among the best, and earning the rewards that come from being the best.'
> **Question:** 'And what would earning the rewards say about you?'
> **Answer:** 'It would say I'd made it on my own merits and am earning the rewards.

Stop questioning when you start repeating the same answers because at this stage you probably cannot go any further. A salesperson whose metaphor for work was 'I want to work in a successful team and be recognized and financially rewarded' answered these questions. He realized that:

▶ *he was already working in one of the most prestigious car sales dealerships in the country;*
▶ *he was already working with a successful team;*
▶ *he frequently gained recognition and felt good about himself, in fact he was one of the best salesmen on the team.*

So what was missing? The financial rewards were missing. He worked for a business that set maximum earnings for their salespeople and he was already earning that amount. He realized a basic truth: in order to earn a higher salary he would have to leave that job and move into an area such as IT recruitment or insurance sales, where it would be possible to attain really high earnings.

The formula for finding out what you really want to do is:

▶ *Identify what is important to you.*
▶ *Clarify what you want.*
▶ *Decide which changes to make.*

All of this means nothing unless you take follow-up actions. Plant this seed in your mind: 'What steps can I take today to lead me nearer to my goal?'

What is the next action you can take today to make the future you want a reality? It may be small but whatever it is – do it.

Find a purpose that makes your heart sing

Insight

If you were doing all the things in life you really wanted to, what would make your heart sing? What would resonate with you so strongly that you could feel it hum in your body, and recognize it as the right thing to do as you breathed in and out.

Remember, the magic formula for being on purpose is:

▶ *Find a need that you care deeply about.*
▶ *Observe what is happening now.*
▶ *Think about how you could do it differently.*
▶ *Fill that need.*

Your purpose, beliefs, values and destiny are all intertwined. As your thoughts and actions flow together and your energy for your purpose builds, you will find that opportunities open up for you in often unexpected ways. It may be a chance meeting, a proposal, a snatch of someone's conversation that alerts your senses and calls you to take actions that propel you towards your goals.

At times like this when some fast-paced decision making is called for, you may feel like a passenger who has arrived on a railway station platform as a train is pulling out. For a split second you hesitate because you are unsure of the destination, then there's no more time to think as you hurl yourself on board.

As the doors close and the train speeds away you realize that things that you strived for are being handed to you now, and events are happening faster than they've ever done before. When serendipity happens, it's best not to labour over how you got your break. Just be joyous that you knew your purpose, and trust that this is another link towards your ultimate destination. You paid for your ticket with all the effort and purpose that has brought you to this point.

First believe you can – then start to do it.

THINGS TO REMEMBER

▶ *Discover your passion, what would make your life more purposeful, and follow it.*

▶ *Notice other people's key to being on purpose, and how they make a difference.*

▶ *Whose purpose are you on? If it is not your own then it is time to rethink.*

▶ *When beliefs, values and actions are in harmony, your energy will flow in the direction of your life purpose.*

....

Sharpen your thinking

In this chapter you will learn:
- *how to build your mental muscle*
- *how to start with your goal in mind*
- *how to improve your results and plan ahead*
- *about flexible thinking skills*

**'Planning without action is futile.
Action without planning is fatal.'**

(Business maxim)

People who become top performers do so by maximizing all the talents, techniques and resources they possess. They have a vision of what they want to achieve with their lives, and they build skills that enable them to improve the way they manage themselves and their working relationships with others in order to achieve their aims.

_____

Learning new skills

Tomorrow's world belongs to the 'core competents'

A survey from the Institute of Directors, which asked Human Resources directors what percentage of their employees they would rehire if they could change all their employees overnight, revealed they would rehire between 0 and 40 per cent of employees.

Purposeful people who are motivated to progress seek to improve their ability to think clearly when making decisions, solving problems, negotiating, in their relationships with others, when generating creative ideas and dealing with incomplete information. They strive to be better equipped to handle ambiguity, uncertainty, risk and errors.

Top performers realize that there is a limit to the relationship between working harder and longer to increase effectiveness. Initially working hard and long may be exhilarating, but over time there is a price to pay in terms of stress, exhaustion and burnout. Constantly relying on adrenalin to get you through a project is destructive and can be seen as self-induced substance abuse.

By working smarter, rather than harder, we can harness more of our thinking ability in order to achieve our aims and look after our future well-being. Standing still in self-development terms is no longer an option, we will always need skills to advance us in our careers.

Remember the motivational skills wheel you completed in Chapter 2? Have you thought of any areas you might like to develop as tools that will bring you closer to your goal?

1 **Motivating yourself to do things.**
2 **Visualizing** – *the future.*
3 **Feeling purposeful** – *can you remember the feeling and describe it?*
4 **Goal setting** – *do you know how to create well-formed goals?*
5 **Getting rid of procrastination** – *can you motivate yourself into action?*
6 **Communication skills** – *how good are your interpersonal skills and could they be better?*
7 **Challenging limiting beliefs** – *beliefs that hold you back.*
8 **Taking risks to move on** – *are you prepared to take risks to move closer to your goals?*
9 **Modelling** – *what have you learned from observing successful people's behaviour and its practical applications?*
10 **Time management** – *how good are you at working within time frames and putting things all together?*

We've repeated the figure here to help you (see Figure 7.1).

(see Figure 7.1)

Thought provoker

Reflect again on your skills wheel outline and how you scored yourself in the different areas of skills development that you require. Ask yourself:

- ▶ *What do I want to achieve with my life?*
- ▶ *What are the main pressures facing me in the course of a working day?*
- ▶ *How does this affect the way that I am thinking?*
- ▶ *What changes could I make to the way that I work that would help me think more clearly about the choices I make?*
- ▶ *Which section of my skills wheel, if concentrated on now, would reap me the greatest rewards?*

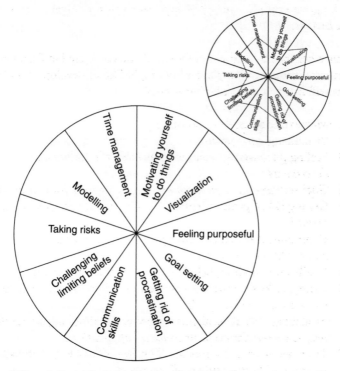

Figure 7.1 The motivational skills wheel: building your skills and abilities.

We never fully develop all our talents

Insight

Adults learn best when they take sole responsibility for their own learning. Being in charge of your own learning is part of taking charge of your life, which is part of your journey to becoming a well-rounded person.

No matter what age we are, we all have talents that are not fully developed. Successful people realize that they are the only people who can improve their results, so they plan ahead. They start with a goal in the future to aim for and then devise a plan of action by systematically thinking backwards to the present time and working out what resources, skills, abilities, tools and techniques they will require to achieve their aim.

Thought provoker
Script your life

If you died tomorrow, what would be missing from your obituary that you would like to see there? What are the things you would like to have achieved? What can you do about it?

Think ahead five years to a time when you have successfully reached a main goal and write the script of what has happened in the interim. Work backwards to the present day, writing down the steps you took to get to where you are now.

▶ *How did you get to your result?*
▶ *What skills and talents did you use?*
▶ *Are you using all those skills now to your maximum potential?*
▶ *List the reasons for the success you have had.*

This will give you more ideas on what you need to do to achieve greater success.

Gain leverage in relation to business goals

Most successful people had a vision of what they wanted and then made choices about how they would live their lives. By beginning with their outcome in mind, they were able to create a step-by-step plan of the things they needed to do and have in order to make their dreams a reality. A really important part of goal setting is to brainstorm until you can find a way to make your ideas or products more desirable to consumers than your competitors' ideas or wares. Goals become really high-powered when you discover how to exert leverage.

Case study – Peter Thomson

At 24, Peter Thomson set up the first of three successful companies and within two years he owned the largest debtor tracing agency in Europe, tracing 4,000 people a month. So how did he achieve his first business success? He says: 'Setting goals is important, I make lists and set goals every single day. But if you are to succeed big time in business you also need a good idea that will give you leverage.'

Thomson continues: 'With my first business we offered a new concept on tracing debtors called 'risk reversal' which meant we only got paid if we found people. On top of that we charged less than our competitors for the basic tracing service, in order to attract more clients.'

So how could anyone make money from a business like that? Thomson explains: 'I found a formula – if you trace someone once but get paid for it more than once – it's called leverage. So if I traced say a shopkeeper, I had that information on file. If he owed money to one confectionery business, he probably owed money to others. So I had

(Contd)

already done the work once and could sell the results again and again. That's where I made my money.'

Similarly, when Thomson decided he wanted to become an audio presenter he used his self-questioning technique. 'I wrote down what I wanted to do – *be an audio presenter*. The biggest audio-presenting company in the world was Nightingale Conant. What got me the foot in the door, because it was different from what anyone else had done, was that rather than going to the company with an idea I went with a completed product.

'The company was approached by hundreds of people every day saying "I've got this idea for a programme." So I wrote and recorded a programme and took it to them as a completed product. I figured there's no shortage of people in the world with ideas – what's in shorter supply is action. They said "we love your voice and your material but we're not heavily into the sales market with our audio products". However, I ended up voicing the Nightingale Conant classic *Lead the Field* and have continued with them from there. I've now written hundreds of tapes and audios.

'People say that information is power, but that's a misquote. I meet a lot of clever people who have amassed a lot of information but are not rich, they may even be working for people who are not as clever as them. It's how you leverage information that gives you power in business.'

Courtesy of MPMG Ltd, *Sales Director* magazine,
© Frances Coombes

GET LEVERAGE WHEN SETTING FUTURE GOALS

When you change a car wheel the leverage exerted by the jack is what allows you to lift an object 40 times your own weight. In business and sales leverage, also known as the 80/20 rule, can come from identifying and concentrating on a critical few customers, rather than applying equal energy and attention to all.

To leverage your time when completing a task, remember that 80 per cent of the returns from your daily 'to do' list will come from 20 per cent of the items you have listed and often from just one item. Avoid falling into the 'busy trap' of racing around completing lots of small tasks that may be easy or insistent or satisfying but ultimately achieve little. Instead focus on the most important task, even though it may not be urgent. Ask yourself: 'Which of these tasks relates directly to my goals?', 'Which will still matter five years from now?'

I asked Peter Thomson how he used his 'to do' list: 'You prioritize tasks – do item one and reprioritize it before you do item two. That way all day long you will be working on the highest priority and if you don't get other stuff done, who cares, because you wouldn't have got it done anyway. Or you'd have been working at the expense of other more important things.'

How effective are you at setting goals?

Many people already set personal and professional goals, but how effective are they? Wherever you are now in life you have reached that place as a result of all the thinking and planning you have done to date. So are you where you want to be, or partly on the way? Vague or ill-shaped goals are no more effective than wishing for the things we would like to happen without taking actions to make it so.

To clarify your intentions when planning ahead you need to know what you want to change. Saying 'I want to make more money' is like saying 'I want to win the lottery'. These statements supply no information on how the goal is going to be reached. Without the power of intention, statements like the above are as inefficient as simply wishing.

Only when you know what you seek to change in your life should you start making changes. It may not just be the present job you are doing that needs to change, perhaps you need an entirely different career. Or maybe there are changes that you can make that would improve your current job. If you do not know what you are looking for then you will not be aware of the conditions that will satisfy you.

Thought provoker

If there was a miracle tonight and you woke up in the morning and everything was just the way you wanted it to be ... how would you know it had happened?

▶ *What would you see, hear, feel and believe that would tell you a miracle had happened?*
▶ *What would achieving your goal give you that you do not already have?*

We all have individual patterns of behaviour that are instantly recognizable to ourselves and to others. Over time our repetitive actions accumulate and we get results. The actions that you have taken over time, have built into the results that you have now.

A QUICK STOCK-TAKE

▶ *Where are you now? Are you on your journey towards your dream?*
▶ *How likely are you to reach it?*
▶ *Is there anything stopping you from achieving your aim?*
▶ *How did you get to where you are now?*
▶ *Is there anything you want to change?*
▶ *What are you going to do?*

What are your criteria for success?

What are your criteria for achieving a better job or a better life? Identify the feeling you want to have when things are working well rather than focusing on the problem.

Negative thinking: 'Things are not going right for me in this job and the situation is spiralling out of control. What shall I do?'

Turn the negative question into one that fits a more positive frame of thinking.

Positive questioning: 'If things could be exactly right for me in this situation, how would they have to change?' Then list the criteria that would make the difference for you.

Having listed your ingredients for the situation to be just the way you want it to be, check that the consequence of achieving your objective does not lead to new problems.

Negative thinking: 'If I get this new job it means I will have to present ideas to my bosses. I don't feel confident about doing this because I am not as clever as they are.'

Once again, turn the negative thinking into positive questioning.

Positive questioning: 'If you knew that you were as intelligent as your bosses, how would you present yourself to them?' Again, listen for the answers your subconscious gives you.

Visualize your goal in detail to ensure that you now have all the ingredients to make it achievable, and notice what steps you will take to make this outcome a reality.

How will you monitor your achievements, so that you will know when you succeed? What evidence do you require to know when you have achieved your aim? Consider:

How will you know you have achieved what you want?
Your evidence might be, 'I will feel more positive in meetings with my bosses, and I will see myself looking and acting confidently, and hear myself contributing to discussions.'

Having done this you can now flesh out your list of intermediate objectives that add up to your goal of a better job. For example, if wanting more money is not your greatest concern in your current position, you should not be tempted by a job that offers more money but will not change the things that are really important to you in a job.

Next think about what actions you will take to ensure your outcome becomes a reality. Consider what you want to achieve and the resources you will need to meet your aims. Self-questioning such as 'What action do I need to take to ensure this happens?' may generate an answer such as 'I need to think constructively about what my objectives are and the actions I will take to be ready for next Wednesday's meeting.'

What will it take to satisfy you that you have achieved your aim and have the outcome you desire?

▶ *What conditions must be true for your plan to succeed?*
▶ *What sacrifices will you (or the people around you) have to make?*
▶ *What must change?*
▶ *What can you do to ensure that these changes happen?*

THESE ARE THE NECESSARY CONDITIONS

Whatever you have answered to the above questions are the necessary conditions for you to create your own favourable winning strategy. Is the challenge too great? Or do you still want to do it?

If you had not undertaken this procedure and found out what your success criteria were, then you could have done what many people do, that is set goals towards your outcome without having enough insight into the situation, and without having put any foundations in place. Often people set a goal and head straight for it without planning ahead all the steps that will be necessary to achieve it. The evidence may be:

- *They start a new venture and are unaware of the costs.*
- *They build an extension to their house without getting planning permission and then have to pull it down.*
- *They may succeed in their business and then find they have changed their personality while their partner has stayed the same. If you are working on a plan that will change your life and is likely to affect other people, then you have got to get them on board with you before you start.*

Strategic planning

The hardest part of developing and employing a strategic plan is having the confidence to use it and the ability to stick to it once you have your plan in place. This is where the real work of building up a combination of the skills of evaluation and taking actions begins. The most common questions that start to arise at this point are:

- *How do you stay on track?*
- *How do you know that you are looking for the right thing?*
- *How do you know when you have slipped away from thinking strategically?*

Only by constantly questioning your ongoing decisions and monitoring your results, both good and bad, can you begin to know what works and what doesn't. Question everything you do.

- *Were your decisions good?*
- *How accurate were your evaluations of situations?*
- *Were the tactics you used sound?*
- *What worked and what didn't? Make a list and keep it to hand for your next plan.*
- *What would you do differently next time?*
- *Was your outcome successful?*

If your outcome was not wholly successful, was this due to:

Lack of skill	Lack of knowledge
Could you acquire this ingredient? Over- or under-estimation of your abilities?	Did you fail to get important pieces of information?
Lack of resources	**Lack of forethought**
Was an important ingredient that is missing necessary to assure a good outcome?	Has something happened that you were not prepared for and had no plan for dealing with?

It is vital for us to be aware of our pattern of strategic and tactical thinking if we are to be able to improve on it. We need strategy to keep our tactics on course, and we need techniques to help us evaluate the deeper consequence of our tactical decisions.

Increase your pattern recognition skills

> **Insight**
>
> Human beings are pattern hunters; at an unconscious level we have always been this way. You hear people say, 'I had a "hunch" or a "feeling" that would happen.' Now more than ever we need to actively practise these skills of pattern hunting, because it will be early pattern recognition and seizing on new trends that will keep us ahead of competition. (See Chapter 13, Model success strategies.)

It is not just our own thinking and decision-making patterns that we need to record, there are patterns going on all around us. Early in life we begin to recognize similar trends, patterns of behaviour, and mental pictures of recurring past events.

> **Insight**
>
> Traders who buy and sell stocks and shares notice trends in buying and selling patterns; mortgage lenders can predict

customer behaviour patterns; we can predict our family's or workmate's behaviour based on what we know of their recurring habits. If we are about to try a new venture we can predict the outcome based on what has gone before and past results in similar situations. All this saves us from having to re-invent the wheel.

If we can recognize a pattern we can:

▶ *evaluate it*
▶ *test it to see if it works*
▶ *isolate the parts of it that don't work and change them for some better tactics.*

This allows us to build up lots of information regarding the things we want to know more about and learn new strategies that will work better for us. Once we see a strategy of the kind we want we can learn how it works, test it to see if it will work for us, and if we are happy with the results make it our own.

If we develop the ability to recognize meaningful patterns, it means when we tackle a problem we never have to start from scratch. Instead we instinctively look for past parallels. We see if we can work out a recipe similar to someone else's from those slightly different ingredients we are working with.

Traders see trends in the graphs of a stock; parents observe patterns of behaviour in their children. When you start to look for patterns you begin to see them in every area of your life.

Develop the habit of using outcome thinking every time you are planning ahead. Anything from a simple to-do list to strategic organizational planning should have planned objectives set.

SET CLEAR GOALS AND OUTCOMES

Setting objectives helps you think through complex and changing situations. Having clear goals and outcomes helps you achieve the results you want. Set goals and keep written outlines which give you a plan of the actions you need to take to achieve your outcomes.

Ensure your goals are SMART. Start with an aim or a goal in mind. An aim is an objective, a marker, an outcome on the way to a final achievement. Every outcome is made up of sub-outcomes which build up to a final achievement. An end is a final outcome or goal.

Your goals should be:

Specific	A short, specific, simple description of the outcome you want.
Measurable	Goals should be measurable, meaningful to you. There should be more than one way to achieve them.
Achievable	Describe goals in the present tense, as if they are happening now and are achievable.
Realistic	Your goals should be responsible, realistic and right for you.
Timeframe	State a timeframe in which you will achieve your goals.

To be excellent in everything you do, your goal must be to become conscious of your thinking processes and the actions you take that spring from them. Notice how successful your results are and then constantly seek to improve them.

Develop flexible thinking skills

To become a flexible thinker capable of focusing on the 'big picture' or whole plan in one instant and 'small detail specific' information in another, it is important that we can 'chunk' our thinking up and down at will. Big picture thinking will let us see what the whole project will look like when it is finished. Setting your objectives requires that you change your thinking and begin to think in detail about how each of your objectives will be met.

Company bosses are usually big picture thinkers; they get the grand ideas for the goal and surround themselves with employees who work out how specific parts around the outcome need to come about. However, if you are working alone on your project then it helps if you have flexible thinking skills in order to chunk your thinking around an outcome up and down at will.

Chunk your thinking

'Chunking' is a process of grouping information into large or small amounts, 'chunks', depending on the type of information we want to obtain. You may hear people described as 'big picture thinkers', which means they are easily able to visualize and have an overview of a whole situation.

Figure 7.2 A big picture thinker sees the whole picture.

The most able thinkers are skilled in changing their thinking patterns at will in order to ask questions that shed light on a task, situation, event, project or outcome in lots of different ways. This type of thinking lets you gain more insight into situations from seeing a subject from lots of different points of view.

CHUNKING DOWN INFORMATION

In computer language a chunk is a description of a piece of information of a particular size. Chunking means to break down information into smaller parts.

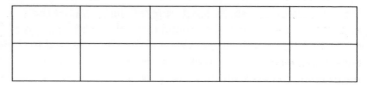

Figure 7.3 Chunking down.

To chunk up when thinking, means to go from small detail-specific questions such as, 'How specifically will I ...?' to big picture thinking which involves how the whole process or project works, for example, 'This wind tunnel is built for the purpose of ....'

To chunk down is to go from seeing the finished project, the big picture, to homing in on individual aspects, small component parts that form part of the whole. Chunking down large objectives into smaller goals makes them easier to deal with.

Having the flexibility to chunk your questions up or down in any situation is one of the most valuable skills you can acquire. Chunking helps you organize your thinking so you can handle more information in different ways.

Thought provoker
You already chunk information when you remember phone numbers. You group the regional part of the number together and then split the rest of the numbers into chunks to make them more memorable.

Chunking up and down at will gives you the flexibility to become adept at categorizing information. You can classify things into groups, and move your thinking from the specific (small chunk) to the general (big picture) to obtain lots of new information which would not be available to you if you stuck to your regular thinking pattern.

SITUATIONS WHERE USING CHUNKING IS HELPFUL

- ▶ *Setting goals*
- ▶ *Negotiating*
- ▶ *Team building*
- ▶ *Resolving conflict*
- ▶ *Intervention or problem solving*
- ▶ *Preparing a presentation and ensuring it is given to the audience in the right 'bite-sized chunks' for them to understand and assimilate.*

HOW TO CHUNK UP YOUR THINKING

To chunk up for solutions to big picture outcomes, ask questions which require people to examine their beliefs, values and what is important to them. Ask:

- ▶ *What is important to you about ...?*
- ▶ *What would motivate you in order to ...?*
- ▶ *What does having this outcome achieve for you?*
- ▶ *What is an example of ...?*
- ▶ *What have you learned?*
- ▶ *For what purpose?*

HOW TO CHUNK DOWN YOUR THINKING

To chunk down to find out about specific outcome explanations, ask questions which elicit small detail explanations:

- ▶ *What stops you ...?*
- ▶ *What is an example of this?*
- ▶ *Who/what/when/where/how ... specifically?*

THINK OF CHUNKING UP AND DOWN

When you have a problem that seems daunting think of chunking it down into smaller more manageable sections. This enables you to focus on one specific area at a time and find solutions, before moving on to the next task.

If you feel overwhelmed by too much detail then chunk up to find the purpose or meaning for what you are doing. Getting the big picture will give you an overview so you can define what you are doing and why you need to do it.

Chunking up and down skills are vital for analyzing problems, finding the best approach to new situations and setting new and more challenging goals.

THINGS TO REMEMBER

▶ *We never fully develop all our talents. If you want to be smart, keep learning new skills.*

▶ *Create leverage in relation to your goals.*

▶ *Know what your criteria for success are.*

▶ *Become a strategic planner, and increase your effectiveness at setting goals.*

▶ *Recognizing new patterns and trends is the key to staying ahead.*

▶ *Learn flexible thinking skills by chunking your thinking up and down.*

8

The power of setting goals

In this chapter you will:
- *create means, motive and opportunity for goals*
- *live your life through decisions rather than habits*
- *break down your goals to make them easier to achieve*
- *achieve a successful outcome in 21 days*

'Saddle your dreams afore you ride 'em'

Mary Webb (1881–1927)

J.K. Rowling who wrote the Harry Potter books ranks among the most successful authors in the world in terms of sales. This divorced, single mother, went from reduced circumstances to become a multimillionaire within a short space of time. Her books have sold millions of copies and her films are doing well, bringing her an estimated fortune of £226 million within five years.

In an interview Rowling was asked if she had any difficulty coping with the obvious changes that success had brought her. She replied 'no', because for five years she had seen the world through the eyes of her main character, Harry Potter, and he was an extremely successful person. Rowling's adjustment to her new lifestyle was not a problem because she had spent years visualizing success. What does this tell you about the benefits of imagining yourself a winner?

> **Thought provoker**
> We may daydream about the things we would like to achieve
> in life, but few people consistently take the necessary actions
> to propel them towards their goals. It is not that we are lazy
> or completely unmotivated, in fact in some cases it's simply
> because we were never taught how to set and achieve goals.

If you've never felt the excitement before achieving a long-desired goal, then it may be difficult to relive previous feelings of exhilaration and pride, and harness them towards making your next experience in order to feel authentic, intense and alive.

Being successful at reaching your goals is the biggest and most exciting gift you can give yourself. To achieve fulfilling goals, you first have to know what you want from life and have the inner awareness of how these things connect to your values and beliefs, and ultimately your life's purpose. Without goal setting there can be no success, so commit your desires to the forefront of your mind to make your purpose a reality.

THE POWER OF SETTING GOALS

While purpose is a long-range target and usually far ahead, goals are shorter. You may have a goal to set up your own business, to run a marathon, get married or increase your learning. Any of these aims might take several years to achieve, but they are all markers along the road to your purpose. You do not stop everything when you get there because these aims are not your ultimate destination.

HOW OFTEN DO YOU SET GOALS?

If you feel bored, uninspired, or that life lacks sparkle then check to see when you last set yourself some interesting goals. It could be that you do not set goals and have got into the habit of going along with the ebb and flow of life's events.

If you do not set your own goals, that doesn't mean you do not achieve targets. You may be part of someone else's dreams and purpose, a cog in your employer's production line or your partner's or family's aspirations.

Do you feel that you do not get the opportunity to have the things you want? Some people lead such an energetic lifestyle, they are too busy doing other things to plan how to achieve the things they want.

If you believe that the breaks that happen for you are luck, then you probably dream and goal set without realizing. Once you begin to plan consciously, you get even luckier.

When you know how to maintain your level of motivation, how you set your goals, and how to follow through with positive actions, you hold the key to success in every area of your life. The art of consciously goal setting is one of the most invaluable mental tools you will ever possess.

Means, motive and opportunity

To set goals and achieve them, you need to employ some of the techniques used by detectives. First you need to know whether you have the means, motive and opportunity to reach your goal.

- ▶ **Means:** *Do you have the requirements such as skill, time, money, connections and knowledge that will help you reach your aim?*
- ▶ **Motive:** *Do you want your outcome enough to pay the price? Are you prepared not to waiver or be distracted from your goal and to follow through until completion?*
- ▶ **Opportunity:** *Do you have the opportunity to go for it, and how much control do you have over the outcome. Although you are unlikely to have complete control over a business or relationship outcome, the more control you have in your power to influence the outcome, the more likely you are to achieve your aim.*

Once you have established that all systems are based on the means, motive and opportunity ingredients, it is your beliefs about yourself and your power and determination to make things happen that will determine how successful you are.

Don't kill your dreams

Your parents may have set a goal for you as a child, perhaps that you would learn to eat with a knife and fork. They showed you how to do it, praised you for eating nicely, and once the habit was established it became easier for you to repeat the process again. Soon eating with a knife and fork became automatic and you could safely place your food in your mouth without spearing your lips.

Could you imagine what might have happened if the first time you tried it you had decided 'No, I'm not doing this eating with a knife and fork stuff any more – it's much too difficult. I'll just never do it again.' Yet that is precisely the attitude some people take to achieving their goals. They kill their dreams by saying, 'I tried that once, it didn't work, I won't bother doing that again.' The fact that you cannot see the means to get something you want doesn't mean you won't find a way if you puzzle over the situation long enough. All it means is that you haven't found the solution yet. Never give up on your meaningful goals, they are your ticket to achieving your purpose in life.

Successful goal-achieving strategies are not just useful for business purposes. They link in to every other area of your life, be it financial, career, social, family, mental, physical or spiritual. How we picture ourselves, whether it's as a success or failure, ultimately affects our level of confidence and self-esteem and our beliefs about the things we are capable of achieving in the future.

Success for many people comes through the career they choose or the talents that they offer in exchange for money and/or recognition.

Make decisions. Live your life through decisions rather than habits. You will have more control over your life, and enjoy greater success.

Peter Thomson

Setting a career goal

You are more likely to reach your goals when they become steps in an overall strategy. For Dela Foster, working in a high-class food preparation and delivery service is ideal because it leads on to her next goal which is to set up her own restaurant and sandwich delivery service to office workers in the City of London.

Case study – Dela Foster

After university Dela Foster, 26, worked for a management consultancy. She says: 'I found the first nine months very exciting, but then began to feel disillusioned. Consultancy is an interesting area, but I felt that it doesn't achieve much – its main role is to validate the opinions of the decision maker in a company. If a chairman has to make an uncomfortable decision they'll often get in consultants. You could argue that it's a valid activity to be reassuring people who are making decisions about millions of pounds. But I didn't find it very satisfying. I also felt the job was too desk orientated; I wanted to be actually running the company rather than simply talking about it.'

One evening Dela was pressed for time; she wanted to order a restaurant meal to entertain people at home and couldn't find a company to order from. She says: 'Later I found there was a new business called Deliverance that offered that service – it seemed just like the sort of business I wanted to get involved with.'

Dela's strategy for finding out if joining the company was the right decision was to talk to the owners and do some evening work taking telephone orders to get a feel for the company. She says: 'It fitted the right criteria, it was a young company, a year old with 60 employees and growing. The atmosphere, quality of life and attitude to work at Deliverance felt good, and it was a new and exciting business area to get into.

'I started as assistant manager, looking at new ways to improve the running of the business. I launched another branch of Deliverance the following year in Clerkenwell and I took over the management of it.

'I find the job really exciting, it's exactly what I was looking for in terms of working with people and motivating them and making things run more efficiently. In the 15 months since I joined, the company has doubled its staff to 120 and is still growing. I have total involvement in the business in terms of the people side, the finances, suppliers, customers and planning for the future. In consultancy that's what I longed to do, to be able to see the whole picture and not just have to focus on one element of a business, such as cost cutting.'

[Courtesy of Cherry Publishing, *Real World Magazine for Universities*, © Frances Coombes]

WHAT ARE GOALS?

▶ *Goals are specific, they are actions you can take that lead in the direction of your purpose.*

▶ *Your goals should be personal to you, although they may link into someone else's goals.*

▶ *Goals should be interesting and inspire you.*

▶ *Goals are measurable, which allows you to judge how much progress you have made towards reaching your target.*

▶ *Goals should be achievable, not so easy that they don't tax you, not so hard that you regularly fail to reach them and so become disillusioned.*

▶ *Your goals should be realistic and fit in with who you are and what you are capable of. If you are a chronic asthmatic then it might be wise to pick a goal other than wanting to run the London Marathon, although there might be benefits of improving your fitness in less rigorous ways.*

▶ *Goals should be set within a definite timeframe. They should also have definite markers along the route so you can tell if you are doing well or if you may need to change some of your tactics.*

Organizations and businesses often fit lots of goals within other goals that align to a purpose.

Align your goals so they flow in the same direction

▶ *Know what you want and in what context you want to excel in.*

▶ *Have a plan or route map for getting there.*

▶ *Have recognizable markers along the way that will let you know whether you are on target.*

▶ *Know that what you are doing is not in conflict with other goals you have. (It's amazing how easily this can happen. For instance do you know people who are food conscious and take supplements to improve their health yet still smoke 20 cigarettes a day?) Work out a way to stack your*

Define your goals

Take a look at your life and ambitions and begin to define your
goals. List the headings under which you want to achieve them,
for example:

▶ *Business*
▶ *Work*
▶ *Money*
▶ *Health*
▶ *Relationships*

Under each heading write a list of things you would like to achieve,
then include a description that covers how you would like things
to change. Do not worry about how you are going to achieve your
goal at present.

Start with a general statement, such as: 'I want to increase my
earnings/run my own business/run a marathon/write a bestseller.'

Now refine your list and make your ingredients more detailed. If you
have said that you want to increase your earnings, then get down to
the specifics, write down by how much and over what period of time
this will happen and write down a target date. Then brainstorm as
many ways as possible in which you could make it happen.

ALIGN YOUR GOALS

Now look at your overall list of goals to see if any might align with
each other and if there are any others that are dependent on, or
could run concurrent with you achieving your present aims.

Our goals are not set in isolation, they are usually connected to and involve other people, things, and situations. Constantly ask yourself, 'When I achieve this outcome, what else might it lead to, where else might it take me?'

CHOOSE A PROMISING GOAL

1 *Think of ten things you'd really like to do.*
2 *Imagine yourself doing each one in turn.*
3 *Now narrow your choices down to the three most possible.*
4 *Don't you just want to get started on one of them right now?*

Set your outcomes

Think about something you really burn to achieve, something that is difficult enough to excite you, but not totally beyond your abilities. From your list of goals is there one that it is imperative for you to reach now, one that hinges to lots of other important aims in your life?

Clearly defining your goals is the first step

1 **What do you want?** *You may already have some definite goals in mind but, if you don't, then now is the time to get them. From your column headings of Business, Work, Money, Health or Relationships, pick something that is important to you in relation to your life's ambitions.*

2 **Imagine you already have your outcome.** *What are the things that you will see, hear, feel and experience that will let you know you have achieved your goal? Athletes practise these sort of actions every day, imagining they have hit the ball, run the race, lifted the weight, lived the experience many times before the actual event. In this way they use all of their sensory apparatus to see things they might not otherwise see, play through and correct different actions in their imagination,*

and feel all the feelings associated with performing brilliantly and achieving success. When they walk on to a pitch, into a stadium, up to a pool table or into a boxing ring, they have success hard-wired into their neurology. When it's time to perform, even in teams, they don't have to think 'Who shall I pass the ball to?' and 'Will he be there?', each person's actions are synchronized to achieving the same outcome.

Check for any side effects you haven't thought of

1 **Context: In what circumstances do you want this outcome?** *Business, work, home, social? Are there any circumstances that you wouldn't want it? For instance, your aim might be to acquire better leadership skills so you can take on a more challenging role in your work. But would you want to carry those skills over to dealings with your friends or family? Be aware that your change in thinking style and behaviour in work, if carried into other areas of your life, might change the dynamics of your relationships.*

2 **Impact: How will having this outcome affect the people around you?** *Business associates, work colleagues, partner, family, friends? Sometimes relationships break up because one partner is striving to be more successful while the other stays the same. If your goal will affect your whole family then involve them and get them to buy into what you are doing at an early stage.*

3 **Cost analysis: What will you gain from having this outcome?** *What do you get from what you are presently doing? Will you lose anything you value by achieving your outcome? Some business entrepreneurs pay the price of losing their first marriage when they undertake a goal because their beliefs and values evolve while their partner's remain the same.*

Have you the control, resources and time you need?

Thought provoker
Whatever it is you want to achieve, don't let being afraid stop you. Fear can cripple or stop you from moving forward, it can also be your greatest motivator.

1 **Control: How much control do you have over this outcome?** *You will probably never have complete control, but the more you can influence the outcome, the more likely you are to achieve it.*

2 **Resources: What skills, understanding, information, time do you need to achieve this outcome?** *Do you have them, or do you know how to get them? Do you need money? Often when you think through a situation you realize that money is only a medium of exchange and that you don't need money. You need what money will buy you – so barter.*

3 **Time: What is a realistic timeframe to achieve your goal?** *Most people work better under deadlines, and if you don't set deadlines then your work may expand to fill the spare time in which you have to do it. Telling others about your plan and announcing the completion date can give you extra motivation to complete if you start to waver.*

4 **Obstacles: What shall you do about anything that might get in the way?** *If you are dealing with other people or events, bottlenecks and delays are likely to occur. Write a list of what these might be and then detail several options you could take to get you past the hurdle. For example, if the delay involves another person agreeing to complete a task by a certain date and you think they won't meet your deadline, ask them at the beginning of the project, 'Can I have your word on that?'*

5 **Bridges: To what is this goal, and your actions, a bridge?** *Achieving goals opens doors to other possibilities, so always be on the lookout for other opportunities.*

6 **Going ahead: What would having this outcome say about you as a person?** *If you achieve this outcome, what else will you get? What is the next step to achieving this outcome?*

Now do you still want this outcome?

FRAME YOUR GOAL PLAN

Your goals should fit into an overall strategy. Write them down so that you can refer to them and modify your methods according to any changes in circumstances.

PERSONAL STOCKTAKING

If you have completed the 'weighing up your values' exercise in Chapter 3 you already know the values which are most important to you. How do your values fit in with your goals towards achieving your big picture plan?

If you value 'freedom' but your goal is to get another job which pays more money, are you really furthering your long-term aims? More money may allow you to take longer holidays in more exotic locations to help you forget about your job, but unless you can tie in the other values you hold about the work you do, will it really make you feel fulfilled or purposeful?

▶ *Think about the successes you have had to date. Which of your attributes have helped you to achieve the things you have done so far?*
▶ *What are your biggest assets in your personal style? Are you an ideas and vision person? Are you determined, energetic, enthusiastic? Do you have an ability to see the big picture or overall strategy (this is an ability that all business leaders should have)? Are you able to home in on small details? Do you have excellent communication and interpersonal skills?*
▶ *Are there any aspects of your personal style that have let you down in the past? You may have got the ideas but need some training to develop the skills required to convince other people how wonderful your ideas really are.*

Strike a balance between seeing what you want, knowing what you have, and acknowledging the training and skills you will need to reach your goals.

Keep things simple to start with and do not over-plan. It is possible to become overwhelmed with the details of how to achieve your goals and to end up feeling disconnected from your final outcome.

Initially practise simple goals, over short timescales. Break them down until you reach an action you can take immediately, which will give you lots of small successes from the outset. If you imagine having achieved your goal and then think backwards in time you can work out the progressional steps you took to get there. From this action you can work out whether you have the resources necessary to start your plan moving and also to know what is the next step to take you towards your goal.

Tips for goal setting

Break down your goals into small chunks

> **Insight**
>
> A complete project, such as breaking into and saturating a sales market, or being slim, supple and active, or earning a million pounds may seem daunting. So break down your steps into chunks and be determined each day to take some small steps towards achieving your goal.

Focus on the progress you are making each day
To write this book and fit it into an already full-time schedule, I kept a time-log diary with a page for each day that I worked on the project. From noticing what worked and what didn't, I decided that I would fit at least five 20-minute segments of time to inputting on the computer in the early morning when I was at my most productive. I also logged each day how easy or difficult I found the progress. Whenever I reached sticking points I was able to look back and remember what I was thinking, doing and feeling when I had been working well and found the going enjoyable.

Think about your goal constantly

See yourself achieving your goal and run action movies in your mind. Use all your senses of seeing, hearing, feeling, taste and smell to associate with your picture more fully. See your movie from different angles, so that if there are obstacles you can view the problem from another perspective.

Commit your goals to writing

Keep your goals simple and use concrete words. 'I want to be thinner' is not a goal, it is a wish. 'I want to be 2 kg thinner in three weeks' gives you a time frame and target. Write down the specific markers you will see, hear and feel, such as 'I will feel fitter and look fabulous in a new outfit', that will let you know that you have reached your aim.

Goals should be time specific

Insight

You may have an overall goal, say over ten years. Then break it down into yearly segments and have monthly check-ups to assess how you are doing. Have regular weekly planning sessions, say on Friday afternoons, where you build your lists for the following week and work on daily improvements.

Dealing with obstacles

When you encounter obstacles to your goals, imagine how people who have already achieved a similar outcome would do it. Take three of these successful people and ask yourself how they would approach this task. Take your time and wait for the answers to come.

Work smarter – not harder

Often it's necessary to work extremely hard to get a project started. But if this means you are constantly working under pressure, working long hours and lacking sleep, your standard of work and ability to think strategically will suffer. Don't get so tied up in your project that you don't have time for anything else. You know where you're headed, so be good to yourself along the way. Take some time to smell the roses, and give yourself some enjoyment and lots of little rewards.

Catch yourself doing things well

Keep a daily events diary of your progress, listing your highs and lows. Look especially for clues to see what triggered changes in your motivation levels, especially the changes that took you from 'can't do' to 'yes, I'm doing it'. When you know how these states were created you can create them intentionally.

Do a look back exercise

> **Insight**
>
> At the end of every project do a look back exercise, and review and write down what worked well and what didn't work. Look at ways of getting better and smoother at what you do, and of improving your efficiency.

Review your goals regularly

Besides asking 'Am I on target?' also ask yourself 'Do I still want this outcome?'. Are you still whole-heartedly committed to the initial goals you set, or have new possibilities arisen that might take you on another course. People who don't review their goals regularly can end up reaching their target and then finding out it wasn't what they wanted after all.

Get into the habit of setting goals and achieving them

Start first with small goals and practise going for them with the same level of determination you will carry through to your larger projects. In the beginning, aim for easy goals so that you can hone your techniques and see yourself as a winner. The more frequently you experience success, the easier it is to expect that you will get the things you want from life and the more likely you are to get them.

21 days to successful goal setting

If you intend to change events in the outside world then a good way to check that your goal setting techniques are working well is to set yourself an inner-space goal on a personal level – one that involves either changing a habit, say slimming, getting fit, giving up something, learning to do something new or making a change.

Your motivation level is likely to drop when you set goals over a long period of time. (I want to be thin in six months' time – but this chocolate bar is beside me right now; I want to run a mini-marathon, but I can't seem to get out of bed right now.) A lot of your initial enthusiasm that bubbled up when you hatched your plan may disappear if you think so far ahead. For a lot of people, 21 days is the length of time it takes to install a new habit, so plan your goal in clearly defined chunks to be achieved over three weeks.

Idea

Select a goal to work on for 21 days. It must be something that you really want to achieve and are prepared to give your attention to for this length of time.

▶ *Take one chunk of your goal that you know can be accomplished in three weeks' time. For example, if your goal is to lose 2 kg in 21 days, then break it down into daily tasks. Initially you might read some advice on nutrition, and work out where and at what times of day your trigger points for eating chocolate cake kick in. Over the first few days you might decide you will spend an extra 20 minutes each morning planning your day ahead and preparing your own lunches, so you are less likely to go off course.*
▶ *As you approach your first hurdle, say the afternoon coffee slot when you suddenly get a craving for chocolate cake, you may decide to come armed for this occasion by substituting a tasty nutritional snack. Once your new habit is securely in place, and your craving for chocolate cake subsides, you might decide to stop your morning journey short on alternate days so you can walk an extra 20 minutes and think about what is working in your new regime. Looking back over the previous*

*days to see what worked and what didn't, you might now
decide how to plan your evening meals when you are satisfied
your new habit has been installed.*

Insight

Avoid 'All or nothing' thinking. If you begin to encounter
obstacles, say your goal is slimming and one day you long to
eat chocolate cake, don't assume because you didn't achieve
that day's target that your whole project is a failure, it isn't
so. Be kind to yourself and allow for two 'relaxation days'
when you can relax your new habit.

▶ *If you are not an avid plan setter then draw large red dots on
your calendar beside each allotted day. Write what you hope
to achieve at the beginning, and on target days write in what
you hope to have achieved by that day.*
▶ *Plan your rewards in advance and treat yourself at the end of
every five-day period, or whenever you are likely to go astray
if you are not pampered in some way. Seeing your goal written
on your calendar in advance will keep you on course. If you
promise yourself something special for staying on target, then
do it, otherwise you might have a relapse.*

Once you have achieved your 21-day systematic approach to goal
setting, check over the next few days to ensure that your new habit
has become part of your regular routine.

THINGS TO REMEMBER

▶ *Set goals and keep them somewhere prominent to ensure you achieve your aims.*

▶ *Align your goals so that they all flow in the same direction towards achieving your dreams.*

▶ *Do you have the control, resources and time you need?*

▶ *If not can you barter?*

▶ *Break down your goals into small chunks.*

▶ *Plan to achieve your goal in 21 days.*

Step to the edge of your boundaries

In this chapter you will:
- *extend your boundaries*
- *get rid of limiting beliefs*
- *choose your patterns for success*

'The real art of discovery consists not in finding new lands but in seeing with new eyes.'

Marcel Proust

Case study – Tim Smit's vision

Tim Smit's vision created a garden called Eden. On a wasteland site he has created one of the most powerful architectural wonders of our time. With the help, energy and enthusiasm of those around him, he turned his dream into one of the most marvelled at wonders of the world. Tim admits he was a dreamer when he conceived his idea for restoring the Lost Gardens of Heligan in Cornwall, England. Yet his dream has become a reality which more than one million people from all over the planet have come to visit.

The interesting thing about Smit is his total belief that the right
people and situations would turn up at the right time. He also
firmly believed that he could be the lynchpin that would be
instrumental in building Eden. Yet if he had written a CV asking
to be the architect of such an audacious plan, coming from a music
background, Smit would probably have been turned down because
he did not fit the criteria for the job.

**'"Come to the edge," she said. They said, "we are afraid".
"Come to the edge" she said. They came, she pushed
them – they flew.'**

Guillaume Apollinaire

FEW PEOPLE EXTEND THEMSELVES

Often people don't extend themselves enough to 'live on the edge'
and find out what else they might be capable of doing, outside their
regular sphere of work. How many other potential Smits are there
out there, serving customers, selling products, making their money
in ordinary jobs?

In this chapter we will teach you how to identify and deal with limiting beliefs that may stop you reaching your potential goals. The aim is to let you try some techniques for countering self-doubt so that you see that these things work in the real world. Ultimately, however, you need to take personal responsibility for trying out, practising and incorporating the ideas that work best for you in your everyday life.

> ### *Thought provoker*
> Arctic explorers say: 'Unless you're the lead dog, the scenery never changes.' If you are the person setting the goals, then everything is new, because you make change happen, so the scenery is always changing.

Once you have positively established the **means, motive** and **opportunity** ingredients described under goal setting in Chapter 8, it is your beliefs about yourself, your abilities and your motivation that will determine how successful you are. Your mission in this chapter, should you choose to accept it, is to bombard your brain with as much evidence as possible that you are a truly competent, confident and capable individual priming yourself like a heat-seeking guided missile aimed towards its goals.

> ### *Thought provoker*
> Of all the things a person can say to themselves when faced with a difficult situation, 'I can't' is potentially the most limiting of all. When you hear someone utter the words 'I can't' you know that person is boxed-in or stuck in a way that is currently cutting them off from finding a solution to their problem.
>
> ▶ *I can't do it.*
> ▶ *I can't get through it.*
> ▶ *I can't see a way around it.*

If you believe you have a problem, then you do have one – whether it's real or not. If you watch the actions of someone telling you they cannot do something, often they will stretch their hands in front of them in a helpless gesture. They are in a state of confusion and are not thinking resourcefully. When someone else offers them a solution to their problem and they are in an 'I can't' frame of mind they are often likely to dismiss sound ideas as being unworkable or turn them down because they simply don't believe that anything will work.

Once we're in a calmer and more resourceful state and we've found a solution, we inform people we've 'got over it', 'found a way round it', or better still have 'sorted it out'. And 'sorting it out' like a computer data sort is often what we do; we sift the available information and look for recognizable patterns. We ask ourselves, 'Has this problem occurred before?', 'How was it tackled', and 'What was the outcome'. If we maintain a state of curiosity long enough we begin to come up with new patterns for solving the problems.

Challenge habitual thinking

If you have ever wondered how a newspaper horoscope can fit your circumstances and also every other 'Leo's' or 'Scorpio's', it is because it uses a technique similar to hypnotist Milton H. Erickson's model of artfully vague language. The horoscope writer uses vague language and the readers interpret and mentally fill in the blanks according to whatever they feel fits their circumstances. The information is accurate to us because we have put our own interpretation on it.

When we speak we **delete**, **distort** and **generalize** incoming information depending upon how we see and feel about others and what we think is going on in the world. If we feel bad about ourselves we may treat ourselves harshly, so that when someone pays a compliment, instead of being pleased, we may be thinking: 'What do they want from me?'

If you questioned your habitual ways of thinking, how many of the everyday statements you make to yourself about situations would stand up to closer scrutiny? Below are a few common patterns of statements you may hear from others or think yourself, with questions beside them to ask yourself in order to generate more information.

Deletions	Questions to elicit more information
'I'm not happy with this.'	*What* are you not happy about? *In what way* are you not happy?
'Nobody listens to what I'm saying.'	Not *one single* person? *Who*, specifically doesn't listen?

Cause and effect	
'She makes me very angry.'	*How* does she make you angry? Has there ever been a time when she didn't make you angry?

Distortions	
'All he does is criticize.'	*Always?* Without exception?
'She doesn't want me in her team.'	How do you know that?
'They think I'm useless.'	*How do you know* they think that?

Generalizations	
'But mum, everybody does it.'	*Who's everybody?* What, every single person?
'Seminars are a waste of time.'	*All seminars?* Every single one?

Assumptions	
'You don't buy me flowers, you don't love me anymore.'	How does my not buying you flowers mean that I don't love you?

If you find yourself thinking 'I can't do it!' ask yourself the questions, 'According to whom?', 'What is stopping you?'

How to confront negative beliefs

Greg Levoy, journalist and motivational speaker, uses this wonderful written exercise for overcoming limiting beliefs in his 'Callings' Heart at Work workshops. For a negative belief that you hold – say 'I can't write a best seller', 'I can't set up my own business', 'I can't be the most successful salesman on the planet' – start questioning yourself about why you can't. Look on it as engaging in a conversation, or a dual between the negative and positive sides of your brain.

Allow Positive and Negative (you might want to call them Pat and Ned for short): one line for each statement. Start with a negative statement, start the next line with a positive statement. Each negative statement should comprise why you can't do something and the following positive statement must comprise something that tells you why you can.

Example – 'I want to write a best seller'

Ned: You can't write a best seller.
Pat: How do you know that?
Ned: Well, you've never written one before.
Pat: That doesn't mean I couldn't.
Ned: Yes it does, you haven't got the discipline.
Pat: I have got discipline in other things, I could organize better.
Ned: You haven't got the talent, or the desire.
Pat: Yes I have, and I've always wanted to write a book.
Ned: When there's time, but you never have enough time.
Pat: I could make time …

Keep this going and don't stop until one side, either Positive or Negative, is exhausted and gives up because it has no more answers. Of more than 80 people at Greg Levoy's workshop who carried out this exercise, most were surprised that they successfully beat their negative 'I can'ts' into submission. We are often afraid to argue with our negative beliefs because we are afraid of being proven wrong.

Experiment with this exercise a few times and see what sort of result you get. You may be pleasantly surprised. Another benefit of listing on paper your negative and positive thoughts about a subject, is that you can spot whether your thinking becomes distorted.

When you can see where your train of thoughts became derailed you can take action to begin questioning your negative beliefs and get your thinking back on track. Most people wouldn't let another person constantly put them down without any substantiating facts. Why should your brain be allowed to make negative statements about you without being challenged to support its facts?

Change your state

Think of a time when you may need to influence others. It may be to put your ideas across, to give presentations, talk to colleagues, ask for a favour or for something which you might not necessarily get, say a contract.

▶ *Think of an activity that you enjoy doing about which you feel confident and proficient? Run your mental movie and associate with the images and become part of them. As you run through them in your happy state you feel your emotions intensify and become stronger. As the colours in the pictures become bigger, brighter, bolder and closer, just sigh and let all the good feelings wash over you.*
▶ *Now shake off that image and put it aside for a moment. Think about how giving your presentation or influencing task will be easier once you transfer your confident and happy, relaxed feelings from your more empowering state.*

> *This time, as you see yourself watching an internal movie of you giving your talk or presentation, notice that you have distanced yourself and are not in the picture – in fact you are actually watching the movie from outside. So you can observe in a detached way more about what is happening from this distant back-row view.*

Associate with the activity you enjoy by running your feelgood movie again to the point where you feel most powerful, confident and alive. As your feelings become stronger, touch your thumb and forefinger together as an emotional trigger and feel yourself leap, taking those strong, feeling good emotions into your less colourful movie. Bring all the good feelings associated with your feelgood movie into a second movie in which you want to experience having a really successful outcome. You're no longer watching a drab or uncomfortable movie, you're actually in it. But you've brought all the strength, determination and confidence with you from your most empowering feelings and images.

Remember the strong feelings you had when you pressed your thumb and forefinger together at the height of your emotional intensity when you changed your mental movie? You can use that action to anchor your good feelings in the future. With a little practice you will be able to recall and trigger this powerful emotional state just by pressing your thumb and forefinger together and bringing your empowering feelings into the next visualization you run.

WE NATURALLY CHANGE STATES

Thought provoker
A person may work at a supermarket checkout counter where they behave in a restrained and predictable way, yet on Saturday night everything changes and they dress up and look fantastic. Before leaving home they engage in rituals to pamper themselves, smell desirable, feel sexy and great and run images of themselves being the best dancer on the floor.

(Contd)

Guess what happens? They go out, enjoy themselves, get noticed, they get talked to and chatted up. What happens then on Monday morning back at the checkout? Do they become invisible? No, they change their state to behave in a way that is appropriate to their job situation.

What would happen if they decided that for just 20 minutes every morning they would go into 'disco chat-up and energy mode' as they served customers? They might get the sack, they might get noticed, they might get promoted, they might get customers enquiring about how they are. They might also start to become more flexible in their behaviour and realize that they can choose how they feel and act. We all have a choice about how we feel and act in any situation, we don't always have to go with the automatic response of the crowd.

Our feelings are the most important things we possess

Figure 9.1 Our feelings.

Our feelings dictate whether we are happy, sad, unloved, hurt, welcome or outcast. We may think that other people influence them, but actually we can choose to manage our internal state and how we choose to feel. How often have you heard someone say, 'she makes me angry'. The truth is they don't make you angry, you allow yourself to feel angry about whatever that person said.

By allowing your state, or how you feel, to be dictated to you by another person you are giving up your power to someone else who can decide at a whim how they will 'make' you feel.

> **Thought provoker**
> As many as one-third of the population of some countries indulge in drug taking mainly because it changes the way they feel about themselves, how vividly and differently they see the world, and how happy, successful and loved they feel – for a short time only. Many crimes committed are drug related, and some addicts are prepared to swap their self-esteem, families, liberty and eventually their lives for tablets or a powder that lets them chase their feeling good state.

Choose your patterns for success

How you choose to feel and the state you choose to operate in can be within your control. I'm not saying it will be like getting high on drugs, it won't be so ruinous and can still feel pretty good. We all repeat patterns for the things we do, even those at which we are repeatedly unsuccessful.

Switching states, that is creating an association between two experiences actively to create a strong mental state, is used a lot by sports and business people, public speakers and musicians and others who need to give a consistently excellent performance each time at peak state.

WE CAN ALL CHANGE STATES AT WILL

> **Thought provoker**
> Most people can recall and associate with a sad experience or bad feelings at will. All it takes to trigger their mental movie is to say to them 'Remember when ...,' and they do the rest themselves. Their eyes will fix on a spot where they see the events happening, their shoulders will crumple, their
> *(Contd)*

breathing will slow down as they relive again the emotions they felt that first time.

So why not choose a ritual that is linked to success? Use it as a trigger to recall a time when you felt truly alive and powerful, when everything you did seemed like magic.

'Losers visualize the penalties of failure. Winners visualize the rewards of success.'

Dr Rob Gilbert

GET USED TO ANCHORING GOOD FEELINGS

Pick a personal moment of success that you've experienced and run through the events several times in your mind's eye until you can recall it with ease.

▶ *Play the actions and feelings through a few times.*
▶ *Then take the associated feelings and memories and save them in your best memories store, like freeze framing a mental and sensory snapshot.*
▶ *When the experience is at its highest point, use a signal such as pressing your middle finger and thumb together to recall the good emotional state.*
▶ *In the future, by repeating the finger press action, you will be able to play your success movie at any time you need to feel powerful, successful and in control.*

Thinking pitfalls to avoid

Avoid 'all or nothing' thinking. Sometimes when we're working hard to reach a goal, things don't always go to plan. When you're tired and working hard to complete a project it's easy to slip into 'all or nothing' thinking. But, if given free reign, negative thinking can fire off a chain of negative thoughts designed to sabotage your efforts, and stop you breaking through your next boundary to success. If you catch yourself slipping into the 'I can't do this', 'I'll never finish', 'Why did I think I could do it?' vein of thought, which is designed to paralyze you with anxiety, depression or fear and make you less effective, then change your thinking immediately.

New projects can take a lot of initial effort and can sometimes be compared with a plane taking off. The plane requires its maximum capacity of fuel for the energy it needs to take off from the ground and become airborne. Once in flight, however, it cruises using only 37 per cent of the fuel it required for take off. Don't assume, because one thing failed, that the whole project is a failure: it isn't.

If part of your plan doesn't work, keep your outcome in mind and try something different. I heard about a pilot who flies from the mainland to a small and difficult-to-get-to island in the Philippines. His flight is off course for 92 per cent of his flying time, but each time the pilot notices he corrects the flightpath and the plane lands on schedule. This is often what happens when we make plans and set targets; we may have to change them a bit, but we still end up at the right destination.

CHANGE VIEWPOINTS

If you are running negative thinking loops you might be too close to the situation you're dealing with to get a rational perspective on what is going on. At times like this it's often good to stand back and distance yourself from the situation for a while – perhaps going to have a cup of tea can help put the situation into perspective.

WHAT TAKING DIFFERENT PERCEPTUAL POSITIONS WILL DO

'Before you can know how another man thinks you must walk a mile in his moccasins.'
Native American saying

By walking in another man's moccasins, we are imagining what it is like to be that person and step out of our own way of thinking.

By purposely taking different perceptual positions, you can step away from a situation you are currently experiencing see things from a different perspective. It allows you to gather different information you might not otherwise obtain. If you have not found a solution to your problem using other means then try adopting different viewpoints and ask yourself questions about the situation. This will give you more valuable information about the situation than you could ever have gained by observing it from only one point of view.

TO INCREASE YOUR FLEXIBILITY IN THINKING

Practise switching your perspectives on a situation at will.

Adopting different perceptual positions can be used:

- ▶ *to imagine how your behaviour may be impacting on others;*
- ▶ *to think about how a being from far away might view your constant bickering with a friend, lover, or colleague, and what they might think is going on;*
- ▶ *to notice what you are feeling inside about a situation;*
- ▶ *to imagine what it feels like to be another person.*

Thought provoker
We adopt different perceptual positions constantly. Sometimes we get involved and are close up and personal, and we feel strong emotions about what is going on. At other times we can distance ourselves from events and this helps us to think more objectively. Each type of observation gives us different types of information about the subject.

Putting it all together

There is a saying that if the only tool you have is a hammer then the solution to every problem will be a nail. Now that you have amassed a powerful toolkit that you can use for problem solving and overcoming limiting beliefs, weigh up each technique and think about how useful it might be and in what kinds of circumstances. When you execute a problem solving technique notice what changes, how it changes, and whether your result was the one you wanted. You have the power to take personal responsibility for motivating yourself and others to make things happen – so use it.

THINGS TO REMEMBER

▶ *Beliefs are your most important tool. The strength of your belief in a plan is what determines whether you will carry it through.*

▶ *Changing your language also changes your thoughts and actions.*

▶ *Use precise questioning as a tool to gather information and confront negative beliefs.*

▶ *Do not allow your brain to make negative comments about you without challenging it to support its facts.*

▶ *Our feelings are the most important things we possess.*

▶ *If you want control over your outcome then learn how to manage your state.*

▶ *Use different viewpoints to help you gather additional information about situations.*

10

Create circumstances for success

In this chapter you will learn:
- *how to move in the right circles for success*
- *how to take risks to extend your boundaries*
- *the tools and techniques to help you on your way*

'Always listen to experts. They'll tell you what can't be done and why. Then do it.'

Robert Heinlein

Chicken soup for the entrepreneur

Case study – Mark Victor Hansen

Mark Victor Hansen is the marketing genius behind the 'Chicken Soup for the Soul' range of books which have sold more than 90 million copies. He says, 'In order to achieve really massive sales you've got to have a dream. You've got to think big – it doesn't cost any more. A miracle starts with a change in your perception.'

You should be able to define the purpose of your product in 12 words or fewer. The purpose of the Chicken Soup

(Contd)

books is to – 'Change the world – one story at a time'. When you've got your product then you look for returns.

The first Chicken Soup book was turned down by 33 publishers, so Mark took it to a book trade fair and was turned down another 134 times. How did he survive in such an atmosphere of rejection? He says, 'You don't give other people the chance to turn you down. You say next please ...' Eventually Mark decided to self-publish. He is co-author of the Chicken Soup for the Soul series comprising 137 titles. His name entered the Guinness Book of Records when sales reached 130 million Chicken Soup books. Mark's aim now, and his strategy is on target, is to sell 1 billion books by 2020.

Thought provoker
Mark tells budding entrepreneurs: 'In order to be really successful at whatever you do you have to have a dream. Think really mega. You've also got to have a team of people with you and working in your corner.' If you are a writer this means getting involved in the sales process, and not seeing your work as finished when you hand your manuscript to the publisher. 'You need to know how successful people have created their dream. So read biographies, lots of them, at least one a week.'

Your motivation does not have to stop when you close this book. In fact, for many people, books, especially biographies, are a starting point that whets the appetite for more knowledge, and marks the beginning of their journey towards mastery of a subject and a more successful self.

There are thousands of different types of motivational talks, seminars and workshops to choose from; the trick is to find one that is right for you. This chapter gives you an overview of an extreme and physical workshop, designed for personal development and to enable people to move through limiting belief barriers that might be holding them back.

The second training method examined uses a combined networking and training approach, and is aimed at ambitious people who are seriously committed to increasing their wealth. The resulting club is founded on the belief that ambitious birds of a feather should flock together for support and encouragement, and then get all the training they need to lead them to success.

The third approach, is a business training method devised by Michael Breen of MBNLP, an NLP trainer and management consultant to blue chip companies, which concentrates on the strategies needed in negotiating skills, to generate options and promote the sort of flexible thinking necessary for problem solving.

Walking on fire

Team building

Team building is a dangerous pursuit these days. Not content with sit-down training sessions and role playing, staff take to white-water rafting, paintballing and absailing in an attempt to aid office communication.

THE FIREWALK

Firewalk leader Simon Treselyan of Starfire training explains: 'The idea of firewalking is very emotive, so people have to overcome the fears they have before they can walk across coals. The firewalk provides a controlled environment where people can make a dramatic change in their lives by moving from "can't do" to having achieved something which they thought was impossible within an incredibly short timespan. Once they've done it they realize they can take that energy and way of thinking, and use it to transform other areas of their life, so they can translate the process directly to whatever they want to change.'

As the flames leap higher, it is a reminder that people have been burned in firewalks. The dangers were highlighted in 1998 when seven insurance salesmen from Eagle Star needed hospital treatment, two of them at a special burns unit, after attempting a firewalk at the end of a motivational training day. In that instance, hot coals were placed in a metal tray which produced extreme heat, like a barbecue. Could that happen at Starfire? 'No', says Treselyan, who uses only wood, with no base or tray. 'Wood is a poor conductor of heat and so long as one walks quickly and is not in contact with the surface for very long, there is not enough time for skin to burn.'

Thought provoker
The psyching-up before the walk also helps suppress any pain, according to John Humberston, Professor of Physics at University College London. It helps people get into a 'mind over matter' state when they take that first step beyond their natural boundaries.

Treselyan, as ex-army special forces interrogator, co-ordinator and operator says, 'Basically the stuff I teach people now has been learned in extreme circumstances. I've moved on from the more negative parts, the aggression, the almost not caring how you do things to get results. I have looked at human behaviour both positive and negative, and ways to be able to influence that behaviour to inspire people to take on new learnings and go beyond their perceived barriers.'

Is the training a bit like tribal initiation? Treselyan states that: 'Some of it has been taken from the rites of passage of many civilizations throughout history. The firewalk has been used by Native Americans and Hawaiians as an initiatory rite. Passing through the fire moves them through a portal into manhood. Breaking an arrow by walking forward against an obstacle with the metal tip against the soft part of the throat, which we did earlier, is taken from the Fijian ritual of bringing women into maturity – so yes, it's tribal. These rituals have been used by mankind for thousands of years and have an historical validity and real meaning for human beings.'

When asked if the training appeals to women as much as it does to men, Treselyan replies, 'Although there is a lot of what could be construed as macho-testosterone stuff, it actually brings out more sensitivity in males and more focus in females. Fifty-five per cent of the people on our trainings are women, so they outnumber the men. Women want what the men have always had – career structure, focus, and the ability to make money and determine their own future. And this is a very powerful mechanism to make sure that they can have that.'

The core issues to deal with before walking on fire

> ### Thought provoker
> What core issues do people have to deal with before they will walk across hot coals? Treselyan believed that 'the greatest instinct of human beings is not survival but to do that which is familiar – like staying in a job or relationship when you know you should get out. Basically people here are learning how to get from one place to another by moving themselves through difficult circumstances.'

Treselyan says, 'When we do things that are unfamiliar we feel stressed, fearful, all of the things which stop us sometimes from moving on. People stay in destructive relationships or unrewarding jobs because they don't know how to do anything else. We even have a saying, 'better the devil you know'. People will trot out lots of reasons to explain why they're staying where they are. The truth is that usually they're just too frightened to move on.

'What the firewalk does very effectively is provide a controlled environment where they can make a dramatic change in their life by moving from "can't do" to having achieved something which they thought was impossible within a few seconds. Once they realize that they have overcome one incredible fear through the power of their own positive thinking then they often start to change other things in their lives that might be holding them back from achieving their full potential.

Having done it they realize they can take that energy and way of thinking and use it to transform other areas of their life, so they can translate it directly to whatever else they want to change.'

Motivation, mental focus and mind storming, goal setting and planning are the core of some of Treselyan's courses. But, in eight hours, can he really take someone who's bored, lacks discipline or has an aversion to structuring or planning ahead and turn him or her into a motivated goal setting individual? Treselyan says, 'Yes, you can do it in an hour if you use the right tools. If you use boring mediocre tools then you're not going to make someone highly motivated and highly productive. But a firewalk is very emotive. It gets people's whole attention – not just on the walk but on every detail of the planning. People's emotions are engaged, they take charge of their personal state management, their energy levels and the goal setting techniques around performing a firewalk.'

But once the firewalk is over and the feet are being nursed, how useful is the exercise seen in relation to work life? For the *Guardian* team, there were mixed reactions. Views ranged from one person who didn't do the walk and saw it as a pointless, painful task, to others who saw it as a life-changing experience.

Isn't firewalking dangerous? Don't some people still get burned? 'Not usually,' says Treselyan, 'but people have to overcome the illogical fear they have about firewalking. They think: "Oh my god, I'm going to get burned". Yet many of them are quite happy to do something like absailing which has a proven track record of killing people. No one has died in firewalking, and the most that could happen is that you'll get a slight blister, which is the same kind of blister you'll get wearing ill-fitting shoes.'

All 20 people who did the walk said it was a brilliant experience. Treselyan says: 'Yes I'm pleased about that. But I'm absolutely delighted that ten of those people also said it was a life changing experience that made them feel capable of achieving much more.'

Why does Treselyan choose dangerous pursuits such as the arrow to the throat ritual, walking on glass and firewalking to move people on? 'I have an unshakeable belief and passion that every person deserves as a human right to be the best that they can be, to raise themselves to their fullest potential and to be absolutely fulfilled. I am passionate about self-fulfilment and will strive to bring that idea to as many people as want to listen to me. I recognize that some people don't want this, they are quite happy to be mediocre and second-rate because it means that they are never going to be challenged. They're always going to have an excuse for not succeeding. But for those people, who actually want to see what they're made of, to be the best that they can be, then I will work with them and make them the best.'

[Courtesy of Reed Business Information, *Personnel Today* magazine

© Frances Coombes]

Club Entrepreneur for top performers

Club Entrepreneur is a forum for sales people who are determined to be the best at what they do – selling. Its founder Alex McMillan, author of the Teach Yourself book *Be a Great Entrepreneur*, published by Hodder Education, believes that attending training courses on its own rarely produces lasting behavioural changes.

He says, 'To master salesmanship you need to feel confident you already have the skills to solve problems, create options and have influence over resulting outcomes. To do this best, people need to see the big picture, to network and to spend time away from work colleagues but in the company of other ambitious sales people.'

Club Entrepreneur is designed specifically for people who want to excel at what they do. McMillan says, 'Here they can distance themselves from work and colleagues and discuss whatever's on their mind. It may be current selling strategies and how to improve them, or how to tackle any obstacles that are blocking them from achieving peak performance right now. The club also has tapes, books and motivational speakers with the type of energy and excitement which ambitious people thrive on.'

One session, 'It's not over until I win', explores how to keep going through setbacks and disappointments by looking at the thinking styles of self-made millionaires and billionaires such as Richard Branson, Bill Gates, Aristotle Onassis, Ray Kroc (McDonald's). As an exercise course participants compare their own mindsets to that of the millionaires and look for any conflicting beliefs held which might seriously inhibit them from achieving outstanding financial success.

So what's the first thing a salesperson would have to do to ensure they earned 100K? McMillan says that rule number one is to be employed by a company where it's possible to earn £100K. He says, 'I was coaching someone who was a top sales performer working for a prestigious car company and he was on top earnings of £35,000. I said, "You cannot make £100,000 a year by staying there." So his next move has to be to get out into whatever sales area he has the potential to earn 100K at the moment, it could be IT recruitment, financial services, whatever.'

'Another simple but effective thing to remember is that people who earn over 100K always take control when they go anywhere and go with an outcome in mind. A sales lead, a tip and ideas, whatever – they don't leave without them.'

McMillan believes that often it's insecurity that drives salespeople – not the promise of the Porsche. He says, They're not moving towards the bonuses, they're moving away from the fear of not selling enough. You often see adverts for salespeople saying earn £60K with a car and offering incentives for hitting sales targets, and many sales people will say that sort of advert is what motivates them – but actually it isn't. When you look at their behaviour the prize isn't what gets them into the office early, what's motivating them is moving away from fear. Insecurity is a powerful motivator.

'When I was selling, if you were in the bottom half of sales nobody gave you any pressure, but managers wouldn't spend time with you, they'd always talk to their top performers, so you wouldn't be in the inner circle, you wouldn't go to lunches with them. The people who were cut out of the inner circle were often motivated to hit their targets because they wanted to move away from that feeling of rejection. Those low performers may have felt bad but it's unlikely that they were consciously aware of the away-from-pain strategy that was motivating them to perform.'

The workshop on 'Managing those Magic Moments' asks: What gets you into your peak performance state? McMillan says, 'Even top salespeople's performances go up and down, it's just the best have learned to have less of a dip than others and to get back on target more quickly. Often when a salesperson is performing badly managers tend to send them on sales training – but these people already have the knowledge and know the techniques of selling. At the 100K Club we have coaches and experts on hand and only have to reactivate their selling state to get them back up. With the right people around you can turn a salesperson's performance around in a day, an hour – sometimes ten minutes.'

So what do top performers do to bring themselves back on target quickly? McMillan claims that, 'The beliefs people hold about themselves affect whether they achieve their aims or not. So a large part of getting back on form is to ask yourself lots of questions and then leave your channels of communication to yourself open so you hear the answers.

'These people have already got all the tools they need to do that job at the top level, and while they're in the trough, something is stopping them performing. They don't need training: they need access to what they've already got. Quite often their problems are emotional ones and we use a whole range of techniques that are brilliant for sorting these things out. For instance, there are some very simple questions people can ask themselves, such as "What would I need to do to get me back on track?", "What's the next action I can take towards it?"

'Our state of mind is geared by the questions we ask ourselves, more than the ones from people around us. We don't do it consciously, but if something went pear-shaped people start to think "What went wrong?", "What did I do?", and the brain gives answers to those questions that may undermine people so that they go into a negative spiral.

'Positive thinking is essential – so rather than letting your brain randomly choose the questions and answers it gives you, start to choose them yourself. Work out half a dozen positive questions, put them on the wall and wake up each day and go through them. For example, on my office wall I've got: "What are the six things that I am really happy about right now?" Next question is "What reward am I going to give myself in the future?" – I go through that every morning, it's simple, doesn't take more than 30 seconds but it gets me thinking positively.'

[Courtesy of Quest Media, *Selling Financial Services*, © Frances Coombes]

Negotiation strategies in business

Michael Breen is an NLP business trainer, consultant and negotiator. He trains people and gives them the tools and strategies they need to generate options and promote the sort of flexible thinking necessary to tackle challenges.

His neurolinguistic programming (NLP) training is based on modelling excellence, the thinking and behaviour patterns of the most consistently effective and productive people in the corporate world. Breen teaches people how to think and to use language as a precision tool to solve problems and implement change. Breen says: 'We first need to recognize thinking patterns, our own and other people's.'

PROBLEM SOLVING

Breen believes, when seeking solutions, you are the central character in the situation, so draw from your experience and viewpoint. Start with a goal in mind: 'What does taking this action get for me?' Draw on all the inner sensory awareness you possess, and the outer factual knowledge in order to frame the situation.

▶ **Events** – *notice what you see, hear and feel. Images and feelings that repeat or form a pattern are particularly significant.*
▶ **Define your boundaries,** *including timespan and the people involved, depending on your goals.*
▶ **Use only elements that can increase or decrease,** *so they can change when they are influenced by another element. If you want to use something that is fixed ask, 'What does this get for me?'*

Asking the above questions will define the structure of the problem. Examine the feedback you've got so far, to determine what new information you have obtained.

Your senses give you immediate feedback

Quiz

Answer these questions for more feedback:

▶ *Is the action you propose based on habit or feedback?*
▶ *What are the results so far?*

(Contd)

- ▶ *Are the results in line with what you want?*
- ▶ *Do you have accurate feedback about the consequences of your previous actions?*
- ▶ *Do you know what effects you have been having?*
- ▶ *How might you Find Out?*
- ▶ *What are you assuming about the problem and the people involved?*
- ▶ *Where do you set your thresholds – how much are you willing to tolerate before acting in terms of your:*
    1. *health and well-being*
    2. *relationships*
    3. *profession?*

Practise outcome thinking

Michael Breen teaches delegates to recognize thinking patterns. Once you have defined the structure of the problem, questions to ask when seeking a good outcome are:

- ▶ *What do I want?*
- ▶ *What have I got?*
- ▶ *What are my criteria for success?*

Think about what is stopping this problem from being resolved.

- ▶ *How is this problem maintained?*
- ▶ *What am I doing that is maintaining this problem?*

Reflect on the mental models you are holding about the problem and ask:

- ▶ *What am I assuming about the problem?*
- ▶ *What am I assuming about the people involved?*

Using these questions will help you to map the situation and pinpoint problem areas, possible actions and change points with precision.

As trainees begin to recognize thinking patterns, their own and other people's, they see the power and control they can exert over situations in which they might previously have felt powerless.

To find out what impact the changes made in the workshop on goal setting and achievement abilities had, I revisited some workshop participants six months later to ascertain whether their early successes had been sustained and how they had applied it to their own areas of work.

Case study – Phil Beardwell

Phil Beardwell, operational manager at Canada Life Assurance, Solihull branch, said, 'I am responsible for managing 40 financial consultants and ensuring they bring in over £1 million in new leads each year. I use the strategies all the time because they get results. We're not a bank, so there are no leads. It's all up to the team, so we need to be focused on what we do. I spend time building positive states in my people, taking them from "can't do", "won't do" problems, and using the strategies to reassess their states and move them on so they have the ability to do it themselves.'

Case study – Ian Harris

Ian Harris, a computer salesman from Hertfordshire, exceeded his monthly sales target by £45,000 by month three of his training. Six months on, his sales figures have stayed on a higher plateau. He says, 'The strategies that
(Contd)

worked for me were calibrating customers' convincer patterns. By paying close attention to the way another person sees the world you become aware of the type of sensory criteria that person looks for and needs to have met in order to make up their mind before buying.

'Some people need to hear descriptions of what a product will do, but their criteria could be that you have to describe it to them three times, twice is not enough, and if you are not aware of this you've lost a potential sale. Others may need to read about the product and some may have to see and touch it before they decide to buy.'

Case study – Steve Harding

For Steve Harding, a property developer, it was the problem solving and negotiation strategies he found most helpful for negotiating property deals. He says, 'I had been putting a deal together while on the training, and a month after completing it, I had tripled my turnover from £200,000 to £500,000 and I know it will be two times higher by next year.

'What worked for me was the state management training; I changed my thinking from, "It would be nice if this deal works" to "When this works". I found the positioning and thinking through strategies that Michael taught us have given me a spatial awareness of where everything is in negotiations that I didn't have before. Now I will think, "Here's what I want on the agenda" and I aim to achieve that. However, if the deal is important to me, I will first find out what the other side wants, and tailor my request to suit.'

When we teach people strategies, the emphasis is on the mental and emotional processes that make them better at what they do. Asking questions, such as 'How will you know when you've become a better negotiator?', 'What will you hear and feel?', clarifies what that person's expectations are. They are the only people who know the criteria they have to meet within themselves in order to visualize themselves successfully reaching their goals.

THINGS TO REMEMBER

▶ *To succeed you have to take risks that take you away from your comfort zone and push you beyond your boundaries.*

▶ *Network and spend time away from work colleagues, but in the company of other ambitious people.*

▶ *Use your senses – they give you immediate feedback.*

▶ *Practise outcome thinking and negotiating win–win situations.*

11

Recognize people's thinking styles

In this chapter you will:
- *recognize thinking styles*
- *use language that increases effective communication*
- *use motivation that fits your thinking styles*

'The most complicated piece of equipment comes with no instructions and performs in a different way every day – it's our people.'

Sir Tom Farmer, CEO Kwik-Fit

Thought provoker
Why do people behave so differently from each other? You ask several people to do the same thing, so why is it that one does exactly what you say, another wants to discuss it and finds fault, or argues with you on each point, while a third person may completely ignore your request?

In a work situation a supervisor may circulate a memo stating that the compulsory manual handling course is coming up but some people will claim they didn't receive it. This is puzzling because these are the same few people who did not receive her carefully crafted missive about submitting annual leave forms a month in advance. What is happening here?

Types of thinking style

Different people run different thinking styles. When the supervisor recognizes the styles those people are running, she will be able to make requests in ways that make it more likely that things will be done, because the requests are addressed to staff in ways that meet their needs.

According to Fiona Beddoes-Jones, management consultant and creator of the training programme 'Thinking Styles', 'People who don't notice the small, to them unimportant things, may be "big chunk thinkers", interested in what we are going to do, not the minutiae of how we are going to get there. They might be people with a poorly developed mental filing system. Or they could be "mismatchers" – people who hate being told what to do.' As part of the programme, Fiona has developed a questionnaire that teaches staff first how to understand their own thinking style, then to apply it to other people's style so they can learn to work together effectively as a team.

Getting teams to work together effectively

Shell and National Westminster Bank have used 'Thinking Styles' to match jobs to the way people naturally process information. British Aerospace used it to allocate tasks among teams of workers. Fiona says, 'When projects cost millions, anything that leads to team effectiveness and shortens the length of a job can potentially save huge amounts of money.'

Some people are visual and see pictures when they think. But if you are an auditory person and hear what people say it may not occur to you that others take in information differently. Fiona says, 'Shut your eyes and listen to the words people use to engage with each other in your department. Someone who says "I see what you mean" is thinking in pictures. To talk to them in their own language and find out if they understand your message, you might say "Do you get the picture?"'

People also have styles of working with others. 'Matchers' are team people who like to work in harmony. They are good communicators and do well in customer relations jobs. Matchers are adaptive and tend to fit in with other people's wishes. They are not normally innovators, simply because they are too nice.

George Bernard Shaw said, 'The reasonable man adapts himself to the world. The unreasonable man persists in trying to adapt the world to him. This is why all change depends on the unreasonable man.' In a team the 'mismatcher' can be seen as the unreasonable person because they think new ideas through by disagreement.

'The first time you talk an idea through with a mismatcher,' says Fiona, 'they usually disagree with you. But when you return they will have thought about it and be working towards an agreement. Mismatchers make good computer hardware engineers because they will be acutely aware of all possible risks involved.'

Insight
We all use combinations of different thinking styles that can change depending on the task we are working on, how relaxed or stressed we feel and where we happen to be. The best type of thinker to be is a flexible one.

Do you recognize your thinking style?

Detail conscious people notice small details. They take in information in small pieces as it relates to them.	**Big chunk thinkers** are able to assess a whole situation. They take in larger pieces of information and key points. Big chunk thinkers are often leaders or responsible for major projects or strategies.
Procedural thinkers follow instructions and the accepted way of doing things. If you interrupt an extremely procedural thinker as he is explaining something, he may go back to the beginning and start to explain all over again.	**Option thinkers** want more choice in their work and to explore different possibilities. They are easily bored.
Matchers like to conform, they're good team workers and communicators, and have a non-confrontational approach.	**Mismatchers** test an idea through disagreement. They often challenge the existing situation and are anxious for change.
Filters for sameness notice what is similar; if you've had piles, they've had bigger ones. They want stability and to find common ground.	**Filters for difference** notice if anything has changed or is different. At the extreme they can be faultfinders, good to have in your team for spotting errors but not to live with.
Process for 'self' see situations in terms of their own needs and priorities and put themselves first.	**Process for 'others'** put other people's needs first, above their own. Women and mothers tend to come into this category more often than men do. A lot of people in the caring professions process for others.

Moving away from people avoid problems or threats by moving away from them.	Moving towards people, especially entrepreneurs, are really proactive and off the scale for achieving their goals.
Reactive people respond to other people's requests or changes in situations or circumstances.	Proactive people initiate change, foresee problems and plan ahead.
Internally referenced people check how they are doing by asking themselves 'How am I doing?' They look inside to check and are not dependent on other people's approval to know whether they have done something well.	Externally referenced need others to tell them they have done a good job. They need praise and reassurance and rely on other people, supervisors, colleagues, friends and partners to tell them how they are doing.

[Courtesy of Associated Newspapers, *London Evening Standard*, 'Just the Job', © Frances Coombes]

Thinking styles examined

WHAT ARE THINKING STYLES?

Thought provoker
Thinking styles are mainly unconscious patterns of thinking we use to sort out all the incoming information that we are bombarded with each day. Our thinking patterns affect what we notice in a situation, how we visualize it, and how we organize and structure it in order to come to a conclusion.

The connections we make and the way we view the world, our memories, ideas and incoming information are all unique to us.

We take in information from the world through all our senses, that is what we see, hear, touch, taste and smell.

If we did not have an internal system which filtered information for us we would be overwhelmed by thousands of unwanted bits of stimulus, such as newspaper headlines, snippets of conversations, bars of songs, labels on food products. Our thinking patterns screen out what does not interest us, so we can pay more attention to the things we are drawn to.

WHAT THINKING STYLES DO

Insight

Our thinking styles give us an automatic way to sort and organize the experiences we have each day.

▶ *By learning to manage our thoughts we can shape them and change them so that we can create the life and career we want.*
▶ *When you know how you think, you understand how you function and you can organize the things you want to do in ways that are most likely to lead to you achieving your outcomes.*

Insight

Although most people share some similar patterns, each person's thinking style will be unique.

Understanding more about thinking styles can help us understand more about people.

▶ *You can understand the thinking styles that are contributing to the beliefs that a person holds.*
▶ *You can organize your time more effectively because you understand how you think and behave and get things done.*
▶ *You can choose a career that is attractive to someone with your thinking pattern.*
▶ *You can select staff that fit particular jobs, based on knowing how they think.*

► *You can build your own personal profile of your thinking habits in order to understand why you do the things you do.*

Bosses and leaders are usually big picture thinkers: they talk in generalizations, but they also tend to balance this by employing personal assistants who are detail conscious. Some people are flexible thinkers and function easily at either end of the thinking continuum; others can learn how to do it.

Managers who are cut off from the grassroots often depend on feedback from others about what is happening at shopfloor level. The messages they receive will have been passed through the messenger's information-filter system and selected according to what that person thinks is important to the employer. An employer who recognizes his assistant's thinking style can more easily recognize the type of information that he may not be getting.

> **Thought provoker**
> Mismatchers may be irritating but they will tell you why your product launch won't work at the beginning, not the end of your project. They will not wait to sympathize with everyone else when it becomes patently obvious why the plan didn't work. Mismatchers may not be the subtlest of communicators, but that's the price you pay for having an employee who is prepared to tell you the brutal truth at the start of your venture.

Flexible thinkers can change their habitual thought patterns at will and operate well at both ends of their thinking scale. For instance, a project manager may be a big chunk thinker, and able to visualize and have an overview of a major plan, say to build a hospital. She will also be good at breaking down the steps required for the outcome into procedural bite-sized chunks. This type of flexible thinking helps she to clarify ideas and understand she role in situations so that she can feel reasonably sure beforehand whether the plan she is implementing will work.

UNCONSCIOUS THINKING STYLES

Insight

Our thinking styles are largely unconscious patterns we use to filter and sort information. They affect what we notice, and how we organize our experience of the world, and make information from it. Witnesses to the same event can give wildly differing interpretations of the same event, depending on what they look for in a situation and how the way that they organize their information differs from others.

People tend to use the same thinking habits and behaviour in similar contexts. You may say about a friend, 'I can read her like a book'. You are indicating that you recognize habitual thinking styles the person uses in certain contexts, for instance some people shop for bargains, others look for quality. If your friend does this you will recognize this behaviour pattern and expect it of her even before you enter the store.

Thought provoker

There are limitations to many of the thinking patterns we run. A bargain hunter may not 'see' quality items in a store, when it may be important that he does so. If we are unaware of our own information filtering processes we may have 'blind' spots and consistently miss important details we need to know about.

Some people are naturally goal oriented – others move away from pain. These are the habitual thinking styles people run in similar contexts. The methods we use to organize information are patterns of thinking and behaviour outside of our awareness. Yet they have a major effect on how we respond to situations in the world, and can limit us in our ability to achieve our aims.

Insight

> People use combinations of lots of different thinking styles but do have traits. Some types of thinker are easy to recognize because they operate at the extreme ends of their scale.

Moving away from ↔ Moving towards

People who move away from pain may be spurred into action to avoid unpleasant situations or when things become unbearable. When you ask people what they want and they tell you what they do not want, you will know they are running an 'away from' style of thinking. To motivate someone who runs an 'away from pain' thinking style, tell them about all the unpleasant things that will happen if they do not reach their target.

When people tell you what they want, and what they want to accomplish, their thinking strategy is to move towards pleasure. Show them the carrot and the rewards they will get for their effort.

Necessity ↔ Possibility

Some people are driven by what must be done, or what they think should be done. 'I must do this,' is their mantra. People who are driven by necessity will often have a preference for procedures and have strong ideas about how things should be done.

People who are motivated by what could be, want options and new ventures, and novel ways to do things. They like to know what the alternatives are and what might be possible.

Focus attention on themselves ↔ Focus on others

People who are self-referenced evaluate a situation from their own perspective, and may not always consider effects on others. At the extreme they may be oblivious to the outside world, and how situations are being experienced by other people. Extremely self-referenced behaviour may be seen as selfish or narcissistic.

Those who focus on others and how situations will affect them are often carers, and may put the contentment and welfare of others over their own needs. They are attentive to what is going on around them and at the extreme may end up trying to please everyone at their own expense.

Sort for similarities ↔ Look for differences

People who sort for similarities notice what is similar in a situation to what has gone before. They want stability and to find common ground with others. The quickest way to get a result from them is to build rapport with them.

Those who filter for differences may notice what has changed or is different from before. They make good colleagues to have in a crisis-management situation because they pick up on every eventuality and possibility that might go wrong. They are good people to have in your team for spotting errors, but not to live with.

Big chunk thinker ↔ Small chunk thinker

Insight

Big-chunk thinkers are able to assess a whole situation. They take in larger pieces of information and key points. Big chunk thinkers are often leaders or responsible for major projects. They may be more concerned with the big picture rather than the fine details of how they plan to get there.

Small chunk thinkers are procedural thinkers, they follow instructions and the accepted way of doing things. If you interrupt extremely procedural thinkers while they are talking, they may need to go back and recount the whole story from the beginning.

Share your people's view of the world

People have preferential sensory systems, visual, auditory and feelings, sensations or emotions for the way they take in information from the world. You can build rapport with them by speaking the same sensory language as they do. Using the same representation system as people builds rapport, and interrupting in another system will break rapport. It's good to know how to be in rapport, but it's also good to know how to break it if you want to move a conversation along.

Thought provoker
If you tell people your message in their preferred sensory style, they will learn and retain it better than if it is given in another style.

Studies carried out with children and adults, looking at how they learn and take in information, discovered the following:

Pictures – People who use predominantly visual senses are good at sorting lots of information at a moment's notice. They may think in pictures and hold and rearrange information in a spider diagram.

Words – People who think in words find it difficult to hold information unless it is structured and the relationship is linear. They often use chants and mnemonics to help them remember things. Auditory is a good system for sorting known information, but is less useful for being creative.

Feelings – People whose dominant sense is feelings may need to physically do an exercise a couple of times before they get the hang of things. We retain a lot of information in our body. If you have not ridden a bike for a long while and you sit on one, your body knows how to ride a bike even if you cannot remember.

People who process through feelings, sensations and emotions are often very bright but may never have learned to process that information in a way that can be checked by others. Once triggered, this system will produce a mass of information at once, leading to a 'flash' of understanding.

How are people motivated to do things?

Below are some reasons why it's invaluable to know other people's
thinking styles when you communicate with them:

▶ *If you are a leader and need to motivate others, then knowing
   how your people take in information and think will help you
   to communicate more effectively with them.*
▶ *When you know how your own internal motivation works,
   you can more easily understand other people's patterns and
   the best ways to guide and motivate them.*
▶ *If you understand more about the way people think, you can
   build rapport and have stronger relationships with clients,
   colleagues and friends on a deeper level than before.*
▶ *You can speak to groups of people using words that appeal to
   a range of thinking styles.*
▶ *You will become more capable of generating favourable or
   win–win solutions. If you can see more sides to a disagreement or
   problem, you are likely also to see more possibilities for solving it.*
▶ *If you are writing job adverts or advertising brochures and
   you want to appeal to a specific kind of reader, you can write
   in language that appeals to the thinking styles you seek in an
   applicant.*

Connect with your audience

Insight
A lot of advertising is aimed at people who run an 'away
from pain' strategy. The messages about the penalties of
not buying the right car insurance or not having the right

internet search engine is that if you do not do these things it will cause you pain. Yet that message may be largely ignored by the part of the population not hung up on the feel-bad factor who quickly move away from heavy guilt trips. If the message is not packaged in a way that fits their criteria, those people will simply switch off and not notice it.

People filter incoming messages by selecting the parts they feel are relevant to them and that they expect to use later. They discard the rest.

HOW DOES AN AUDIENCE WANT YOU TO COMMUNICATE WITH THEM?

Your audience wants you to make them a promise and expects you to fulfil their expectations. They want you to use linked information, stories and jokes, give handouts and exercises that will make your talk memorable. If you present your message so that it is appealing to several types of listener, you can ensure that everyone in your audience connects with and remembers what you said.

Communicate in people's thinking styles

If you are presenting to a general audience and you don't know their background then consider this:

▶ *The biggest part of the population, 35 per cent, want to know 'why' they should listen to you. So you have to win their hearts and minds and tell them at the start why what you have to say is important to them.*
▶ *One-quarter, 25 per cent, of your audience are thinking 'So what?' They want to know how useful whatever you are saying to them is.*

(Contd)

- *Just under one-quarter of your audience, 22 per cent, are wondering 'How do I apply this information? Show me how to use it.'*
- *And the remainder, 18 per cent, of the group are thinking 'What if ...' – What if I took this information and customized it? What does it mean to me and what can I do with it? What might it lead to?*

[Statistics from Bernice McCarthy, author of the COLB Learning Styles book *The 4-MatSystem* (Excel Inc., 1987)]

If you are speaking to a group and you want to influence people, glance at your notes to see whether your talk will satisfy the sort of questions that a general audience would want answered.

Technique

A useful tip for increased focus while preparing a presentation is to cut out magazine pictures of people who represent your typical audience. Stick them on the wall and glance up at them as you write.

If you give each person in your pictures a name and then write the words, 'Why?', 'What?', 'So what?' and 'How?' under each one you can converse with each part of your audience individually at any brief sticking point. You can simply stop and say to 'So what?' – 'Well Dave what did you think of the way I put that?' – and wait for the answer.

Manage your state of leadership

Insight

If you are going to take somebody to a new level of understanding then you have got to go there first yourself. In order to convey information to a group of people your energy level, state, motivation and enthusiasm must be higher than your audience's. It is your internal state and level of motivation that determine how well your talk will go.

To connect with the group and to get them into a participatory mood:

▶ *Start by asking a question that requires people to raise their hands, for instance: 'How many people are here today because they want to be?' To encourage them to do this, raise your own hand in the air when you ask the question and keep it there until you're ready to have them lower theirs.*

▶ *Look at the people with their hands raised and briefly make eye contact with each of them. Then ask another question that will encourage the rest of the group to raise their hands. 'And how many people are here because they have been sent?'*

▶ *Summarize what you have learned from the questions you have asked: 'It looks like 90 per cent of you are interested in the mating habits of the snail, so we're going to have a really interesting time tonight.' Glance round the room making eye contact again as you make this statement.*

THINGS TO REMEMBER

▶ *If you are communicating with others make sure you recognize their thinking styles.*

▶ *Recognize how your motivation and thinking styles work together.*

▶ *When you present to groups of people, use language that engages all styles of thinkers and increases effective communication.*

▶ *Manage your state of leadership.*

12

Take control of how you think

In this chapter you will:
- *take control of how you think*
- *create your own thinking blueprint*
- *change unhelpful pictures to change motivation*

For maximum impact notice listeners' thinking styles

Canadian Shelle Rose Charvet is an international communications and influencing skills trainer and author of *Words that Change Minds* (Kendall Hunt Publications, 1997). She has trained sales groups in large companies on how to get the edge in selling, and helped political parties design campaigning strategies based on understanding how differently people think and decide how to take actions.

Charvet says, 'The better you understand someone's thinking strategies the more able you are to influence and predict their behaviour. If you are a team leader then you need to know which of your people are motivated by external circumstances, that is praise, rewards, recognition, and which are motivated by their internal beliefs and values.'

Thinking style tips

If you are selling your product or idea to someone, the better you understand how people think and comprehend their internal drivers, the more able you are to influence and predict their behaviour.

▶ *There are people who move 'away from pain' and at the other end of the scale those who are motivated to move 'towards pleasure'.*

▶ *Some customers want a new product to be 'different' and others look for 'sameness' to whatever they are using now.*

▶ *There are also 'sameness with exception' people who like to know the product is similar to the one they had before and then to hear words such as 'improvement', 'better', 'more', 'less'.*

Shelle says: 'It's not just individuals, professions also have "towards" or "away from" attitudes. If you're addressing salespeople, they tend to move towards goals. While doctors move away from sickness and prefer speakers who take a similar cautious approach.' She continues, 'Can you imagine rushing in to see your doctor about a medical condition to be greeted by a cheerful "towards" person who ignores your symptoms and instead, asks you, "What are your health goals?"'

As people listen to others they select the parts of the conversation they feel are relevant to them and quickly forget the rest. A lot of advertising is aimed at people who run an 'away from pain' strategy. An advertising message about the penalties of not buying the right car insurance may suggest that if you do not buy the insurance it could cause you pain. The message may not be heard by people who move towards pleasure and quickly move away form heavy guilt trips.

If you are an individual seeking that extra energy and motivation you require to move in the direction of your heart's desires then you need to know whether your habitual thinking pattern is to move 'towards pleasure' or 'away from pain'.

Questions to elicit what motivates a person

Shelle says, 'You can find out what motivates a person by asking them a question such as:

▶ *Why did you decide to change your last job?*
▶ *Why did you change your last partner?*

Choose a question where they tell you why they changed something.'

People who move towards pleasure will tell you, 'Well, I saw this great job, it offered a lot of potential for me to do the sort of things I wanted', and they will offer a list of criteria.

People who move away from pain will say, 'Well, I couldn't stand my job anymore, and so I left'.

When it comes to partners the story is similar. People who move away from pain will say, 'Well, I couldn't stand it anymore so I got out.'

The person who is motivated towards a goal might say, 'Well, I found a better partner, so I grabbed the chance to be happy.'

Don't assume that people who run 'away from' strategies will do any less well than those who run 'towards' fulfilment, both types can be phenomenally successful but are motivated towards their goals in different ways.

WE RUN SIMILAR THINKING PATTERNS IN SIMILAR SITUATIONS

Some people naturally move towards goals – others move away from pain. These are recognizable thinking styles that people run in similar contexts. These methods of organizing information are patterns of thinking and behaviour which are outside our awareness, yet they have a major effect on how we respond to situations in the world.

Knowing how habitual thinking patterns work will give you a better understanding of how you are motivated. This is useful information for

- *when you are setting your goals*
- *knowing other people's thinking styles*
- *building rapport with others.*

RECOGNIZE PEOPLE'S DIFFERENT THINKING STYLES

Recognizing your own and other people's thinking styles can help you understand better how you are motivated; it can help predict your future behaviour in recognizable circumstances.

Understanding thinking styles allows you to plan ahead how you might interact with other people, and alter your behaviour to get the best results from others and the outcomes you desire. The list below shows the characteristic behaviour of people who fall within each thinking style.

Checklist of thinking styles

Move away from pain
- *Focus on problems.*
- *Talk about what they do not want to happen.*

- *Are motivated by negative consequences.*
- *Often have difficulty defining their goals.*

Move towards pleasure
- *Respond to incentives.*
- *Are motivated by achievements.*
- *May find it difficult to recognize negative consequences.*

Motivated by necessity
- *Often display driven behaviour.*
- *Strong ideas on how things should be done.*
- *Motivated by clearcut, recognizable methods.*

Motivated by options and possibility
- *Want choices, lots of options.*
- *Good at thinking up new ways of doing things.*
- *Motivated by new challenges.*

Internally focused
- *Respond to the content of the communication.*
- *Do not notice or respond to others' emotional behaviour.*
- *Do not easily build rapport with others.*

Attention focused on others
- *Respond to the people around them.*
- *Good rapport builders.*
- *Take responsibility for the way that other people feel.*

Sort for similarities
- *Will notice what is the same in a situation.*
- *Will often repeat a story similar to the one you tell.*
- *Use words like, 'just like me', 'the same', 'similar'.*

Sort for what is different
- *Notice what is different.*
- *Sort for what is missing.*
- *Can be fault finders.*

Big chunk thinker

- ▶ *Takes a global view of an idea or situation.*
- ▶ *Does not pay attention to the small details.*
- ▶ *Can overlook things that do not fit into an overall plan.*

Small chunk thinker

- ▶ *Good at remembering and handling details.*
- ▶ *May lack an overall framework to relate an idea to.*
- ▶ *Want to be familiar with the process of doing things.*

Identify your thinking patterns

Look at the checklist of thinking styles descriptions above and mentally replay some recent situations in your head and how you reacted at the time. Ask yourself which type of thinking you habitually use – that is your thinking style.

Check where you are on the continuum using the thinking styles patterns below. Draw an X on the line at the point where you think you function in that particular thinking style.

Away from pain	⟷	Towards pleasure
Necessity	⟷	Possibility
Self-referenced	⟷	Respond to others
Sort for similarities	⟷	Look for difference
Big picture thinker	⟷	Small chunk thinker

Thinking styles are useful predictors of behaviour, and recognizing and understanding them allows you to make crucial distinctions about how to interact with people. They are guides to behaviour only – no one is exclusively programmed to behave in a certain way. And we can all, with practice, learn to change unhelpful or irritating behaviour.

Where do your decisions come from?

Where in your body do you make decisions? Internally referenced people gather information from outside sources and then they decide about it, based on their internal standards. External people need other people's opinions to help them make up their mind. It's vital to know where you make decisions because it will determine the way in which you are motivated.

Action

You can find out how people make decisions by asking them, 'How do you know when you have done a good job?' Ask this question of a good number of people, say the next six people you meet, so that you get a selection of answers.

▶ Some people will say, 'Oh, I just know when I've done a good job. It's a feeling.' These people are internally referenced and look inside themselves for the answers.
▶ Others will say, 'I know I've done well when my supervisor/friends/colleagues tell me I've done well.' These people are externally referenced and they seek confirmation from people outside.
▶ Some people will say, 'Well, I suppose that really I know when I've done something well. But I like somebody to tell me so too.'

Shelle says, 'Whenever I am called into a large corporation and I keep hearing similar statements from employees: "The bosses keep us in the dark and don't tell us anything." I can predict that I am dealing with an organization whose managers are mostly internally focused, and a workforce who are predominantly externally referenced and need to be told they have done a good job. Because the managers don't need someone else's approval on how well they think they are doing, they can't see what the problem is for the staff.'

Knowing the habitual thinking patterns which you run will give you a better understanding of how you are motivated. This is useful information for when you are setting your goals. Knowing other people's thinking styles is useful for building rapport with them.

'Away' and 'towards' problem solving

How do the people around you react when confronted with problems?

▶ *'It's here so let's deal with it.'* (Towards resolution)
▶ *'Oh no, not again, let's ignore it and see if it goes away.'* (Away from pain)

These are extremes on the scale of reactions, but are pretty much how people think. People tend to run patterns of behaviour in similar circumstances. Although you can often predict how they will behave in one situation, this does not necessarily mean they will run the same behaviour in another context.

Thought provoker
Understanding other people's behaviour will let you know what really motivates and triggers them to perform at their best.

Understanding your own habitual behaviour lets you realize there are choices you can make, and a variety of different ways of doing things.

You don't have to keep repeating the same behaviour if it doesn't get you the results you want.

We all use habitual behaviour patterns in everything we do, from the way we get out of bed in the mornings, to choosing our next life partner. Understanding how our behavioural patterns work can be the key to understanding how we are motivated to set our own goals in life and succeed at what we do.

Take control of how you think

Suppose I said that you could record and store your own feelings and thought processes in a systematic way, using nothing more high-tech than a pen and paper. You might say, 'What would I want to do that for?'

If it would enable you to compare past sensory blueprints of how you thought and felt and behaved during peak performances or when overcoming problems, and you could recall precisely what the triggers were that moved you on to greater heights – would that be interesting? Once recorded you could review past scenarios and refine your future strategies, based on what you had learned, so that you didn't have to repeat unproductive old types of behaviour any more – would that surprise you?

Until recently it has been mainly athletes and businesspeople with the help of professional sports and personal achievement coaches, who have learned to record, store and refine their past sensory impressions in an amazing way that leads them to achieve world class performances in their field.

HABITUAL THINKING

The way you brush your teeth, use your knife and fork, choose the hand to drink your cup of tea with, are all habits you've formed. Try brushing your teeth or swapping your fork to the other hand next time and see how different it feels initially. Most of us also think in habitual ways and there is a multibillion pound global industry engaged in finding out about how we think in order to get us to buy into ideas, beliefs or products.

When people are stressed, they often reconnect to past feelings of panic and dread experienced in childhood. It may be 20 years later and the person is a successful executive, but when faced with a deadline or a bigger challenge the old feelings of panic re-emerge just as when handing in a classroom essay and expecting to receive bad marks.

That is why the facts that people give us during conversation are often less important than the sensory (seeing, hearing, feeling, smelling, tasting) language they use. Often it is the throwaway remarks, the ones we miss when listening to others, that hold most of the vital clues to their attitudes to stress or to bigger challenges.

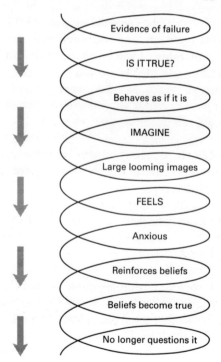

Figure 12.1 Downward progression of a negative belief.

Create a blueprint of your thinking habits

Can you remember the last problem you had that you successfully solved? How were you experiencing the problem? What were you seeing, hearing, feeling, about the situation? What was stopping you from moving ahead?

How to measure your thinking habits

The context we will use is the behaviours and attitudes that you run when you have problems.

Jot down your thoughts and feelings about your last challenge sequentially, paying attention to feelings from just before you realized there was a problem until just after you realized it was resolved.

Take a highlighter pen and colour all the descriptive language you used to describe how you felt. Look at the thinking habits chart and mark an X along any of the continuum lines at the point you believe your phrases demonstrate that you were displaying a recognizable type of 'thinking behaviour'.

Away from pain   ⟷   Towards pleasure
Necessity   ⟷   Possibility
Self-referenced   ⟷   Respond to others
Sort for similarities   ⟷   Look for difference
Big picture thinker   ⟷   Small chunk thinker

WHAT ARE YOU SAYING TO YOURSELF?

Away from pain vs. Towards pleasure   Did I see this problem coming but put it off until it could no longer be avoided? Or did I see the possibilities in the situation and move towards making changes?

Necessity vs. Possibility   Is this a problem because **I think it is**, or because **someone else has told me it is**?

Self-referenced vs. Respond to others   Am I worried about the consequences **for myself**, other people or both?

Sort for similarities vs. Look for difference   Is this problem **similar to** or **different from** other problems I've faced before? If so, how is it similar/different?

Big picture thinker vs. small chunk thinker   If you are thinking 'this **always** happens to me', you are generalizing. Asking yourself why this specific thing is happening is a more useful question that will generate more answers.

Now think about what happened to make you change your mind and decide that you could reach your goal. What changed in the sights and sounds and feelings you were experiencing to help you achieve your outcome? Highlight those sensations in another colour and transfer to your blueprint.

Once you understand your own behaviour patterns when faced with problems and how you solved them in the past, you can record this information and let it work for you to propel you more quickly towards your goals.

Gill Shaw, NLP executive and brand coach of Fresh-look Experience says, 'Beliefs are our driving principles which give us a sense of certainty, realism and direction particularly in decision making. Positive beliefs are necessary to achieve our outcomes, and may even become our purpose. Beliefs work in conjunction with our values, which are the standards which frame how we live and provide the juice to motivate us.'

There are three parts to changing beliefs:

1 **It's possible.** *To be able to change a negative belief to a positive one you need to reframe and believe that it is possible to achieve (so that you can model success).*
2 **You are able to do it.** *You are able to achieve your goal with the resources you have available, and you deserve to achieve it. Otherwise you will have no commitment to your goal, or worse, you will sabotage your outcome because you don't believe you deserve the goal.*
3 **You must believe that your goal is realistic.** *You can change from a downward progression of a limiting or negative belief, to an upward progression of a positive belief when you know that something is possible because someone else has done it. Then it is possible for you to achieve if you believe you can do it.*

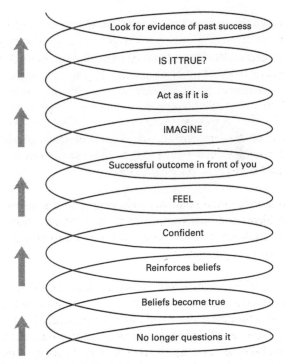

Figure 12.2 Upward progression of a positive belief.

Changing beliefs

DOES CHANGING PICTURES MOTIVATE YOU?

One of the most useful things you can know about yourself is how you become motivated to do something. If you can't get motivated enough to perform a necessary task, perhaps it's time to change your view.

Case study – Claire

Claire wanted to change her career and work for a City stockbroker. On three occasions she had reached the interview stage and then been turned down. She felt that there was an extra piece of information she needed to produce at her interviews to make her a serious contender for a job.

Claire knew:

▶ *what she had to do*
▶ *when she had to do it (she had an interview the following Wednesday).*

Yet she couldn't quite get around to doing the task.

Claire said she needed to produce an analysis of the top 100 share price projections for interview, but kept putting it off. As she spoke her hands seemed to keep pushing an imaginary object down towards her left foot.

'What's the hand gesture about?' I asked.

Claire replied, 'I guess that's me pushing the task away. I don't want to do it, so I keep pushing it away so it stays small and dim and distant down there.' I asked her what would happen if she turned up for interview without the share projections. Claire looked uncomfortable and fell silent.

Elicit your strategy for being motivated.

I asked Claire if she had ever done a similar task well and how was it different from this time. She said when she had done the task successfully she was motivated and saw the task as 'big and bright and throbbing in intensity, colourful and up close' to her face. And what motivated her, I asked. She realized it was the fact that others wanted her to succeed at it. Emerging now is Claire's motivation strategy for doing a similar task successfully. I asked Claire to pretend I was a temp come to fill her role, and to describe what she was 'seeing', 'feeling', 'saying' to herself that motivated her to finish the task successfully.

The main difference between Claire's 'motivated' and 'unmotivated' state was in how colourful and close she pictured the task. She practised switching her unmotivating picture from 'small' and 'dim' and 'distant' to seeing it as 'big and bright', 'colourful and up close' to her face. She really felt motivated to do it now and was able to describe every part of the procedure linked to performing the task successfully.

(Contd)

Finally, I asked Claire if she had a timescale for completion and she said confidently, 'Yes, now I'm motivated to do it, I will complete it by Monday afternoon.'

Changing unhelpful pictures changes motivation

▶ *Changing what you 'see', 'hear', 'feel' and are 'picturing' around performing a task will change the way you feel about doing it.*

▶ *Identify the feeling that comes when you think of performing the unwanted task; often it is a feeling that needs to be changed.*

Case study – Emma

Emma experienced a 'feeling' like a dark, heavy cloud over the back part of the left side of her head each time she felt stressed and had to write a piece of copy to deadline.

First came the feeling, then she saw pictures of lots of pages of paper in front of her face so that it obscured her view. Each paper represented a different project and it made her feel as if the work was never ending and that she could never focus entirely on one piece of work alone.

Change the feelings to an organized picture of you performing the task well.

I asked Emma what would happen if the projects were not all screaming for her attention and directly in her face. Suppose each project was a sheet of paper which was laid in a neat row from left to right at floor level.

Emma said that she would be motivated if she could choose one sheet of paper labelled 'project' at a time, and bring the image close enough to be within her vision, but not enough to block her view. She would focus on only one task at a time, make sure she knew the procedure for doing the task before starting, and give herself a reward for completing on time.

If you can't get around to doing a task you really know you should, ask yourself, 'What are the "picture's" and "feelings" I associate with doing this task?' 'How can I change them and make them more motivating for me?'

['Does Changing Pictures Motivate You?' courtesy of *Positive Health* magazine, (PH) issue 132, February 2007, www.positivehealth.com, © Frances Coombes]

To change a habit look at what holds it in place

Thought provoker
Limiting styles of thinking and behaviour make life more difficult because they can lead to stuck situations. If we can notice and categorize the sort of habitual thinking that may be stopping us from reaching goals, we can replace it with something new that will keep all the benefits of the old habit and still get us the outcome we want.

THINGS TO REMEMBER

▶ *When selling your ideas, notice your listeners' thinking styles.*

▶ *Use questions that elicit what motivates a person to comply with your wishes.*

▶ *Take control of how you think.*

▶ *Notice the downward progression of a negative belief and the upward progression of a positive belief.*

▶ *Create your own thinking blueprint.*

▶ *To change a habit, look at what holds it in place.*

▶ *Change unhelpful thought pictures to change motivation.*

13

Model success strategies

In this chapter you will learn:
- *what the main attributes of successful people are*
- *about new ways of doing things*
- *how to gather the habits of successful people*

'There are a couple of universities around. There's Einstein's university you go to and you stand on the shoulders of others. Then there's the University of Life, and anyone who's been there has learned by his or her own mistakes. And that's okay, there's nothing wrong with that – it's just that it takes a hell of a lot of time.

'There's a way of speeding up getting to where you want to go simply by looking at other people and seeing what works for them. When you really model other people it's not just a question of going to the "experts". If you've ever bought diet or healthy eating books, check out a picture of the author. Need I say any more about experts? There are questions about who and how we model. The mantra is "adding to the choice we have".'

Martin Goodyer, motivational trainer, Reach International Associates

Noticing successful strategies

Success is seldom achieved by individuals working alone; it comes from working with others, entering their worlds, building relationships and recognizing the exceptional things that people do that work well and contribute to their success.

You might want to be thin, get promotion, be a better shopper, lover, businessperson, sportsperson, entrepreneur or host, you might want to do almost anything! Chapters 11 and 12 looked at habits and behaviour patterns that people display and why people do things; here we look at how they do them.

All professional athletes have coaches who teach them to notice and build on other successful sportspeople's strategies. Many of these strategies are also adapted and used in business to enhance people's teamwork, sales performance, negotiating, or communications skills. Every franchise outlet that opens on a high street is modelled on the successful practices of businesses elsewhere.

You may not know what they are but you also repeat strategies for everything you do in life – from the way you comb your hair, do your shopping and decide what to eat when you are hungry. You run strategies for the things you do well, and also for the things you do badly. The good news is that by modelling what works for other people, you can explore a variety of different strategies that get successful results for other people, and make them your own.

HOW DO YOU DO THAT?

capitalize on the magic of understanding why people do the things they do. Get the action habit – you don't need to wait until conditions for learning new skills are perfect. Whenever you see somebody with a really good skill, one that you'd like to acquire, get into the habit of asking, 'How do you do that?'

Knowing what motivates other people to make their choices can help you change your life to be just the way you want it. Suppose you want to be slim, trim and active: you could model a range of slim people's thinking and behaviour and find out what it is about their strategies that keeps them slim. Ask them how they decide when it is time to eat.

Similarly, if you want to be a successful entrepreneur, spend an evening at an entrepreneurs' gathering and build up a picture of what makes them different from the rest of the herd. Entrepreneurs tend to be proactive, they make decisions quickly and are also prepared to take the sort of risks other people might not. They tend to think big and aim high.

How do you score as a high achiever?

To find out how you score as a high achiever, for each of the statements below rate yourself on a scale of 1–10.

High achievers have a passion for what they are doing.	
Their goals are supported by their emotions.	
They believe their actions can make a difference.	
Life is about seizing chances and learning from experiences.	

(Contd)

The successful person's goal is overcoming challenges.	
They have the ability to observe, identify and adapt other people's strategies for their own uses.	
Their energy and enthusiasm comes from being on purpose and working towards their goals.	
Successful people are master communicators.	

If you commit to improving your skill, talents and abilities, you can increase your score for any of the above.

YOUR BELIEFS ABOUT WHAT YOU ARE CAPABLE OF DOING GIVE YOU LEVERAGE

We have looked at how your beliefs, values and motivational drivers influence what you believe you are good or not good at, and what you think you can and cannot do. Your beliefs about your capabilities are your leverage to whether you achieve little or, like Superman, you burst through every obstacle and achieve a phenomenal amount. Stop and do a spot check on your beliefs now.

Thought provoker

▶ Write down ten positive beliefs that you hold about yourself which have supported you (i.e. I'm a good ..., I will be successful because ..., I can do this because ....)

▶ Now write down ten negative beliefs that you have held which have limited you (i.e. I'm not smart enough ..., I'm not good enough ..., I can't do it ....) Think about devising a simple modelling project which will provide you with the next step towards 'doing it', and repeatedly ask yourself 'What would happen if I could do it?'

Keep your list and throughout this chapter think about what type of skills you might want to acquire that would help you move any items in the negative column to the positive. Systematically seek to improve your skills and performance capabilities and confidence in those areas.

Modelling success at work – blueprinting technique

Do you know someone whose first job position was lower than the office cat's, and they now head an entire section? We've all seen it happen but can we ever hope to emulate it? If you think the person got there because they're brighter than you, have more qualifications, or managed to be in the right place at the right time, then you may have mentally shut down all possible routes that could make you a success.

Ann Fuller-Good, of training consultancy FOCUS Group, runs workshops where management and staff discover what makes people excel at work. She says, 'If you want to be successful find a successful person and find out how they did it. If one person is good at a task because they have an interesting idea, that may not necessarily be a great way to do things. But if ten people have done the task in the same way, and they are all successful, you are getting close to excellence.'

Eurostar has used this success blueprinting technique to train control staff who managed the rail terminal at Waterloo in London. Fuller-Good says, 'The aim was to find out what made excellent terminal controllers, and then give their colleagues the opportunity to try out the same thinking styles.'

Blueprinting excellence is more than taking on someone else's habits. You need to understand the beliefs that person holds that makes them outstanding. At workshops in other companies Fuller-Good studied people who make excellent leaders and discovered that the overriding belief they held was: 'There is more than one way of doing things'. She says, 'They believed that if they didn't get the result they wanted they could try a different approach. This belief manifested in the way they paid attention to achieving results.'

Fuller-Good says, 'If you're an admin person who would like to become a manager, then find someone who has the skills you'd like to be good at, say multitasking, or organizing things in chaotic situations. The questions to ask that person to bring out their underlying beliefs are: "How do you do this thing you're good at? And when you do it, what is important to you?"'

Thought provoker

You may be in a position where you are expected to react to other people's needs, but if you want to become a manager you must become proactive. Imagine holding a successful manager's overriding beliefs for a day, such as: 'I can overcome all challenges.' Then notice the difference it makes to your thinking as an administrative worker.

Before adopting someone else's belief, it is important you choose it consciously, and practise holding it for a while. Ask yourself, 'How will holding this belief benefit me? Can I accept and feel comfortable with it?' If you can, then one of the best ways to make a belief your own is repetition. Stick the message somewhere prominent and repeat it ten times a day. It usually takes three weeks of repetition for a new belief to become embedded. Notice how quickly the belief begins to alter the way you think when dealing with work situations.

Are some people born with a success gene? Fuller-Good says, 'No, but some people have early life experiences that seem to motivate them to achieve more than others. These are people who believe they will be successful and work towards that vision. They don't fear failure, they see it as a challenge, and believe they will overcome all obstacles.'

Is success worth the effort? You bet it is! Why not aim for it and see?

[Courtesy of Associated Newspapers, *London Evening Standard*, 'Just the Job', © Frances Coombes]

Start with simple observable skills that are easy to acquire

> ### *Thought provoker*
> What sort of skills could you use that would motivate you and enhance your beliefs about your abilities or advance your career and take you to the top? You don't have to re-invent the wheel and come up with totally original ideas. Start mining the attributes you see in the people around you, initially learning skills which are relatively easy to acquire.

SOME TYPICAL OBSERVABLE SKILLS YOU MIGHT FIND AT WORK

There are bound to be people in your workplace who have talents for particular aspects of their job. Modelling skills requires that instead of thinking 'I wonder why they're good at that?' or 'I wish I could do it like that', you move to a point of active curiosity and find out exactly *how* they do it.

EVERYDAY EXAMPLES OF WHERE YOU CAN START TO MODEL SKILLS

There will be people all around you who are displaying the skills you would like. Regard your colleagues and isolate particular skills you might like to have. Some simple, easy and worthwhile skills to acquire from the people around you might be:

▶ *how to make good decisions*
▶ *techniques for solving problems*
▶ *drawing spider diagrams to aid your creativity*
▶ *taking control of a situation*
▶ *how to ask for help*
▶ *how to say 'no'*
▶ *handling interruptions*
▶ *tips for saving time*
▶ *chairing successful meetings*
▶ *structuring reports*

- *speed reading techniques*
- *organizing your email system*
- *asking precision questions*
- *listening for what is really important*
- *dealing with a cluttered desk*
- *how to organize yourself*
- *planning situations in advance*
- *dealing with the unexpected.*

Modelling

When you start to model a new skill or behaviour, you should keep a note of the things you will see, hear and feel when you achieve your success. Chart your progress by consulting and updating your attributes list regularly to see which of your beliefs have moved columns.

NOTICE SMALL SKILLS THAT ARE EASY TO ACQUIRE

Choose ten small practice skills that you really want to acquire from your colleagues. Acquiring these skills will make a visible difference to your overall performance at work. The question to ask to elicit people's strategy for doing the things they do well is 'How do you do that?'

If a strategy can be described, it can be taught and learned

Thought provoker

The more we know about how a person who demonstrates the kind of excellence we want to have, the easier it becomes to follow their way of working and incorporate their strategies into our working life. Simple physical, observable skills are easiest to start with to learn and practise the process. Modelling shows us that it is not simply an accident, or good luck, that some people can do some things exceptionally well, while others may find it difficult. Modelling an excellent practitioner is a wonderful way to learn.

Easy skills to acquire

▶ **Find anything fast** *How does a colleague in a busy environment manage to lay their hands on a memo, document, or anything that is required by a telephone enquirer immediately? If you have got a strategy for this then it is easy; if you do not have a strategy then it is worth acquiring. Look around you and see which of your colleagues already has this skill, then find out how they do it. A successful strategy may involve labelling files, and putting contents lists on front covers, but look around you and take note of what people who have the skill are doing.*

▶ **Tidy desk** *How does a colleague with lots of different aspects to their job manage to keep their desk tidy, despite lots of interruptions that draw their attention to other things? If you already have this skill you may think, 'So what, I do that already.' If you do not have this skill then it might be a quick and easy strategy to learn. You will reap rewards in that the payoff for acquiring it will be immediate, and you will use the strategy for the rest of your life.*

▶ **Where did I leave off?** *Many people write lists and notes to themselves to remind them of what they have to do next. However, last-minute bag, purse, trouser or plan changes can leave them bereft of their to-do list. One of the simplest ways of ensuring that you have your list to hand in any situation is at the end of the day write a to-do list and email it to yourself for next day. A simple easy strategy, but see how* *much it changes the way you work and feel, knowing that you already know what you have to do today.*

▶ **Staying calm** *If you are good at staying calm in a difficult situation, ignore this. If you become flustered and you would like to find a simple strategy for remaining calm then this would be a really good strategy to learn from a colleague. The benefits of learning this strategy if you do not have a successful one, are that you can put it into use immediately and use it every day, which will also increase your confidence.*

Stay calm strategy

Repeat the mantra 'calm' and breathe deeply, then go through the following thought processes slowly:

▶ *Focus on the situation.*
▶ *Collect your thoughts. (Imagine yourself on a seashore slowly and calmly collecting shells representing thoughts and putting them into a basket you are carrying.)*
▶ *Seek advice from anyone else if you need to. If you are dealing with a telephone caller, tell them you will call them back.*
▶ *Deal with it. Take the action necessary to resolve the situation.*

This is a very simple strategy. Practise it a few times to find out whether it does or does not work for you. Notice how colleagues around you who are good at becoming 'calm' do it, and become curious about their different strategies. Find two or three different ways for doing 'calm' and practise each to see which one works best for you.

Do it now fever. You may have a colleague who, when given a task, takes-off like a whippet at the starting gate to complete it. If you are not as highly motivated, but would like to be it may be worth noticing what is happening when this person is given a command. If you are a person who thinks, 'Do I really need to do this task, is it absolutely necessary?', 'I will sit on it for a day or two to think it through,' then get curious enough to ask them 'What happens in your brain, what do you think when you are given a new task?', 'How do you do what you do?' Find out what is going on mentally and physically for them when they are given a new task to perform. Notice particularly, and write down, the beliefs they hold about doing tasks straight away.

Make it a habit to be curious about how people around you get the successful results you want to have, and then begin to acquire these simple new strategies in every area of your life. Think about which strategies would enhance your performance, then find people who already using these skills. What are these people thinking and doing when they perform a task really well? Study their process from beginning to end, then capture the essence and make it your own.

ACQUIRE SMALL INCREMENTAL SKILLS

....

Insight

Acquiring small incremental skills, like the everyday ones that are being performed well all around you, can change your performance from average to outstanding. If you become proficient at a dozen new strategies along with 'do it now fever', you are much more likely to be noticed and to accelerate your career path.

....

Once you have the hang of acquiring simple, easily found skills it is time to move on to the next chapter, and the skills that require greater focus on your part, that will really improve your performance – and ultimately change your daily experience to that of being a successful performer in every aspect of your life.

When you understand what causes successful behaviour and can repeat these patterns of thinking and behaviour at will, you will become consistently better at gathering effective strategies and making them your own.

EXPERIENCE HAS STRUCTURE

> ### Thought provoker
> If someone else can do something that you want to, then find
> that successful person and model him or her and how they
> do it. Modelling becomes exciting once you realize that a skill
> that might have taken months to learn can be acquired in a
> very short time.

There is a story about the actor, Sir Laurence Olivier, playing
Hamlet. He gave an extraordinary performance which the audience
raved about and returned for ten curtain calls. Later, the stage
manager went backstage to Olivier's dressing room and found him
in a rage.

'What's the problem?' the stage manager asked, 'you gave a
fabulous performance.'

'I may have been fabulous,' Olivier stormed, 'but I don't know
how I did it, so I can't repeat it again.'

Most of us have had those magical moments where we did
something stunningly well, yet when called upon to repeat it, we
do not know how we did it. Without knowing what is the formula
for success we cannot repeat it. Modelling makes the transfer of
skills possible because, if we know how someone does something
well, we can learn to do it too, provided we have enough detailed
information. Once we know what they are, we can repeat the
person's patterns of thinking and acting at will.

WE HAVE ALREADY BEGUN OUR MODELLING CAREER

We all begin modelling skills at a very early age. The child who
walks around in their mother's high-heels, or talks like their
parents is modelling their parents and learning about empathy and
what it might feel like to be another person. There are all sorts of
methods of acquiring skills and abilities.

How modelling differs from textbook learning

You may have learned to cook by reading a cookery book that gave you a list of ingredients to use and the process to follow to produce a recipe. Or you may have preferred to learn the same skill by observing a television cook perform the task. This gives you more information than a recipe book, because you can see the whole cooking process being performed, but it leaves out the taste, smell and touch of ingredients.

If you are a person for whom authentic atmosphere and taste and smell of food is important, then you may prefer to attend classes, or watch a relative cook so that you can appreciate the full sensory experience of cooking. Modelling other people's skills is a whole learning sensory experience; we take in not just the process of what the person is thinking and doing, we also notice what they are seeing, hearing, feeling, tasting and smelling that contributes to making them so exceptional at a particular task.

What sort of skills would be most useful for you?

What sorts of skills could you use that would motivate you and enhance your beliefs about your abilities, or advance your career and take you to the top? These may be skills that you have tried to acquire before and either given up with or decided you were not good at. You do not have to reinvent the wheel and come up with totally original ideas. Start mining the attributes you see in the people around you.

> **Thought provoker**
> Modelling other people's success skills and winning strategies will expand your potential to bring about similar successes. It will give you a deeper understanding of how people achieve excellence than textbook learning ever could.
> *(Contd)*

You also acquire new insight into the behaviour, beliefs, state of mind and sensory awareness that make up the whole experience when a person is engaged in the process that leads to their successful outcomes.

Think of modelling when you:

▶ *want to be able to repeat a past performance when you have done something well and do not know how you've done it (self-modelling);*
▶ *want to learn a new skill or improve an existing one;*
▶ *meet someone who is exceptionally good at a particular skill or talent and you want to find out more about how they do it;*
▶ *want to emulate other people's successes;*
▶ *want to change parts of what you have done, which might not have been successful, and keep the other parts that worked well.*

Reflection

Think about:

▶ *what sort of initial project would be most beneficial to you?*
▶ *what would possessing this skill say about you?*
▶ *what would it let you accomplish?*
▶ *to what goal is this ability a stepping-stone in your future?*

The creative part of modelling requires you to stretch your thinking by taking on the beliefs, physiology and strategies of another person performing a skill you'd like to acquire and adapting it for your own uses.

Choosing a skill to model

Look around you – whatever environment you are in, there are bound to be people whose talents you admire and would like to acquire. Below are some examples of how patterning the successful way people perform tasks has been used in the sales and education fields. Hopefully it will spark some ideas for your own new applications.

Some of the first skills that participants of a PPD Personal Development training company course modelled were: capturing the essence – the ability to simplify complex information; improved speed at mental arithmetic; the ability to assemble flat-pack furniture; making decisions in a timely manner; choosing the next move in a mountain climb; stopping mind-chatter and remaining focused; establishing immediate credibility in a sales situation.

Case study – modelling sales success

Understanding strategy is crucial for success in sales. Some salespeople are instinctively good at selling but few can consistently generate new business. Consultant John Joint was asked by a large City firm to find a way to develop more people who could generate new business as opposed to just doing the sales.

John says, 'For the modelling I talked to 15 people who had this skill to understand some of the key things about how they did it well. So we were looking at what were the successful people's drivers, what were their skills, what were the tools and techniques they used and what were their personal beliefs around what they were doing.

(Contd)

'We identified what the really good sales generators did that was different. And the key findings were that the motivation was not what people expected. Each person has a very strong driver that wasn't necessarily money or winning. It ranged from being interested in other people, to being interested in the subject, and it was the driver that motivated them to win, and they earned money as a result.'

Modelling other people's success skills and winning strategies will expand your potential to bring about similar successes. It will give you a deeper understanding of how people achieve excellence. When you understand and replicate what makes a person truly outstanding at what they do, you gain new insight into the behaviour, beliefs, state of mind and sensory feelings that make up the whole experience a person feels when they are performing at their best.

YOUR MODELS ARE ALL AROUND YOU

Thought provoker
Is there someone with a really useful skill that you would like to model? One person might be a good organizer, another good at making quick decisions. You don't have to find someone who's a genius and excels at everything, only someone who excels in the activity you choose to model.

Begin to notice what it is that other people are doing when they are performing at their best.

THINGS TO REMEMBER

▶ *Increase your success strategies by finding out how other people achieve the results you would like.*

▶ *Once a strategy can be described it can be taught and learned.*

▶ *Begin by acquiring small incremental skills.*

▶ *What sort of skills might it be useful for you to acquire?*

14

....

Pick a skill you want to acquire

In this chapter you will learn:
- *what to look for when modelling a skill*
- *about eye accessing cues*
- *how to acquire a strategy*

> **'Life is like a combination lock; your job is to find the right numbers, in the right order, so you can have anything you want.'**
>
> Brian Tracey

Success strategies that work

Whole industries such as sports performance enhancement, therapies, education, business management, sales, coaching, team development and just about any area of endeavour where people seek tools and techniques to enhance human performance, use techniques to model human excellence. Yet there is little written for the general reader who might want to self-improve in a few chosen areas using modelling techniques.

Choose a skill

Once you focus on a skill you want to acquire you get new insights into the behaviour, beliefs, state of mind and sensory experiences that make up the whole experience when a person is performing a task at their best. There are thousands of skills' permutations you can model. It is important that the skill you choose to model is one that you really want to learn, rather than something on which to practise. Being curious about the process you want to learn about will make it more interesting and memorable to you.

Some everyday abilities that people around you may display, one of which you might like to model, are:

- *how to pay or receive compliments*
- *making good decisions quickly*
- *capturing the essence of a book or a complex situation*
- *the ability to assemble flat-pack furniture*
- *sorting clutter*
- *stopping mind-chatter and becoming focused*
- *leadership skills.*

If you want to model someone's skill, you want to know exactly how they go about it. This involves observing not just what they do and the order they do it in, you also need to know what they believe about it, what they are thinking as they are doing it and the things they say to themselves before, during and after they do it.

There are many practical applications for modelling. The trick is to learn new strategies which you can replicate and adapt, then use these new abilities to enhance your everyday live.

Modelling is a practical skill

Case study – Frances Coombes

When I felt twinges of RSI in my wrist I decided to model the skills of someone who wrote equally well with both hands, so I could lessen the strain on my left arm. Finding
(Contd)

an ambidextrous person who had acquired the skills in adulthood was difficult but also illuminating. James, an architect, had broken his right arm at university and taught himself to write fluently with his left hand in order to gain his degree.

I asked James to imagine the first time he had written automatically with his non-dominant hand and to re-enact the process. By modelling his behaviour and sensory processes around writing, I discovered that the quickest way to master hand control and writing legibly was from a standing position. The body weight should be evenly balanced on both legs to give a feeling of being grounded, and for poise and control of the pen. The writing surface should be at kitchen surface level, or some convenient height to aid writing in an upright position.

I had never heard of such a writing strategy before, yet as I listened to James I was struck by how obvious it seemed. Interestingly, James had not been consciously aware, until now, of how he made his initial breakthrough or what his actual strategy had been.

Installing a new habit

I set my intention to spend six to ten minutes each morning for 30 days writing for either clarity, speed or flow. I maintain my new habit by spending two minutes a day writing to-do and shopping lists, while standing up. Within a month I could write fluently with either hand.

If you want to enhance your performance in any sphere then the best way to do this is to model the behaviour of the people around you who already possess these skills.

- ▶ *What are the person's beliefs that support the skill?*
- ▶ *How does body language and demeanour change as a person recounts or runs their strategy?*

▸ *Don't ask people 'why' they do things, instead ask 'how' they do them. This is a clean way of questioning which does not impose on people's own model of the world. 'How' will elicit the person's process for how they do the task.*

Eliciting a strategy

Ask the person to carry out or re-enact the behaviour imagining they are actually performing, rather than observing the task.

▸ *Find out the very first thing the person is aware of as they enter the cycle of behaviour.*
▸ *Note which representation system they are using to enter the loop by listening for 'I see', 'I hear', 'I feel', 'I need to'. This will tell you the initial state the person needs to be in to start the process.*

If they need to be prompted, then ask:

▸ *Did you see an image in your mind's eye?*
▸ *Did you say something to yourself like 'that's a job well done'?*
▸ *Did you have a feeling about it?*
▸ *Are you triggered by something internal or external? Do you here an inner voice, a memory or feeling?*

STRINGING THE STRATEGY TOGETHER

Ask the person what they noticed next (picture, sound, feeling), and again identify the sensory representations. Keep asking the question, 'Was there anything you were aware of before that?' until the person's description of their strategy appears. Carry on until you get the complete sequence of thoughts, pictures, feelings and actions that the person runs to perform this task.

['Modelling Success Strategies', courtesy *Positive Health* magazine (PH) issue 120, February 2006, www.positivehealth.com, © Frances Coombes]

Case study – Janette Hurles

Information obtained from a neurolinguistic programming (NLP) modelling project: 'Capturing the Essence of a Book or Report' (simplifying complex information)

Janette Hurles, an advanced modeller, did a lot of research reading for work and wanted to find a way of distilling the essence of what was in the books. She chose three people to model who were excellent at this skill.

Through modelling these people she discovered that: 'They all thought systemically at a very basic level. They believed that all information was connected and part of a bigger picture.' Detachment and objectivity seemed to be key to all three people's strategies.

'If they are distilling information from a book, the people all hold the information in a map within their senses and they'll create a picture of the issue, and come up with a premise. So they'll think, "Okay, so this is what this is about."'

'One person said their picture was a "spider" with tentacles where different sorts of information was held. Another person said their picture was "Almost like a globe of the world". There were bits where they would say, "This fits into this and that into that". So as they're going through a meeting or book, what they're doing is looking for connections and relationships to their own internal model.'

Modelling requires you to take on the beliefs, physiology and strategies of another person performing a skill that you'd like to acquire. Start looking for people who display talents you admire and would like to have. Begin modelling by asking them, 'How do you do that?'

What to look for when modelling a skill

There are three things to look for when modelling someone's strategy.

▶ *What are their beliefs that support the skill they are doing? Listen for words like 'I believe', 'I think', 'it's important that ...'. These words indicate that whatever they say directly afterwards is important to that person and it is what they believe.*
▶ *Pay attention to how their body language and demeanour changes as they recount or run their strategy. Notice any change in their manner, posture and the way they hold themselves as they begin to relate their account and associate with the task.*
▶ *Notice at what point the strategy begins and ends. Once you have the person's strategy and know what makes them feel confident and competent about their abilities around it, you need to try on their beliefs.*

Sit or stand as they did and adopt their body postures. Run through the strategy yourself saying it out loud as you perform it. Repeat whatever your model has shown and told you in precisely the same language they used. They will correct you if you're wrong because you have plucked this strategy from their world and the slightest mistake you make will jar with them.

At this point you have acquired the strategy. If you run it through and nothing happens for you, ask the person to do it again and talk it through because something may be missing.

▶ *Listen and look for consistent patterns of behaviour.*
▶ *Pause to check out your insights.*
▶ *Relax, and then reach your conclusion.*

Sometimes when people are so familiar with a process that it becomes a habit, there are parts of it that are so obvious to them that they fail to explain them. And the missing part is actually the most crucial piece of information that you need to make sense of how the strategy works.

Run through the strategy several times until you know you've got it and then practise using it over a few days. Decide whether the beliefs that this person holds around their strategy fit well with your own beliefs before deciding to adopt their strategy.

['Success Strategies', courtesy of *Positive Health* magazine,
(PH) Issue 120, February 2006, www.positivehealth.com
© Frances Coombes]

Eye accessing cues

If you ask a close friend if they want to go with you for a meal, you can probably intuitively tell whether they want to or not before they utter a word. You are familiar with the person and have picked up information from their non-verbal cues.

People's behaviour tends to be remarkably consistent in similar circumstances, including how they move their eyes to locate different types of information.

HOW EYE ACCESSING CUES ARE USED FOR MODELLING

Understanding eye accessing cues will give you information on whether a person performs a task using an auditory or a visual strategy. Knowing whether a person performs a task in a particular sensory way can be useful, because if what they are doing is not working you can help them learn a new strategy for performing the task in a different sensory mode.

Cricket Kemp's speciality is modelling and strategies (see also Chapter 6). She teaches children who cannot spell how to use a visual strategy which she learned from observing what excellent spellers did. She is researching how her Magical Spelling strategy changes the right–left brain co-ordination patterns in learners and enhances literacy learning for them.

Case study – Cricket Kemp

Magical Spelling is educational consultant Cricket Kemp's name for her visual spelling strategy with which she has taught thousands of non-spellers, aged from 5 to 67, how to spell.

She says, 'While learning a list of words rote fashion may help a child spell these words, it does not make them a good speller or increase their capability to spell. Good spellers tend to repeat an automatic internal process to spell a word correctly.

'Most teachers in this country teach using visual methods. Children who are predominantly auditory (hear words then spell them) or kinaesthetic (able to feel that a word is correct) are distinctly disadvantaged in a visual learning setting. We hold Magical Spelling Days to encourage children to learn a visual spelling method that they can use throughout their lives.'

Set up a good state for learning

It is important to find a level of rapport with each child in order to get their state right while teaching the strategy, and it is important that children know how to access their best learning state.

Storing the correct spelling

Teachers write the correct spelling, using lower case letters, on a piece of card. Once the children have seen

(Contd)

the word in front of them, the teacher walks to the right-hand side of the classroom and holds the card high.
'We do this because the upper-left visual quadrant is where good spellers fix their eyes to spell and file their visual words.'

Trying it out

Removing the card, she asked children to keep looking at the space it was held in and to still 'see' the word, then write it down. The children then count how many letters are in the word, and tick above each letter they got right. The most important thing is not getting the word right but to notice the good feeling that having written the correct spelling gives them.

Practising the spelling strategy

If your word is not yet the same as the correct version, simply repeat the process another time.

Jenny Morgan who taught children with special needs, particularly children with dyslexia, learned Magical Spelling from Cricket and taught it to her pupils in Kirkby Stephen Grammar School. She believes the spelling strategy 'is the most amazing teaching tool I have ever come across'.

She recorded pupils' spelling ages at the beginning of the school year, and the average gain in spelling ability within six months of learning the strategy was two years. Many pupils made gains of four to five years in spelling age within the six months.

[Courtesy of *The Teacher* magazine of the National Union of Teachers (NUT), © Frances Coombes]

Thought provoker
People tend to look up when they are making pictures in their head. They look down when they are experiencing feelings and remembering past events. They may look from side to side when they are hearing sounds. They may even hang their head to one side so they hear better in one ear. You can communicate better with people when you know how they filter and take in information from the world.

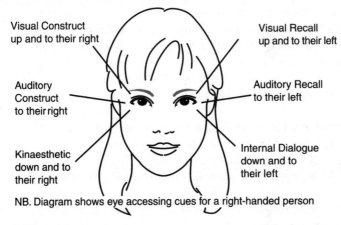

Visual Construct
up and to their right

Visual Recall
up and to their left

Auditory Construct
to their right

Auditory Recall
to their left

Kinaesthetic
down and to
their right

Internal Dialogue
down and to
their left

NB. Diagram shows eye accessing cues for a right-handed person

Figure 14.1 Eye accessing cues.

Ask the person some visual, auditory and kinaesthetic questions and notice their eye accessing cues, that is where they look and their eyes move to in order to retrieve different sorts of information.

HOW TO ELICIT CLUES TO HOW PEOPLE HOLD INFORMATION

Visual recall (Vr) – most people will look up to their left (your right) when they are recalling an event.

▶ *What colour is your front door?*
▶ *Picture a friend's face.*

(Contd)

Visual construct (Vc) – most people will look up to their right, when they are constructing the events of what might have been.

▶ *What would you look like with purple hair?*
▶ *Imagine a brass band made up of orange and green cats.*

Auditory recall (Ar) – most people will look sideways to their left when they are recalling what was said.

▶ *Hear your favourite piece of music.*
▶ *Listen to the sound of water running.*

Auditory construct (Ac) – most people will look sideways to their right when they are constructing unfamiliar dialogue.

▶ *Compose and play in your head a short tune.*
▶ *Hear the sound of a seagull barking.*

Auditory dialogue (Ad) – most people will look down to their left when they are internally talking to themselves.

▶ *What do you say to yourself when you have done something well?*
▶ *What do you say to yourself when you can't decide what to do?*

Kinaesthetic (K) – most people will look down to their right to access their internal emotions and feelings.

▶ *Think of the last sad thing that happend to you.*
▶ *Think of the last joyful thing that happened to you.*

Being able to code someone's sensory strategy is useful because it lets you see where they hold different types of information and whether they are using a predominantly visual, auditory or kinaesthetic strategy.

Coding a strategy

One benefit of codifying behaviour is that sometimes people who feel unconfident will run a strategy over and over again, a hundred, or a thousand times, over a day, a week or months before they finally take an action.

A motivational trainer who works with that person can help them identify that part of their thinking and remove their looped behaviour patterns so they take the actions that produce the results they want much more quickly than before.

Learn a tidy strategy

So a tidy person's strategy might be:

▶ *First, imagine a tidy environment, which is a visually constructed* **(Vc)** *image.*
▶ *This leads to an inner feeling, maybe of pride, pleasure, relief, which is kinaesthetic and internal* **(K)**.
▶ *This may lead to the person thinking some internal dialogue, such as 'Won't this place look brilliant when I've finished', which is auditory internal* **(Ai)**.
▶ *Then the feeling* **(K)** *which motivates the action of performing the task.*

So the code for that strategy is **Vc, K, Ai, K – ACTION**.

The tidy person automatically runs the same strategy each time they tidy up because this is their habitual code for performing this action. When you can codify actions you can change very minute parts of the process later to find out what works best for you.

Case study – Michael Breen

Michael Breen is a motivational trainer and head of MBNLP, a training, coaching and consulting company. He teaches participants on his NLP business practitioner course how to code their sensory images and thinking, in order to see and remove the repetitive looped behaviour that many people engage in before they perform an action that makes them feel nervous.

'Managers may put off making difficult decisions. Salesmen may indulge in other behaviour to avoid making calls to customers where they feel their sales pitch may be rejected. For many participants, once they see their own behaviour coded on a flipchart they say, "Oh yes, that's exactly what I do and that's where my time goes!"

'Once people recognize the unproductive energy sapping behaviour they indulge in, they can often change their habits within a few minutes by practising and removing the loops.' He adds, 'Then I say, "Now what are you going to do with all that extra time you have saved by identifying your unproductive behaviour loops and removing them from your life?" And that really motivates people to keep the new less stressful, more time saving, behaviour going.'

Learning strategy

You can hone your skills at observing other people's eye accessing cues by watching television quiz games. First, note the type of question asked, then which direction the contestant immediately moves their eyes in order to access the information.

USES FOR EYE ACCESSING CUES

If you were modelling how to be a successful salesperson, or how to be successful at interviews, or how to chat up someone on a date, being familiar with their eye accessing patterns gives you an indication of whether the person is actually listening to what you are saying. It also indicates how they are processing the information, in pictures, sounds or feelings. If they are mostly looking up and use visual descriptions, then if you paint your ideas in pictures, you will be talking their language and building rapport with them.

WHERE DO PEOPLE LOCATE TYPES OF INFORMATION?

If people are pointing and waving their hands around in front of you as they talk, begin to notice where they locate certain types of information. If you ask them, 'Where is the past?', they might point and tell you it's behind them. If you ask, 'Where is the future?', they might point and tell you it's in front of them. All of this is relevant if your job is to influence people to buy goods, perform tasks or agree with you.

What can you do if you know where in space people locate different sorts of information? Say you're a salesperson and you want to sell a customer your brand of computer, but they have another type in mind. While the customer describes the computer they want, they may look and point at a space in front of them. This is the place where they store their picture of their ideal product. As the salesperson you spot the ideal product location and may wave your hands around in that area as if to disperse the existing image and then make movements of pushing the rival computer off to one side. You then start talking about your company's product, and place it neatly in the customer's 'ideal product' space. You will see some salespeople, who know where customers locate their 'new purchase' space, use this strategy subconsciously.

ACQUIRING A TIDINESS STRATEGY

If you are a disorganized person and you'd like to be tidier, then find a tidy organized person who agrees to let you model them.

Tidy people tend to be organized in their minds as to where they store information. If you ask them a question such as 'What colour is your front door?', they may look up to their left, which is a place where people commonly hold their visually remembered images. If you ask them, 'What would a melon look like if it sprouted legs and turned into a caterpillar?', they might look upwards and to the right where they construct their visual images, because they would have had to make that picture up before they could imagine it.

Insight

People tend to be consistent about where they store types of images and information. Organized people usually hold a model in their heads of what 'tidy' looks like, and have a good storing and sorting system for placing and retrieving things.

If you ask someone who does not have an organized retrieval system for how they store information and images, 'What is the colour of your front door?', their eyes may dart all around the place, up, down, round and round, as if they are searching for the location of the information. If you ask them, 'What does "tidy" look like?' they may tell you they can't imagine it, or that an image of 'untidy' may dart through their mind first. By modelling and practising the precise sensory, eye accessing cues and thinking strategy of the organized person, the messy person can begin to bring order to their world within a short period of time. Sometimes the person just says... 'Oh, I get it!' and it can happen within 15 minutes.

Getting the picture

How much do you know about the way a friend or colleague, who you've known for years, actually differs from you in the kinds of mental pictures they see, or don't see, and thus the way they view the world?

▶ *Those who think in colour and can recall a person's face as clearly as watching a colour television will think that everyone else sees images in colour too.*

▶ *Those who see in faded colours, or black and greys, will be surprised that someone else can imagine seeing a familiar face as clear and colourful as if it were on television.*

▶ *Some people can't see anything at all when they imagine people, all they get is a sense of people. There must be some sort of recognition process going on because otherwise they wouldn't recognize their own front door or people when they see them. So if they can't picture people, what do they do to record images?*

Can you imagine how differently someone who does not see pictures or words on a page when they shut their eyes to imagine would have to think to devise their own strategy to learn how to spell?

Modelling skills in teaching and learning

Cricket Kemp, trainer, of Learning Excellence says, We tend to see and teach from our own model of the world. Teachers tend to teach in their own dominant sensory profiles (often visual), and may not understand enough about how someone who is auditory or kinaesthetic takes in or stores information to be able to adapt their teaching methods to meet a child's learning needs.

> 'To help, say, a child who is having difficulty with spelling you have to put your own model away in order to understand their world and how they perceive it and develop strategies that will work for them.'

'We're hoping to tackle problems like this by bringing an understanding of neurolinguistic programming (NLP), the study of modelling excellence, into education and modelling how people who do things well do those things. We need to understand the thought processes and beliefs that a person is holding while they are performing a task excellently, and be able to incorporate it into our repertoire of thinking styles in order to understand it and teach it to children who use predominantly non-visual representation systems, and who are often left behind in education.'

Visual learners can hold pictures in their mind, and find it easy to move and rearrange information around in their head at will, because they can see it all happening before them.

Auditory learners find it difficult to hold information unless it arrives in a structured way and the relationship is linear. If I want to do my accounts I do them in auditory, and I will have them laid out in an ordered fashion. It is a good system for sorting known information and following an established process; it is not good for being creative.

Kinaesthetic learners are often bright but may not have learned to translate that information to a form that a teacher can mark. It's a system where there are triggers that will give the kinaesthetic learner a lot of information at the same time, which initially may be confusing. Kinaesthetic people may often make the leap and solve a problem without knowing the steps they took to get there.

Kemp says, 'We are encouraging children to switch between sensory representation systems to perform different tasks. So if I have a whole bunch of information how do I make sense of it? Visual is a good system to be in to view and arrange the information, and then maybe to structure it you want to switch to auditory and write it down.'

Modelling is all about adding flexibility to the choice of skills and abilities we already have. There are many ideas here to start you thinking about planning your own modelling projects. Look at each of the ideas and ask yourself, 'How could I adapt that for my uses?'

You can't control the future or decide what you will be doing on a Tuesday morning five years from now when overnight success knocks on your door. You can decide on the next steps you will take today, and tomorrow, to make the successes you want a reality.

If you master modelling skills you will never be bored again. Each new person possesses hidden talents, and becomes the most fascinating person you could meet. It is your job to unwrap them and find their hidden talents as quickly as possible. Discover any skills they have that you do not yet possess but would like. Are any of their skills, interesting, challenging, awe inspiring, mind blowing? Then it is up to you to decide how you will model these skills and acquire them.

So get motivated – start increasing your modelling skills and taking the actions that make successes happen much more quickly.

THINGS TO REMEMBER

▶ *Notice other people's success strategies that work.*

▶ *Choose a skill that you want to acquire.*

▶ *Elicit that person's strategy.*

▶ *Question for clues to how people hold their information in place.*

▶ *Remove any looped repetitive thinking habits you run and replace them with more efficient time and energy saving strategies.*

▶ *Keep modelling and acquiring lots of strategies.*

15

Strengthen your completion drive

In this chapter you will learn:
- *about time in relation to goal setting*
- *about disorganized space – disorganized time*
- *how to bring your next goal nearer*
- *which time zone you function in*

> 'Time, like a snowflake slips away, while you are deciding what to do with it.'
>
> St. Louis Bugle

Where do you keep time in relation to goal setting?

If you set a goal but have no sense of time passing you are unlikely to set it within a time frame for completion. Whatever the reason you give – 'I don't want to put pressure on myself', 'I am a perfectionist and want to wait until everything is just right', 'I don't have time right now' – you are unlikely to achieve your outcome.

I know people who have missed some really big chances, mainly because they do not realize that although sometimes a window of opportunity opens up for them, it opens for a short period in time only. If you're not motivated enough to be standing by, ready to seize the chance and run with it, the window of opportunity closes again. Suddenly, the offer that would have led you nearer to your heart's desire disappears. No matter how much you want to kick yourself, it does not alter the fact that you are too late.

> **'Regret for the things we did can be tempered by time; it is regret for the things we did not do that is inconsolable.'**
>
> Sydney J. Harris

There are only three ways in which decisions are made:

- ▶ *You make decisions.*
- ▶ *Someone else makes decisions for you.*
- ▶ *Time passes and makes the decision for you, the opportunity like a snowflake is gone.*

Getting time on your side

You do not use time, it uses you. Whether you race to complete tasks as quickly as possible or you sit at a desk and do nothing at all, time still passes at the same rate and you can't have any of it back. But what if you could strike a balance and complete more things, more of the time?

Time doesn't fly. It doesn't drag by. We have a relationship with time – one we can change for the better. Wendy Sullivan, of Discovery Works Limited, an in-house workforce trainer, says, 'If you need better time-management skills the solution is not actually about "managing" time because time cannot be managed. Time just "is". The question is how you choose to manage yourself in relation to time.

'People do things for one of three reasons:

> ▶ *They are drawn to the task and want to do it.*
> ▶ *They have no choice, they must do it.*
> ▶ *They do things that allow them to put off what they most want to avoid.*
>
> Then afterwards they may feel guilty, frustrated or resentful about the way they've apportioned their time.'

Time-management techniques do help us to take more shortcuts, stop wasting time and become more productive. But it's possible to have an even better relationship with time by knowing how you think about it in relation to your work. Are there times when time 'drags'? Or do you see time 'flying by', only noticing and possibly regretting it when it has gone. Knowing how you relate to time and listening to what you say to yourself about it is the first step to understanding why you do things the way you do. It also gives you an option to change how you think about time.

How do you relate to time?

Answers to the following questions will vary if you change the context to work, home, or social situations, so choose only one context. Tick a statement on the left OR right, whichever is most applicable to you.

Are you often surprised by how much time has passed when you look at your watch?	Do you usually know the time within a few minutes?
Is your diary filled with loose papers all ready to fall out?	Is it well organized and tidy?
Do you ignore deadlines others give you and avoid setting deadlines for yourself?	Do you set yourself deadlines and treat them as being important?

(Contd)

Do you delay making decisions so that you can be flexible and keep your options open?	Do you like to make decisions well in advance?
Can you focus easily on what you are doing so that everything else is blocked out?	Do you find it difficult to concentrate when you are in a hectic environment?
Do you get caught up in what is happening so that you forget about other things you need to do?	Do you automatically keep track of things other than that in which you are involved at the moment?
When you talk to someone is it usually the other person who ends the conversation because you are so involved in it you don't realize it is time to stop talking?	Are you often the one to end a conversation?
Do you prefer to be spontaneous?	Do you prefer to plan beforehand?
Do you sometimes arrive late without realizing that you are late?	Do you usually arrive on time and know if you are even a few minutes later than the agreed time?
Do deadlines seem to creep up on you without you noticing?	Are you aware of deadlines moving slowly closer to you?

▶ *If you ticked six or more boxes on the right, you probably live life in an organized, methodical way. If you want to become more flexible, ask yourself, 'What will happen if I don't know what is planned?'*

▶ *If you ticked six or more boxes on the left, you probably lead a flexible life with a minimum of forward planning. You may end up rushing to get things done or feel guilty about things that you have not done.*

▶ *If you ticked a mixture of boxes you may be someone who is flexible when managing yourself in relation to time – congratulations!*

[Courtesy of Associated Newspapers, *London Evening Standard*, 'Just the Job', © Frances Coombes]

'When you feel passionate, hungry and enthusiastic about achieving your goals then time flies. Your energy level, enthusiasm for life, belief in your abilities and commitment to your calling is what shapes time for you.'

Peter Lewin – motivational coach

Do you make time work for you?

▶ Are you **'in time'** *and live for the moment and 'right now'?*
▶ Are you **'through time'** *and plan each moment, and know precisely where you will be and what you will be doing in ten years' time?*
▶ Are you **'behind time'**, *remembering the past and how different things are now?*
▶ Do you live **'in the future'** *at some joyous point where everything will be wonderful, but shut down on the present?*
▶ Are you drifting through life as a casual observer, or did you just wake up one day and wonder **'what has happened to all your time'**?

Action

List the types of tasks you are doing:

▶ *when you notice you have* **too much** *time*
▶ *when you experience* **too little** *time*

(Contd)

▶ *when you say to yourself,* **It's just the right amount** *of time*

Through time

A 'through time' person plans ahead, has a schedule, and may know pretty much to within ten minutes what time it is.

In time

If you ask an 'in time' person, 'What does the future look like?', or 'Where do you see yourself in ten years' time?', they may say: 'I can see a picture of me sitting on a beach somewhere and living a comfortable life, but I have no idea how I got there or any other details'.

What has happened to the time

Someone who does not have a sense of time passing, or feel any urgency about performing tasks in a related timeframe, may live a disorganized life and not notice clutter until it threatens to engulf them.

CONFLICT ARISES BECAUSE WE ALL DO TIME DIFFERENTLY

People may clear out clutter on two levels:

▶ *On an* **environmental** *level, for example in the office where files and computer software that is no longer needed is encroaching on space.*

Figure 15.1 How do you relate to time?

▶ *On a time level. This may be due to procrastination by you or the people around you who waste your time.*

A visible mess in a cluttered office, kitchen or house is easier to organize than a cluttered time schedule. Because time is invisible, and there may be no messy piles of papers lying around as evidence of cluttered thinking, people who eat into large portions of your time unnecessarily often take longer to detect and deal with. However, organizing time is not that different from organizing your office environment.

Disorganized space	Disorganized time
Untidy drawers	Cluttered time schedules
Lack of space	Lack of thinking time
Excess baggage you don't need	More tasks than time to do them
Items jammed into space	Tasks moved because of any lateness

Solution

One solution for 'through timers' who need to work with 'in timers' is to explain, when you meet people with whom you are going to have close involvement, that your time is very important to you. 'In timers' may not understand what you're fussing about, so give a couple of examples of the sort of **behaviour** you want to see, such as:

> 'I expect people to turn up on time and give as much prior notification as possible if they need to change meetings so that I can schedule something more productive to do with my time.'

If they are still not responding then move on to explaining your beliefs around other people and time, such as:

> 'I believe that people who don't turn up on time are not showing respect for me', or 'are stealing my time'.

If you are a person who has to work with a space invader or time invader, think about the behaviour that they are demonstrating and the types of things that might be influencing the situation. If you can't take control of your paperwork or time schedule then ask these questions of yourself.

Is the problem:

- ▶ *an environment problem* – **Where is it happening?**
- ▶ *a person's behaviour* – **What are they doing?**
- ▶ *your capabilities to manage your time or space* – **How is my unstructured behaviour sabotaging my outcomes?**
- ▶ *your beliefs and values* – **What do I believe about why the situation is like this?**
- ▶ *identity* – **'What does my behaviour say about who I am?**
- ▶ *part of the system* – **Who else or what else affects the situation?**

Be aware of the invisibles – beliefs, values and identity

The table below shows the route by which we change our thinking when we change our beliefs. If you start at the bottom with Environment and work upwards to Identity you will notice that while Environment, Behaviour and, to some degree, Capabilities can be seen, Beliefs and values and Identity are like the tips of icebergs under the water, largely unseen. However, they are there and can affect the outcome of all that we do.

If you choose to make any permanent changes in your environment clutter or want to use your time more effectively and your decision is to be a permanent one, you will need to think it through and make a change in your thinking at a 'beliefs' level.

Identity	**Who?**	
Beliefs and values	**Why?** Does it fit with your beliefs?	Is this a belief you hold about clutter? Perhaps you don't know how to deal with it in the way other people do?
Capabilities	**How?** How capable are you of dealing with it?	Is this a skills and capabilities thing? Have you been trained in the skills to deal with clutter?
Behaviour	**What?** Whose behaviour displays the problem?	What is the problem? Someone else's behaviour/ your own/the result of both? How is the behaviour manifesting?
Environment	**Where?** Business? Home? Location?	Where is the problem? Your sourroundings/head/ both?

[Adapted from Robert Dilts (and others), *Neurological Levels of Thinking*]

Action

Ask a group of people to explain to you how they perceive time. Ask each person to stand in the middle of a large room, or outside in a clear space.

▶ **Ask them to point to where they locate 'the past'.** *They may turn round and point behind them. Some people see time as a straight line that runs from behind them, through them and straight out in front of them.*

▶ **Then ask them to point to where they see the future.** *They may point to somewhere in front of them. However, others hold feelings of time differently; they may sense time around them, or through them, and others construct time as a circle. There are all sorts of alternative ways in which people relate to time. Ask a roomful of people to point one finger to their past and another to their future, and to hold the pose, and you will be amazed at how differently they all see time.*

If you are going to solve a problem with time, your own or other people's, then you need to know how individuals think of and relate time.

Time in relation to goal setting

Mike Treasure, a physicist and NLP trainer, says, 'Understanding how you relate to time in relation to goal setting and problem solving increases your awareness and flexibility with time. Plan ahead and tidy up the mental clutter around unmade decisions that can rob you of total commitment to your goal.'

'If you are going to solve a problem with time, your own or other people's, you need to have an overview map of how individuals think of time.'

A systematic way to find out how someone considers time is to ask them to pick a location and stand where they want their 'now' to be located. Then ask them to point and walk to where they see their past and future.

By getting people to walk along their time continuum and explain their thinking about how they will complete a difficult task at various points, you can achieve a sense of how they perceive the problem in relation to time.

SORT OUT YOUR COMPLETION DRIVE

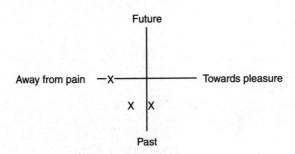

Figure 15.2

This is a simple feelings-based exercise, so you really need to just do it, rather than read or think about it too much. You will experience an instinctive realization instantly as you stand on different parts of your timeline.

▶ *Find a large, clear space and write the words* **Away from pain, Towards pleasure, Future, Past,** *on large sheets of paper.*
▶ *Stand where you consider yourself to be in relation to the problem. (This might be: 'I want to ask for a pay rise', 'I want to change my job', 'I want to take on more business or go for a really big contract', or 'I want to ask someone for a date',*

'I want to write a book'.) Then place the sheets of paper
on the ground in the positions you feel represent your Past,
Future, Towards pleasure and Away from pain (Figure 15.2).

▶ Stand on your 'now' at a place where you feel most
comfortable in relation to time and the pain and pleasure of
achieving your goal. Think about the challenge you want to
undertake and close your eyes and breathe deeply. As you do
so, notice any thoughts and feelings you are experiencing.

▶ Step outside your model for a moment and move to the edge
of the room. You may even want to stand on a chair to
look down and get another view of where you chose to stand
in relation to time and pain and pleasure. Looking down
on the situation, are you surprised at where you positioned
yourself?

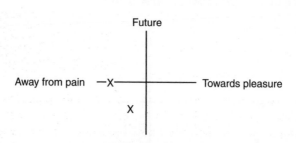

Figure 15.3

▶ Now step back onto your model to where you feel most
comfortable on the 'Away from pain–Towards pleasure'
thinking style line. Are you standing closer to one extreme
than the other? Notice what you think and feel about yourself
in relation to the project.

▶ Now move along your thinking style line a little at a time,
towards the other extreme of thinking that you normally shy
away from when planning ahead. Describe what you feel as
you get closer to the other extreme. It may be uncomfortable
standing closer to pleasure if you habitually motivate yourself
with pain. Nevertheless, describe out loud what you are feeling

and any new insights you have received from imagining the pleasure of the successful completion, and the celebration and recognition that comes with it.

▶ *Notice what you are feeling about the project as you stand at different points.*

▶ *Then move along the 'past' and 'future' line, as before.*

▶ *Experiment with where you stand and what you feel at different points on your model. Notice and carry back all the extra information and insights you have collected about your future undertaking.*

This type of exercise releases information about the reasons why you might be feeling anxious or blocked, and also offers unexpected solutions for ways of overcoming obstacles.

Case study – sorting out a completion drive

Lynne wanted to write a book, a project that would take a couple of months, but had lots of obstacles in the way. By standing where she felt most comfortable on her Away from pain–Towards pleasure timeline, she realized that she was very close to the pain extreme and had not connected to the pleasure part of the goal.

Pain............X...Pleasure

The inner dialogue that she was running was connected to familiar feelings she experienced when standing near to Pain on her timeline:

▶ *time restraints*
▶ *other commitments*
▶ *cannot see where I would find the time*

(Contd)

> ▶ *big project, didn't know how to do it*
> ▶ *might fail, and would have wasted a lot of time.*
>
> By standing on a chair and looking down at her completion drive problem space, Lynne reflected and realized she was allowing herself to experience only the negative things associated with what she wanted to do.
>
> As Lynne moved along the continuum towards the other extreme, towards the good things about her experiences, she experienced the pleasure of completion and what that would feel like, and acquired a set of pleasurable thoughts and feelings.
>
> Pain...X.....Pleasure
>
> Lynne says, 'Initially I did not think I could move in the direction of Towards pleasure. My thinking changed and I experienced unfamiliar feelings each time I took a step nearer to pleasure.
>
> ▶ *I felt excitement, this was a challenge and a chance to move towards a really worthwhile target.*
> ▶ *I thought, if I succeeded I would grow as a person and probably move towards other even bigger targets.*
> ▶ *I realized there was a chance for financial success and recognition. The project suddenly seemed really worthwhile.'*

How you 'see' time affects how you use your time and what you can achieve over a period of time. So if you are not getting the results you want, challenge your current model of time and choose one that gives you an opportunity to succeed and feel good about what you are doing.

Action

Choose any one of the habitual patterns you run when faced with new challenges. Pick one for which you would like to become more flexible in your thinking, say **Necessity vs. Possibility** or **Away from vs. Towards**.

Necessity ....X...Possibility

▶ *Walk your continuum line between the extremes of Necessity and Possibility, stopping at points along the way to close your eyes, breathe deeply, relax and experience how it feels to use a different frame of thinking, and utilize the information and insights you collect on the way to sort out your completion drive for your next major goal.*
▶ *Question: Have you learned anything new or unexpected about yourself or your project that will help move you towards successful completion?*

Procrastination: the art of keeping up with yesterday

Procrastinators will go to great lengths to convince themselves and those around them that they are engaged in productive activities, while avoiding the main task they want to achieve. They are often frustrated people who never realize their aims or potential. Although procrastinators can make excellent critics and may help you tremendously by telling you where you went wrong and how to improve your work, lifestyle, romance, finances or weight loss, they may not make much headway in these departments themselves.

When pressed for results procrastinators will assure you they know that the deadline for completion is the weekend but they have lots of other important tasks competing for their time. They just have one or two more details to collect. They need to speak to a couple more people, and play an extra game of tennis this afternoon because exercise is really important for them when they are under pressure.

When a procrastinator says they have a great idea and wants to talk to you about it, one way to stop them in their tracks is to say, 'Great, go and work out a plan. Then come back to me with something on paper that we can both look at.' If they are a real procrastinator, nothing will happen after that because the procrastinator's timeline stretches only as far as thinking, not as far as doing. Success is doing, not wishing.

PERFECTIONISTS

There are many reasons why people do not produce results on time. Perfectionists can't let go of anything until it is perfect. A deadline comes and goes, and the task is completed days later – perfectly.

Choose a better approach to time

Can't prioritize
The important task looks daunting, so some people do other smaller tasks, but do not make much headway with the most important part of the project. Inability to prioritize can also be a 'time' problem if you're an 'in time' person and have no sense of how time passes in relation to getting things done.

Break your workload into small chunks
Making lists that prioritize tasks and which move you forwards each day can help. Assign a level of importance to each task you do:

- ▶ *URGENT – your immediate tasks that must be done now in order to make things happen in the future.*
- ▶ *IMPORTANT – the things you are setting up to happen next.*
- ▶ *TO DO – the standard things you must do around tasks and events to make things happen: book a room for an event, thank a speaker, check a date.*
- ▶ *NOTE – things that are coming up in the future that you need to be aware of, and maybe gather information and prepare for.*

Sense time moving

Deal with things straight away
An invitation to an awards ceremony arises. Decide whether to go or not. Make a decision about what you intend to do and deal with that piece of paper straight away.

Follow your natural rhythm cycle
Notice how you perform at different times of day and fit your tasks around your natural rhythms of working. If you are best in the mornings, attack the big tasks then and leave letter opening and phoning people to later in the day.

Things that go wrong are not disasters
Analyze what happened and what if anything, you could have done to save the day. Work out a plan of how you might do things differently to get a different result, and file it away for future reference. In all areas of life, disappointments sometimes precede success. 'It's not a crime to make a mistake,' Walter Wriston, former chairman of Citicorp once said. 'What is a crime is failure to learn from a mistake.' If what you're doing isn't working then try something else.

Insight

When situations are moving quickly it's sometimes difficult to get a handle on what is actually happening. At times like this, the best thing may be to stand back and become detached from the situation. Ask yourself, 'What is at stake here? What is important? What will matter in ten years' time?' Imagine you're an alien and see things and ask questions from a different point of view.

Get sorted

Finally, find some really organized people and model their strategies for organizing themselves in relation to time and clutter. Take what you've learned from modelling successful time and space users and use their strategies to perform one small clutter-clearing task. Resolve to do this task really well and complete it within a realistic time frame. Then take some time to celebrate and feel really good about your achievement.

Action

Wendy Sullivan advises, 'Discover the things that are really important to you by asking yourself as you perform each task, "How will doing this help me achieve my goal in life?" Now choose some of the new time strategies you have learned that reflect the way you would like to operate.'

▶ *If you are a perfectionist for whom things are never right, then drop your standards. If you wait until things are perfect you may never finish tasks.*
▶ *Do the important stuff first.*
▶ *Practise saying 'No'. Just because you can do something does not mean you have to do it.*

▶ *It takes a lot of time to procrastinate, so stop doing it. One way is to change your self-talk from 'I should' to 'I'd like to finish this by ...'*

▶ *Make decisions more quickly. Ask a few good decision makers around you how they do it and practise for best results.*

THINGS TO REMEMBER

▶ *Find out where you keep time in relation to goal setting.*

▶ *Question people's assumptions about time.*

▶ *Learn how to handle people who have different relationships from your own.*

▶ *Organize your time the way good planners organize their physical clutter.*

▶ *Sort out your completion drive using your timeline.*

▶ *Choose a better approach to time.*

16

Listening and questioning skills

In this chapter you will learn:
- *CRAFTY listening to increase your listening abilities*
- *to use questions which challenge existing assumptions*
- *AEIOU questions to draw out explicit information*
- *T-GROW coaching questions to help someone move on*

> 'I listen a lot and talk less. You can't learn anything while you're talking.'
>
> Bing Crosby

Getting the right tone – listening skills

Whether it is to motivate, manipulate or magnetize others to you, the most important skill that a self-motivated person can possess is the art of listening. If we are not attuned to listening for the whole message another person is giving us, we may focus on the words they use and ignore voice tone, how the person is breathing or displaying distressed body language. The result may be that we give the person all the information they requested and still they are not appreciative of what we have done for them. Or we feel they have not been as forthcoming with information as they could have been. The situation has arisen because we have not built rapport with that person.

NOTICE VOICE TONE AND BODY LANGUAGE

Face to face with someone you can see how interested they are in what you are saying and how they are reacting to you. Most people have a similar listening ability which they have used since they were born. Mothers listen to tone and can distinguish a baby's 'I'm hungry' or 'I'm tired' cry from an 'I'm wet' wail very quickly.

Actively listen and recognize more about people's tone of voice, modulation and anxiety levels. By understanding how someone is feeling you can assess that person's mood. Listen to the way the person speaks; is their voice slow and rhythmic, or high-pitched staccato? Do they carefully pause to construct their next sentence, or do the words tumble out fast and furiously without pausing for breath? Does their voice have a light melodic tone to it, or is it single tone and monotonous?

To build rapport with someone using your voice, notice how they breathe and use their voice, then match your breathing and tone with theirs. If they speak slowly, then slow your speaking, if they speak fast, speed up your speech.

Pay attention to people's sensory language
People tend to think in pictures, sounds and feelings and you can build rapport with them by noticing what their dominant sensory style is, and matching it.

Seeing pictures (visual) words and phrases

Looks, appears, clarify, clear, dark, focus, gaze, glance, hazy, hindsight, illuminating, illustration, image, mind's eye, notice, observe, opaque, outlook, picture, reveal, see, dim, vision.

Hearing (auditory) words and phrases

Loud, shrill, call, harmony, rings a bell, hear, listen, say, shout, tune in, voice, wavelength.

Feeling (kinaesthetic) 'touchy feelie' words and phrases

Cold, soft, crash, crawl, get a grasp, grip, hassle, lukewarm, sharp, solid, stress,

Listen to people's dialogue for sensory language clues:

▶ *I feel uncomfortable when I am around her.*
▶ *I see your point of view.*
▶ *I get the picture.*
▶ *I sense it is not going to work.*

Meeting outcome tips

Jot down the outcome you want to achieve as a result of the exchange with the person.

▶ *Is it to gather information?*
▶ *Is it to get the person to do something?*
▶ *Or is it the way you want them to feel as a result?*

Keep your paperwork so you can check afterwards whether you achieved your aim.

▶ *Focus your attention on the person, particularly if they are new to you. They will give you cues on how to behave.*
▶ *Build rapport by matching breathing, pace of language and voice tone. Match body language in some small way.*
▶ *Finish off by informing them of the next action that will follow as a result of your meeting with them.*

['Listening to others' courtesy of Associated Newspapers, *London Evening Standard*, 'Just the Job', © Frances Coombes]

'Do you have the patience to wait till your mud settles and the water is clear? Can you remain unmoving till the right action arises by itself?'

Lao Tzu

Why can't we listen?

Why do so many of us feel the need to interrupt others when they are speaking? Even when we appear to be listening we often think we already know where the person's conversation is going and we are merely going through the motions of listening, nodding politely having switched our thinking to other things.

Action

Think back through all the conversations you have taken part in during the last week.

▶ *How many times do you feel you really communicated with another person in a way that made them feel valued and listened to?*
▶ *How often did you feel that the people listening to you were really present with you without being hurried or having their mind elsewhere?*

Why do some people have such a pressing need to jump in and finish people's sentences, or tell them what they think they are about to say? Is it really so hard to let people finish their own sentences for themselves?

Some of the reasons given for why people needed to interrupt others were:

▶ *Interrupting people saves time.* (**I know what they are about to say.**)
▶ *What they were saying is not new.* (**Nothing about their idea will improve if I listen to it.**)
▶ *I am more important than they are.* (**So my ideas must be better than theirs.**)

▶ *What they said sparked a good idea* **(and I wanted to finish their sentence because I am more articulate and will express it better than they can).**
▶ *I am too busy to listen to them.* **(Their words are not important.)**

Not listening to other people is insulting. When people show impatience by finishing someone's sentence they are assuming that the person cannot finish it themselves. Not listening to other people breaks rapport and inhibits feelings of connection or goodwill that might be built between them. Not paying attention to other people can also mean that you lose out on valuable information, that tiny key to a puzzle you might need to have in order to understand a situation.

How well do you listen?

Paul Burns, Organizational Development Consultant and Psychotherapist, uses the Psychology of Mind (POM) method to show people how most of us think while listening to others (Figure 16.1). 'First, we listen at a high level to understand what the person is talking about, then our listening level drops as we begin to think about the implications and applications around what they have said.' Gradually our attention drops below the level of listening, to 'I agree/disagree with what you are saying'. We may interrupt at this point to do a comparison and say 'Here is my story'. After that we resort to nodding politely and not listening.

Much of what we learn from other people when we talk to them does not come from listening to the actual words they use; we sense it with our whole being. In studies carried out at the University of Texas to assess personality traits of 2,000 managers, it was found that, without exception, senior executives scored higher than middle managers when it came to thinking intuitively. Part of what is termed intuition comes from people's ability to listen and take in information in ways which may seem magical to other people who don't possess the same degree of listening skills.

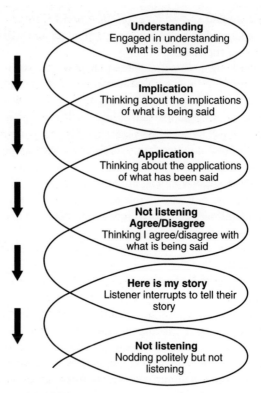

Figure 16.1 Psychology of Mind (POM).

Action

Decide before the next conversation you have with someone that you are going to listen to this person in an understanding way, then see how easy or difficult this is for you.

TYPES OF LISTENING

There are different types of listening:

- ▶ **Random thinking** *Thoughts just come into our heads, similar to internal dialogue.*
- ▶ **Process thinking** *A learned way of thinking where we sort and evaluate, using past memories for comparison.*
- ▶ **Flow mode** *Comes from a clear mind. The depth of thought is variable and it may appear random but it is not.*

Flow mode is the best style to be in when you are listening to other people; you are relaxed and trust that the information you want will come.

Can you control the way in which you choose to listen to another person for a full five-minute period? Or does your listening just happen for you?

Action

Choose a person and decide you will listen completely and be present with them for at least eight minutes. During this time you will listen in an interested way, not interrupt them to describe your own story, or say how you feel about what they have said or how it is like what happened to you.

(Contd)

Soon afterwards, write your answers to these question on a piece of paper:

▶ *How difficult was it for you to listen?*
▶ *What was going through your mind as you listened?*
▶ *How comfortable were you with not interrupting?*
▶ *How did the speaker react to your uninterrupted attention?*
▶ *Did the speaker say anything that you did not expect them to?*

Case study – quantum listening

Michael Mallows, life coach, organizational trainer and workshop facilitator, teaches quantum listening skills. He says, 'Good listening is a skill, a craft and a gift. Exquisite listening requires the ability to ask incisive, purposeful questions. Done well it can open closed minds and reveal the untold and untapped potential of the people we are attempting to communicate with.

'Many people who ask questions think that they already know the answer, so they are seeking confirmation not information. Or they are not really asking the question, they are telling the answer. Someone might say: "Have you spoken to him about that?" which means, you should speak to him about that. And so even when listening, we have this urge to tell, to instruct, to rescue, and to feel we know best.

'Quantum listening is listening at every level, paying attention to what's happening inside us, maybe noticing that our stomach is a bit tense. You're paying attention to your internal self-talk and what is happening around you. You check out your assumptions but you allow the intuitive process to happen and you notice any subtleties.'

Listening to yourself

Make a stream of consciousness recording by talking out loud. Just say whatever comes into your head and notice how random and non-sequential are your thoughts. Repeating this exercise a few times makes you aware of the internal chatter inside you which can make it difficult to listen attentively to other people.

Listening to others

If you have the urge to interrupt someone, make sure that the interruption is proceeded by a recap by saying, 'Let me just check I'm understanding' or 'Let me just recap on what I have understood you to say', rather than jumping in. This gives the person a chance to say 'No, I didn't say that,' and it gives you a chance to reflect. It also lets people know that even if you are going to interrupt and counter what they have said, you have heard and understood them and are including them in your thinking process.

How to listen

Michael Mallows runs workshops in organizations and teaches participants to listen using his CRAFTY listening model. He says: 'Effective listening is an essential skill'.

Effective listening means that it has an impact on both speaker and listener and that the effect it has is both desired and desirable.

It is important, especially when we are at odds with each other, to be able to listen with a sense of wonder, to listen with care and concern rather than anxiety or indifference, to focus full
(Contd)

> attention as thoughtfully as possible, without being knocked off
> balance by a word or a phrase, by a look or a facial tic, or to be
> reactive or restless because of a rude gesture, intended or not.

Listening with good will and great skill involves asking questions that are targeted and 'tight'. This skill is also useful when working with, or talking to, people who want to explore and expand on creative ideas, or ambitions and achievements. Good listening is a rare gift! It lets people know that their thoughts and feelings, their dreams and disappointments, hopes and aspirations, really matter to you.

CRAFTY listening is much more than just good listening because you focus all your attention on another person in the moment of their sharing with you. It involves self-awareness, self-management, empathy, courage, intuition and generosity of spirit. CRAFTY listening creates space for people to think more clearly and gives them time to reflect more deeply.

CRAFTY listening can be much less comfortable than 'ordinary' listening because, for some, it doesn't seem like listening at all. It is devoid of the usual interruptions and challenges. When not demanding justifications, not discounting beliefs they disagree with, are not interrupting all the time, many speakers find it difficult to handle that quality of attention.

When people are attempting to communicate their distress, the listener often tries to 'rescue' the speaker from the sadness, anger or fear that they are trying to share. 'It'll be alright tomorrow, cheer up!' or 'There's no need to get upset, I'm sure they didn't mean it the way you think.' Or, 'Don't be silly, there's nothing at all to worry about!'

The listener/rescuer wants to alleviate their own distress and in doing so discounts the feelings of the speaker. Someone who seeks to rescue the listener is not listening very well. Rescuing inhibits the sharing of deep-rooted anxieties and concerns and prevents old hurts from healing. Rescuers believe they are doing it for others but they are meeting their own needs.

If you use CRAFTY listening skills it will encourage greater disclosure from the person you are listening to and stimulate more profound insights from them into the situation.

CRAFTY listening

CRAFTY stands for Curiosity; Respect; Attentiveness; Fearlessness; Thoughtfulness; Yes!

Curiosity
A sense of wonder. It can be difficult to keep on wondering what another person will say or do next when they are full of sadness, fear, rage, confusion and frustration. With CRAFTY listening, you will never be bored by another person's boredom or whinging. When people feel that they are seen as fascinating beings even if they are not entertaining, amusing, pleasing or compliant, or if they are shy, timid, angry, sad or scared, listening with compassion can reinforce their self-esteem and sense of belonging.

Respect
Respecting other people's feelings can be difficult, especially if your own feelings are churned up. It is difficult to stay focused if, for example, we find something offensive, or if aggressive, threatening or alarming behaviour in some way has an emotional or physiological impact on us. Stay respectful by building and maintaining rapport.

Be prepared to give time and attention to exploring the speaker's beliefs and values, even if they differ from or clash with your own. This demonstrates that you respect the listener.

Attentiveness
Pay attention to what's going on for you when you see or hear other people's distress. Listen to your own inner voice, breathe deeply, be aware of the bigger picture and develop the will and the skill to elicit information gently, skilfully and sensitively.

Fearlessness

People can be so full of hurt and pain that we are afraid to approach, challenge or upset them by speaking our truth in a direct and forthright manner. People need to know that they are safe – and we need to be prepared to listen – really listen – when they are trying to explain and to make sense of the feelings and thoughts that distress them. When we try to cheer them up, distract them from any hurt, it is usually to meet our own need not theirs.

Thoughtfulness

Hold other people's pain and potential in your mind and think deeply about how you respond when you are together so that your responses can assist them on their journey from hurt to healing.

Yes!

An affirmative assumption that you and the other people in your life are 'all in it together'! Approach each conflict, argument, struggle, obstacle and set-back believing that, together, you will come through.

Having well-formed outcomes makes it easier to stay focused and positive, to ask questions from a place of hope rather than hopelessness, with curiosity instead of carelessness and always – always! – with loving respect for what is created in the space that grows between you and the people whose lives you touch.

Ask questions with a purpose

Insight

Every question that you ask a person steers their thoughts and attention in a slightly different direction. To help free-up another person's thinking, keep a set of high-quality questions to ask them. Give the questions a recognizable structure so that you have a framework you can construct around any situation that needs clarifying.

Structure your questions to elicit more information, insight, or to move on the person's thinking in a clearer direction. Choose a simple question construction style to start with that progresses the person's thinking by clarifying cloudy issues and moving towards a solution.

YOUR QUESTIONS MUST BE DEFINED BY PURPOSE

As you listen to what a person says notice the language the person is using, and the beliefs and assumptions they hold about the problem.

- *Identify what the person perceives to be a problem.*
- *Listen for the assumptions they are making about the situation.*
- *Then ask yourself, how must this person have perceived this situation as a problem until now?*
- *What are the beliefs and assumptions they must hold?*
- *Construct a question to challenge their beliefs and assumptions.*

You might hear the following type of statement, that uncovers a person's way of thinking about a situation:

Problem thinking: I haven't made any progress.
Challenge with: You haven't made any progress, **until now?**

Insight

This challenge presupposes that there is more than one way of looking at what they have been calling a problem. That assuming it is a problem is just that, an assumption. In addition, you have put a timeframe around the perceived problem. The 'until now' implies the problem was in the past and that things have changed.

All change takes place at a subconscious level and the mind processes information by presupposing what it believes to be true, until a different interpretation is put on the matter that challenges the previous belief.

Problem thinking:	It is difficult for me to make changes.
Challenge with:	**But not if you have help?**
Problem thinking:	I don't seem to be able to do this.
Challenge with:	You don't seem to be able to do this, **yet**. I am curious about how soon you will notice your increasing skills.

The 'until now', 'but not if you have help' and the 'yet' will cause the person to compare and reconsider in different ways the meaning of what they have said. You can try the exercise on yourself by stating a limiting belief you hold about your ability to do something and then get someone to repeat your sentence with the 'until now', or 'yet' appended. Notice what happens to the way you think about the problem.

Questions change the way you see things, and the perceptions of the people with whom you communicate. When your perceptions change, your reality changes; that is why questions are one of the most powerful tools you can use.

SELF-QUESTIONING

....
Insight

Think: What is the purpose of my question? What is the outcome I want to achieve.

▶ *Choose something you have identified as a problem, until now.*
▶ *Ask yourself, 'How have I seen this as a problem, until now? This question presupposes there is more than one way of viewing what you had been calling a problem.*

By asking this question you are steering your attention in another direction and inviting your subconscious mind to review the evidence.
....

Challenging existing assumptions

Our beliefs affect our performance in everything we do. Our confidence influences our beliefs about how well we will perform a task. To make sure that we successfully achieve our outcomes, we need to identify any thinking patterns that may be holding us back, and replace them with a positive alternative.

The most common patterns of thinking that undermine us are:

▶ **Self-sabotage** *This involves having a pessimistic outlook, expecting things to go wrong, or assuming things are hopeless, and there is little chance of getting what we want.*
▶ **Over-competitiveness** *Some people tend to become obsessed with winning. One problem can be that the person sacrifices other aspects of life, then the neglected areas bite back and undermine the person. They may experience stress, 'I don't have to do anything else' complaints, or punish themselves if things go badly.*
▶ **Dithers between two alternatives** *This leads to tension and fogged thinking, which in turn leads to poorer performance. As a result nothing is achieved.*
▶ **Stuck in a rut** *Some people have a particular way of doing things and may continue with the same technique, even when the strategy no longer works. They can become locked into the pattern and be oblivious that they are behaving in this way, even when it is obvious to other people. Your job is to free up their thinking, and make the person aware of the pattern they are stuck in, then offer alternative choices.*
▶ **Dreamer** *Some people spend a lot of time visualizing the future, but they take no action. They then become demotivated by their lack of progress. The aim should be to clarify their cloudy thinking and formalize some positive actions that will take them closer to their outcomes.*

Notice how a person usually frames their question. They will tell you what they want to do, and then give all the reasons why they feel they cannot do it. The structure goes:

I want to do this ..., ... but I can't because ...

Precision questions to challenge their thinking are:

▶ *What would happen if you could do it?*
▶ *What stops you?*
▶ *How would you know if what you are saying is not true?*

Precision questions are framed to cause a person to re-examine their interpretation of a situation, and often their thinking will change.

CHALLENGE A LIMITING BELIEF YOU HOLD

Thought provoker
How do you react when you make a mess of something? Write down the internal dialogue that goes on in your head and all the things you say to yourself. List all the reasons you gave for the mess and then challenge them, one at a time.

I want promotion ..., but I will never be chosen ...

▶ *Why is it like that?*
▶ *How do you know that?*
▶ *How does X cause Y? (for example, how does not having a degree mean that you are stupid?)*
▶ *How will you feel when the problem is no longer an issue?*

Framework for listening and questioning: AEIOU

Knowing the right question to ask someone, or what order to ask questions in can be quite daunting. So it is a good idea to have a simple model to follow to gather information and direct the conversation. The AEIOU listening style is useful because it gives you an effective and systematic approach to listening and questioning.

The five key points you are listening for are: **A**ssumption, **E**vidence, **I**llustration, **O**pinion, **U**nique.

Assumption
- *What assumptions is the person making?*
- *Are their assumptions correct?*
- *Have they missed anything out?*
- *Have they made a sweeping statement backed up by an isolated incident to support their conclusion?*

Evidence
- *What is the evidence for what they are saying?*
- *Are they using facts or opinions?*

Illustration
- *What is an example of this?*
- *Does what they are saying fit with what I know?*

Opinion
- *Is what they are saying fact or opinion?*

Unique
- *What are the unique points in what they are saying?*
- *What is new and important to know?*
- *What is just padding?*

Whatever is unclear, or has not been drawn out while you listened can then be put to the person as questions.

[Strategy adapted from *Master it Faster*, author Colin Rose, published by the Industrial Society]

T-GROW coaching, a gentler approach to questioning

For clarifying thinking and goal setting, the T-GROW model, developed by Sir John Witmore, is widely used as a coaching for performance outline which is particularly effective. Using it may seem rather strange to start with, but as you become competent at using it you will not realize you are following the process.

T-GROW COACHING SESSION STRUCTURE

Theme
Let the speaker lead the conversation and define the theme. At this stage you are not looking for detail, just a broad picture. You are looking for the scale of how important the topic is to the speaker. Typical themes may be career, business, life–work balance, self-confidence, relationships, health, money. Select only one theme to work on.

Goal
Work with the speaker to define what the goal will be for the session in terms of what will move the speaker forwards towards their long-term goals.

Reality
When you have a clear goal you can begin to help to understand all the factors which are impacting on that goal. You are looking at ways of understanding the current situation, to understand how it impacts on any progress towards the goal.

Questions to ask might be:

▶ *Where are you now in relation to this goal?*
▶ *How great is your concern?*
▶ *Who else is affected by this issue?*
▶ *How much control do you have over it?*
▶ *What action have you taken so far?*

- *What stops you going further?*
- *What other resources (skill, time, money, support) do you need?*
- *Where could you acquire them, and by when?*

Options

Once you have clarified the issues dealt with in the reality check you can explore the options for reaching the goal. If there are several ideas in the frame you can lead the speaker back to look at each idea in turn. Useful questions might be:

- *In how many different ways could you approach this issue?*
- *Which solutions seem best to you?*
- *How will doing that give you the result you want?*

Way foward

At this stage we move from exploring possibilities to deciding on actions. Having worked through the T-GROW model, any actions taken will be based on a clear understanding of the issues. Finally, ask the speaker to define how success will be measured.

IN A NUTSHELL

Theme

Let the speaker lead. Pick up clues on what is important to them. Learn to think on your feet about what is going on in their mind.

Reflect and summarize

Whatever the speaker says to you, make sure you understand and ask for clarification, do not make assumptions. Consciously work to empower the speaker.

Reality

Remember the 'big picture'. Ensure the speaker commits to clearly defined and agreed actions. Be aware of how the results of their actions will move them closer to achieving their goals. Be careful to focus on the results of the actions, not the actions themselves.

Way forward

Find out what is preventing the speaker from taking the action by asking, 'What needs to change, so that you do?' Good questions are:

- ▶ *How will this help us move forwards?*
- ▶ *I noticed you've not mentioned .... Is there any particular reason for this?*
- ▶ *What would be the right action for you?*

Research shows that performance is linked to goal setting. Your goals are indicators of what you hope to achieve and indications are that people with well-thought-out goals are most likely to achieve their aims.

THINGS TO REMEMBER

▶ *Listening skills: actively listen and build rapport with the speaker.*

▶ *Know in which type and level of listening you are engaging.*

▶ *Listen for sensory language.*

▶ *Check how well you listen; practise listening*

▶ *Quantum listening and CRAFTY listening will increase your listening abilities.*

▶ *Ask questions with purpose to enable you to challenge existing assumptions.*

▶ *Use the AEIOU framework to draw out explicit information.*

▶ *Use T-GROW coaching structure to help a person move on.*

17

....

Coaching your inner team

In this chapter you will learn:
- *who is in your inner team*
- *about building self-confidence*
- *to think on different logical levels*

'No matter what our circumstances, we have the power to choose our directions.'

Author unknown

_____

Is your inner team really working for you?

Inside us we have lots of different components that make up our inner team and contribute to the way we think. We might have a team member who says, 'I wake up each day and I feel good, and I expect good things to happen.' We may have another part of us who alerts us to things that are coming up in the future, who says, 'We must be prepared in case something unexpected happens.' We may have another team member who takes care of our welfare and says 'It's time we took a holiday'.

There may be other team members who, although trying to help us, actually undermine us. We may have parts of us that say, 'I can't do this' or 'I will never get it right', 'It's time for me to panic'. Their purpose is to help us and keep us safe and away from imminent failure, but the other function they unintentionally perform is to stop us reaching our full potential and being successful.

Your inner team strengthens or weakens self-confidence

Self-confidence relates to actions and how we view ourselves when we perform those actions. If we feel confident when facing an unfamiliar or difficult task we will expect to perform well. We review our memories of how we tackled new challenges in the past, and if we feel that we performed them well then we carry those confident feelings with us and expect that our success patterns will repeat themselves.

How confident are you?

▶ *Can you accept a compliment gracefully, without saying, 'it was nothing', or something else that will lessen the impact?*
▶ *Are you afraid that this success was a one-off and that somebody might find you out as not being as good as they think?*
▶ *Can you list six qualities you like about yourself without hesitating?*
▶ *How do you react when asked to try something you have not done before?*
▶ *What do you say to yourself when you are about to do something difficult or challenging?*

Do your answers suggest you like yourself?

To feel supremely confident, we need to hold a store of strong mental images of seeing ourselves doing phenomenally well at the tasks we undertake. If we do not hold strong images of our successful outcomes, then we may be more prone to fail, even though there may be evidence to suggest that we have the same skills and experience as people around us who expect to do well.

We undermine our ability to perform tasks well when we have low self-confidence.

Examine your beliefs

If we want to do something which opposes a current belief we hold about our abilities, we set up an inner conflict. Are you aware of any beliefs or attitudes you hold that might block or limit your chances of success. You may want to have more fun, for example, but do you also believe that work justifies your existence? How might holding this belief affect the way you participate in doing tasks that are considered creative and fun?

Signs of low self-confidence

Think about the things you constantly say to yourself about new situations or tasks you consider strange or difficult. Do any of the following common undermining beliefs keep coming up?

Thinking
- ▶ *I can't do it, I wouldn't know where to start.*
- ▶ *It is too difficult for me.*
- ▶ *I don't think I can handle this.*
- ▶ *What I do won't be good enough, other people can do things better.*

Feeling

▶ *Worried or anxious and not knowing why.*
▶ *Apprehension about future difficulties.*
▶ *Being frustrated and angry with yourself.*
▶ *Fear of the unknown, or of new situations.*
▶ *Anger because other people seem to find things so easy to do.*
▶ *Easily discouraged and demoralized.*

Behaviour

▶ *Seeking reassurance.*
▶ *Not participating, but staying in the background.*
▶ *Hesitation and repeatedly needing others to say you are doing alright.*
▶ *Avoiding taking on new situations, or making changes in your life.*
▶ *Procrastinating, or being a slow starter.*
▶ *Passive, waiting to be told what to do, not a self-starter.*

Sort out your inner team members

Thought provoker

On a piece of paper, draw a line down the centre. Reflect on the thoughts and the things you most constantly say to yourself in work, testing experiences or difficult social/relationship situations.

On one side of the line, list the types of thoughts that support you and categorize them into which type of team member they are. On the other side, list the members whose types of thinking do not support you, and give each one a name, for example:

Support	Team leader
I will do it!	Inner cheerleader
I am a good team member	Good supporter
I must hurry up	Team organizer
I know how I will do it next time	Inner strategist

Do not support	Team member
I will never do it	Inner critic
I can't get it right	Underminer
It is all my fault	Blamer
I will never get the chance	Pessimist

WHO IS WORKING FOR YOU ON YOUR INNER TEAM?

Think back to the last couple of situations when you did not do well. Write down the things you were saying to yourself about what was going on in your mind. List the things you said to yourself that supported you. List the things you said to yourself that undermined your confidence.

Look at your team and decide which members you want to keep, and which members you want to replace.

- ▶ *Team members I will keep are my …*
- ▶ *List of qualities each member brings that support me …*
- ▶ *Team members I want to replace are my …*
- ▶ *List of qualities that do not support me …*

TEAM MEMBERS' INTENTIONS

Action

All of your inner team members do the best they can for you, regardless of how helpful or unhelpful they are to you.

- ▶ *List the team members you want to replace, and underneath each heading write what you feel was the positive intention behind their undermining behaviour. (For example, Procrastinator, saved me from failing at anything because I never completed anything in time, so nobody judged me as having failed.)*

▶ *List the new team members you want to replace them with, and the type of thinking, that would support you and be more helpful to you?*

Actively work to replace each unhelpful team member with another with the type of thinking that would bring about a positive change for you.

Our self-confidence impacts on how successful we feel and how we enjoy life; it is concerned with how we feel about our abilities. We can strengthen our sense of self-confidence by learning strategies for doing things we particularly want to achieve, and holding images of ourselves performing tasks particularly well. If we do this often enough we will eventually see ourselves as natural born winners at everything we do

We can overcome our fears by changing the way we think about an experience.

Case study – Howard

Howard was a project manager for a large telecommunications firm. He knew he was good at coming up with ideas that worked and implementing them. Yet he was puzzled as to why, when he presented his ideas to senior management, so many of the projects he proposed were often dismissed or turned down in what seemed a perfunctory manner. Senior managers conceded his ideas were good and relevant yet they seemed lukewarm when he presented them.

Howard's self-confidence was shaken. He had become so used to putting up new ideas and having them knocked down that he said, 'I can feel myself "shrink" as I get nearer to head office and feel "diminished" as I open the meeting

(Contd)

room door.' Howard was wary of showing or sharing his emotions so no one else knew just how bad he was feeling about the situation. He noticed that other project managers who were more enthusiastic about their ideas seemed to get them accepted, but that was not Howard's style. He felt that his ideas were 'strong' enough to stand on their own without the benefit of razz-a-mataz.

How we see and feel about ourselves affects our self-confidence in any situation from boardroom to bedroom. For Howard, what he enjoyed most and made him feel most powerful was being on his own driving in his car, when he played loud, rousing classical music that engaged his emotions. This made him feel powerful and stirred his passions. He said, 'when I get out of the car after a burst of music I feel strong and able to deal with anything.'

As music engaged his strongest emotions and made him feel in control he decided to use it as a way of managing his state when he entered the meeting. As he drove to his firm's head office he would listen to the music and imagine himself conducting an orchestra. Then he would visualize running through his presentation to the board a couple of times with his appreciative audience nodding their heads enthusiastically and applauding. He stepped out of the car feeling powerful, and as he put his hand on the meeting room door handle he imagined a great burst of music coming from the room.

Howard decided that his inner team members would comprise his orchestra and he would be the team leader. When he waved his baton his team members would come together and be working in harmony towards his goals. Howard swapped team members:

| I can't do it | for | Feeling in control of his thoughts, his actions, and taking the situation in the way he wanted it to go |

| Afraid of being ridiculed | for | Team leader, whose appearance said, 'I am in control' |
| I'm feeling inhibited | for | I am in control |

He introduced his psyching-up sessions, and within two presentations Howard could see his ideas were being discussed with enthusiasm and followed up. There was also a change in the way the board engaged with him; there was now more banter and goodwill. He says, 'On a logical level I already knew my ideas were good but the change in the board's acceptance of them only came after I dropped my inner critic so I could be excited without feeling inhibited, and show them that I was enthusiastic about the things I wanted to do.'

Our beliefs may be positive and powerful, enabling us to do whatever we want, or negative and limiting causing us to do badly or fail at new challenges.

_____

Get yourself a cheerleader

If you hold any of the limiting beliefs in the left-hand column below, think about how you might bombard your inner team member who holds that belief with so much evidence to the contrary that they give up in favour of an alternative more positive belief. Get yourself a cheerleader from the positive right-hand column to take their place.

Negative team's belief	**Positive team's belief**
Failing at anything is painful	I can do that
I can't do this	I am good at this
I am no good at this	I achieve what I set out to
I always get things wrong	Learning a new skill is exciting
I am too fat, thin, short, tall	I like being me

(Contd)

Negative team's belief	Positive team's belief
This is too difficult	I ask for help and get it
People will not like me	Strangers are just friends I have not been introduced to yet

ANCHOR A GOOD FEELING

Howard used the powerful technique of anchoring all the positive beliefs he had in order to anchor a good feeling to what would normally be a stressful situation. By taking all the images, sounds and feelings of joy and heightened awareness that he recalled vividly and attaching those feelings to a situation about which he felt apprehensive and did not enjoy, he changed his frame of thinking to one where he was confident, upbeat and expected to have his ideas accepted.

OUR LANGUAGE DESCRIBES OUR INNER WORLD

The words Howard used indicated not just how he felt about the situation but also how he held a picture of the problem in his mental landscape.

People unconsciously describe the colour, clarity, size, shape or density of the picture they see in their mind's eye. They may talk of 'having a bright future', 'a dark cloud hanging over' them, 'it feels like wading through treacle' or 'walking on air', 'it's all very hazy to me'. These patterns of description for the most part go unnoticed yet they are familiar enough to us so that we recognize if they are out of place. You don't hear people saying they are looking forward to a 'dim and distant future' or 'in the emptiness of time'.

Thought provoker
Each person is unique in the way they see the world, but a pattern we tend to follow is that we give clarity, colour and nearness to things with which we feel strong emotional attachment. Things that are less interesting we send to the

dark, dim, distant and hazy pictures box. We describe people we like as 'colourful' and 'larger than life', and those in whom we feel less interested in as 'drab', 'colourless', 'a grey little man in a suit'.

The way we view the people around us, and our ability to interact with them comes from how we view ourselves. If you see yourself as 'drab' or 'colourless' or feel 'small' in areas of your work, then changing how you view yourself when performing in such a situation can enhance your performance.

ANCHOR YOUR GOOD FEELING

To achieve peak performance in a situation that makes you nervous, **anchor a good feeling.** An anchor is any stimulus that changes your state. (Remember Pavlov and how his dogs salivated when they heard the bell?) Anchors are fired when we think of associations or past successes when doing things we enjoyed or did well, which made us feel good about ourselves. By remembering a time when we did something particularly well and felt good about our performance, we can harness that good feeling and carry it with us when we enter a more challenging situation.

Insight

Use anchors when:

▶ *you do not feel confident and want to draw on your inner resources;*
▶ *you find you are responding in a familiar way that did not achieve good results before, and you want to change the way you feel and respond;*
▶ *you are in a situation that puts you under pressure.*

We gain confidence and our sense of self-esteem increases when we build up images of ourselves engaging in actions that may be challenging and excelling at what we do. The more good experiences you can anchor and use in potentially difficult situations to overcome them, the more powerful the anchor becomes and the more successful you feel.

Thinking strategy

Think of yourself undertaking some future challenging tasks, but this time with five of your new positive thinking inner team members working with you. Act as if you have already got them embedded in your thinking and they are working towards your goals.

Notice what phrases of encouragement you are saying to yourself that encourage you to perform at your best. Collect these phrases and stick them up in prominent places in your home, so you can see them all around you and embed them in your mind.

Then see yourself performing new tasks effortlessly and incredibly well. Your brain cannot tell the difference between reality and fiction, so the more often you run these success making images, the more often your brain will light up with pleasurable feelings.

Logical levels give structure to thinking

Thought provoker
Who taught you how to think? Most of us just picked up our own thinking habits, whether useful or not, as we went through life. We all have blind spots in our thinking, and repeat behaviours that people close to us instinctively recognize that enable them to know how to 'push our "hot" buttons', to get a predicted response.

If you want to acquire a systematic way of thinking and problem solving that asks questions you may not cover in your habitual thinking process, then learning more about logical levels will pay you dividends in terms of gaining clarity and insight, and more information on situations.

The NLP logical levels of change model is a good way to help you discover your own, and other people's, underlying thinking patterns in relation to any subject, event, relationship or organization. Understanding from what logical level a person is talking to you, gives you the chance to build rapport and engage more deeply with them in conversation.

Being able to think flexibly and at lots of different levels on a subject provides us with a powerful framework for thinking through change. We can problem solve, uncover hidden information and gather extra insights about a situation from several different viewpoints and build-up a 'big picture' view of events.

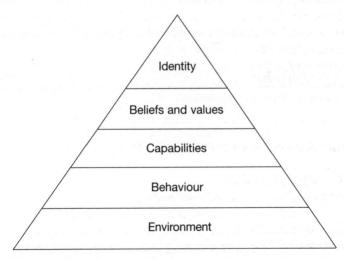

Figure 17.1 Logical levels of thinking.

Logical levels of change is a model devised by Robert Dilts, based on the 'neurological levels' proposed by anthropologist Gregory Bateson.

We can think ideas through on a different level or category at a time, and capture all the additional insights gained that would otherwise have escaped.

There are five main logical levels. Below you can observe how the levels are connected with each other. A change in a belief made at one level will influence other areas of your thinking. The effect is like throwing a large stone into a pond and seeing the ripples spread out.

Logical levels can help us clarify the way we see a situation, and reveal what are the real blocks and issues behind a situation. The core questions to ask are 'Who?', 'What?', 'Where?', 'When?', 'Why?' and 'How?'.

Environment: Where? and When?

Where and when does this situation occur? Is it a place, at work, at home, with colleagues? What is the setting and context when the problem arises?

Behaviour: What is happening?

What is being done, by whom, to whom? Equally what is not being done, is this about inactivity? Behaviour is what you actually do.

Capability: How is this being done?

Capability is about how someone does something, or how confident they feel to do it. Having capabilities is what makes people feel competent and in control of situations. If you feel you lack capabilities you may anticipate and find a task really difficult.

Beliefs and values: Why?

Our beliefs and values are personal to us, and what we think shapes our understanding of what we believe is or is not possible for us. Beliefs and values provide us with a rationale and drive our actions.

Identity: Who?

Who do you think you are? This is your identity, who you think you are. All your actions derive from your sense of who you are. You will hear people say, 'I am not the kind of person who does that ...'

WHAT DO LOGICAL LEVELS LET US DO

▶ *Logical levels clarify our thinking about ourselves, our friends and colleagues, our workplace or any other entity with which we engage.*
▶ *They can let us work as a team to recognize on what level to concentrate to make breakthroughs.*

If you are a therapist charged with helping people to give up smoking, it will be much easier to help someone to give up what they see as an unwanted behaviour than it will be to help someone who sees smoking as part of their identity.

'I am a smoker'	The person making this statement is telling you that smoking is part of their identity. It is who they are.	IDENTITY
'I smoke'	The person making this statement is telling you what they do. They are describing a behaviour.	BEHAVIOUR

EVERYDAY EXAMPLE OF LOGICAL LEVELS

Thought provoker

You might hear someone say, 'On one level, not passing any exams was terrible; on another level I would never have built my own successful business if I could have got a paying job.' That person has given you information about the levels in which they are thinking.

In one sentence in the paragraph above, a person has discussed their thinking about their:

- ▶ *capabilities (they did not pass their exams);*
- ▶ *beliefs, (they would never have built a successful business, if they could have got a paying job);*
- ▶ *identity (they see themselves as a successful business owner).*

It would be difficult to glean this much information about a person from a sentence, without applying some sort of structure to the way you think.

When we talk we are unaware that all sorts of information, besides the content of what we say, is leaking out. We discuss things on different levels:

- ▶ *On a behaviour level, what we or someone else did.*
- ▶ *On a capability level, how we, or someone, did, or should do, something.*
- ▶ *On a beliefs and values level, why we should do something, and what we believe is and is not possible for us.*
- ▶ *On an identity level, who we think we are and how we fit into a bigger system. This can be spiritual and takes us into exploring our bigger purpose and mission in the world.*

LOGICAL LEVELS OF THINKING

People will differentiate between different logical levels when discussing events or actions they want to take. Each of the levels gives us a different kind of information.

Learning strategy

Think of a problem you would like to work through, or a situation with yourself or others in which you feel constrained and would like to clarify. Define the problem in one sentence, using this structure:

'I want to do ..., but I can't because ...

Take six pieces of paper and write the headings on each one, (Environment, Behaviour, etc). Space these pieces of paper on the floor and stand in front of each one in turn, starting with Environment. For each heading ask the relevant questions from the list below. Ask the questions aloud and wait for the answers to come to you. Get used to having regular open dialogue with your inner self, and gaining information on every level on how you feel about situations. Work your way through the logical levels of thinking to Identity. Then go back and pause at each level, gathering up the new insights and information you collected at each stage and carrying it with you to the next. By the end of the logical levels thinking process you will have insights into your situation that you did not have when you started.

Identity

▶ *Who are you in this area of your life?*
▶ *Who are you at your best in this area of your life?*

Beliefs and values

▶ *What's important to you about doing/wanting/having this?*
▶ *Why does it matter?*
▶ *What's most important about it?*

(Contd)

Capabilities

▶ *What capabilities do you tap into in this area of your life?*
▶ *What skills do you put into becoming proactive?*
▶ *What areas of expertise do you draw on?*

Behaviour

▶ *What do you do (activities) when you engage in this area of your life?*
▶ *If someone was watching you, what would they see you do?*
▶ *What would they hear you say?*

Environment

▶ *Where are you when you engage in this area of your life?*
▶ *What do you see and hear?*

WHAT DOES LOGICAL LEVELS THINKING ENABLE YOU TO DO?

By questioning your thinking and beliefs about a topic, using one of the logical level questions (above) at a time, you can find out more about a situation and how someone thinks about it than you could otherwise have done. You can ascertain:

▶ *what sort of information you are dealing with, whether it is about the person's environment, behaviour, capabilities, beliefs or identity;*
▶ *on what level a person views a problem originating, whether it is about the environment, behaviour, capabilities, beliefs or identity;*
▶ *on what level the problem is being experienced;*
▶ *what the real issue is about. People are often afraid to challenge another person's identity as it may end in conflict. We tend to start with something small, on an environment level, and if an*

argument ensues, proceed through the logical levels by taking the behaviour and attaching it to the person's identity.

Environmental	He has left his socks on the floor again. (*An environmental observation*)
Behaviour	He will not pick up his socks. (*Describing his behaviour*)
Capability	He does not even know how to pick up his socks. (*He is not capable of picking up his socks*)
Belief	I don't think he cares. He won't pick up his socks. (*He expects someone else to do it for him*)
Identity	Who does he think he is? He won't pick up his socks. (*He thinks he is too important/busy/ different to pick up his socks*)

Flashpoints

Often when we have what seems to be a small disagreement with someone over something that seems trivial, it escalates into a major fall-out. You will hear people argue with each other from different levels of thinking, or points of view.

He:	'What's the matter with you? It is only a pair of socks.' (*He sees situation as an environmental*)
She:	'No, you're always leaving your clothes on the floor for someone else to pick up. Who do you think you are?' (*She is arguing on an identity level, and attaching his behaviour to the type of person she believes he is*)

When people are arguing on different levels of thinking, they are more likely to reach agreement if one person recognizes the level at which the other person is speaking, and then matches that level before attempting to reconcile the situation.

Learning strategy

The next few times you watch people disagree on television news, dramas, in debates, or at home or in work, ignore the content of the argument and instead identify at which of the logical levels each person is operating.

▶ *Notice whether they are on the same level of thinking as each other.*
▶ *On which level are they talking? Environmental, someone's behaviour, capabilities or skills, beliefs and values, or identity?*
▶ *On which level do you think the real issue belongs?*
▶ *Think about what sort of question you could ask that would have both parties discussing the matter on the same logical level.*

ALIGNING OUR LOGICAL LEVELS

When everything we think, do, say and believe about our capabilities to take on challenges and win aligns in the same direction as our goals, we become truly powerful.

THINGS TO REMEMBER

▶ *Examine your inner team and weed out members who weaken your self-confidence or do not support you.*

▶ *Anchor confident feelings.*

▶ *Use logical levels when you want to engage in a structured way of thinking to gain more clarity and insight into situations or problem solve.*

Tips for staying motivated

In this chapter you will learn:
- **tips for staying motivated**
- **things to do to keep you connected**

Belief in yourself, belief in your purpose is the mantra of the self-motivated. But often it is hard to stay motivated when things are not going to plan. At times like this we need to plumb our inner resources and here are some tips for people who want to become and stay motivated.

Stay connected

The way you think determines what you feel. And staying motivated, especially if you are working alone, or are the only motivated person in your vicinity, can mean that you cut yourself off from the people and stimulus you need. It is important to take time out from your project to look around and smell the flowers, otherwise you may find you lose contact with friends.

Insight

If you are starting a long project then tell people in advance. Say, 'I will be busy for a while, I will stay in touch with the odd phone call and I am really looking forward to having a celebration meal with you at the end of my project.' Planning the event in advance and imagining meeting up again with friends is a way of feeling connected with them. Knowing that you have already put the wheels in action by stating what you will do to make it happen is also reassuring.

Create a 'buddy' system

Have someone in your corner routing for you. Choose someone who is going through a similar life journey and between you decide on the best way to press each other's 'hot' buttons that will motivate you on to greater things.

I know of two friends who ring each other up, each with a list in hand of five specific things they must say to each other during the conversation that the other person wants to hear. Comments may range from, 'You are a really excellent public speaker and deserve to be heard worldwide' to, 'You have perseverance and I know you will get there'. These 'whoop-em-up' conversations are really powerful because although your best friend might now and again hit upon the words you want to hear, your buddy will do it every time you speak to them.

Have a mission statement and revisit it often

Insight

When things get tough and you feel your resolve wavering have pictures and diagrams of what your finished projects will look like. Spend time visualizing in technicolour your success, the events leading up to it and receiving your reward. Visit your mission statement often and note your progress so that you keep a positive outlook. Have some sort of indicator, such as gold stars, that you can use to stick on a chart to indicate your progress to date. Sometimes just seeing how far you have come will be enough to spur you on to your goals.

Have a clear sense of purpose that describes who you are and what you are about. Commit it to memory and recite it like a poem.

Decide to be happy

Deciding to be happy is a decision that only you can make. Let what makes you happy be a pointer for the direction you take in life. Make happiness your goal and avoid losing yourself in busyness. Stay in touch with yourself and feel for your inner joy. When you are happy you are creative, and all of your talents bubble up and come to the fore.

Have a mentor and be a mentor to someone

Mentoring will give you a powerful feeling of connection to others. Also, at a skills level, explaining how things work with other people builds your own capabilities. A survey of top UK bosses revealed that 70 per cent of UK males heading UK companies have had at least twelve mentors.

Stay in touch with yourself

Our beliefs are constantly changing in relation to the sights we see, and thoughts and feelings we experience. But sometimes we can get so caught up in busyness that we are not aware of the changes going on within us until something happens that startles us, and we are forced to take time out to re-evaluate our beliefs. Be open and aware of the subtle changes that happen within.

Insight

Focus on what is important and do not let other things get in the way. Calmly review your schedule for the last week and decide, what did you really do that was worth mentioning? Allow yourself 20 minutes each day to reflect on how you can use your time doing more of what is of value to you. Decide that in future you will cut out anything that was busyness masquerading as important.

To help stay in touch with yourself practise early morning writing. Ask yourself a question about whatever is foremost in your mind, and follow up with ten minutes of really fast writing allowing whatever is on your mind to tumble out. Let the pen fly down the page followed hastily by your hand. A phrase by E.M. Forster sums up the technique: 'Think before you speak is criticism's motto. Speak before you think is creation's motto.' Early morning writing lets you stay in touch with yourself, your goals, your needs, your desires. It also shows you how creative you can be when you are free thinking.

Be fully present with people

If you are busy you may not be able to spend a long lunch hour with someone, but you can spend ten minutes. Pick one or two people a day and decide to make the time spent with them special.

Insight

Show the person that you are listening to them and that what they have to say is of interest to you. Most people do not experience being wholly listened to by another person very often, so this is one of the most powerful things that you can do with someone to build up a shared relationship with deep rapport.

Congratulate yourself

Thinking an occasional thought about how well you have done lately will not do as much good as if you put it in a framework and make it significant and visible. Write a list of all the things that you have achieved and made happen in the last few months, then read them aloud with gusto and as you do so, feel really proud. To embed your success, print the achievements of which you are really proud in large letters on A4 paper and stick them inside cupboard doors so you can see them several times a day. Get that feeling of vitality and powerfulness that comes with knowing that you are a person who constantly makes things happen.

Things to do to help you feel grounded

Affirmations

Affirmations are a lovely way of focusing on what you have in life, and the things that you want to bring into your daily living. There are thousands to choose from and if you read a book of affirmations you can choose the ones that resonate with you each day.

You can change your affirmations whenever you want to, depending on what you want to draw into your life. Some favourites are: 'I have abundance, joy, love and fulfilment in my life', 'I am the teacher I never had'; 'I embrace all living creatures, and the whole of nature in its beauty'; 'Thank you for everything that comes into my life'; 'Thoughts become things. When I can see it clearly in my mind, I get to hold it in my hand'.

Find people on the same journey as you

> **Insight**
>
> There is nothing so exciting as meeting someone you click with and finding out that they are interested in the same things as you and are on the same life journey. Treasure these people. If you are networking, find two people in the room and discover what is special about them and what is important to them. This is one of the best ways to find life-travelling buddies.

Keep your sense of humour

A sense of humour can often free you and those around you from automatic responses to situations, as this letter from a student to her parents demonstrates:

> Dear Mum and Dad,
>
> I'm sorry I haven't written to you for a while, but the fire that engulfed my flat also destroyed all my writing materials.
>
> Fortunately, one of the firemen that helped put the blaze out was a nice young man called Wayne, who kindly let me stay with him in his flat. I do so hope you will like him when you meet him, as we got married last week. I did want it to be a surprise, but as I've started telling you all the good news, you also might as well know that you're about to become grandparents. I'm sure you're both delighted.
>
> Your loving daughter, Sharon
>
> PS My flat didn't burn down, I'm not married and I'm not pregnant. But I did fail my maths exam. I hope this puts everything into perspective for you.

Insight

Keep things in perspective. Do not blow things out of proportion. Something that you might have viewed as a major catastrophe can seem like only an irritation in a week's time. A walk in a cemetery on a sunny day will let you know that nothing really matters that much because we all end up in the same place eventually.

Gratitude

Before getting out of bed each day, ask yourself, 'What was good about yesterday?' You will find something worthwhile about even the worst of days. Then list all the things that you are grateful for having, and carry the feeling this gives you throughout the day. A quote from Lydia Child says it all: 'Gratitude is the memory of the heart; therefore forget not to say often, I have all I ever enjoyed.'

Have a breathing mantra
As you breathe in roll your tongue under your top teeth. As you breathe out bring your tongue down behind your bottom teeth. Hold your hand lightly on your stomach and ensure that this is where your breath is coming from, rather than shallow breathing from high up in your chest. Breathe deeply and repeat your own special words as you breathe 'in' and 'out'.

Learn to live in the present
If you look closely at your worst fears, you will find they tend to be of the 'what would happen if' variety. Accept that you will have periods of stress, and work out where your stress level lies. At least 90 per cent of the things we worry about never happen; worrying over whether they will or not will bring a cocktail of stressful hormones spiralling through your body.

Happiness
A Chinese proverb says that 'happiness is something to do, something to love, and something to look forward to'. Make sure you are working on at least one each of these aspects of yourself to lead to self-fulfilment, and that you plan many more for the future.

['Tips for Staying Motivated', courtesy of *Positive Health* magazine (PH) issue 142, December 2007, www.positivehealth.com © Frances Coombes]

The pink bubble meditation

The pink bubble meditation is a good way of calming yourself when you experience stress triggers.

▶ *Close your eyes and sigh deeply. Become aware of your body, and gradually relax any tension you may feel in your neck, shoulders, forehead and the rest of your body.*

- Slowly begin to focus on your breathing, how the air is being inhaled and exhaled, in and out of your body. Imagine your mind as a glass full of pink bubbly champagne.
- Fix your gaze on the champagne and allow any thoughts that come out of it to be encapsulated in a pink bubble that slowly rises and floats away. The bubbles may be irritations, frets and worries about future circumstances; let them all float away. Encapsulate each thought as it appears, then watch it float away. Gradually your thoughts will become calmer and you will achieve a still, clearer mind. Take some time to stay in this place and be aware of the stillness and calm.

THINGS TO REMEMBER

▸ *Stay connected to the people you care about.*

▸ *Create a buddy system and have people routing for you.*

▸ *Have a mission statement and revisit it often.*

▸ *Congratulate yourself on the things you have achieved.*

▸ *Use affirmations to focus on the things you have in life.*

▸ *Use meditation and have a breathing mantra.*

19

Model success to master change

In this chapter you will learn:
- *simple steps to master change*
- *how to borrow other people's 'strategies'*
- *to be aware of your behaviour patterns*
- *to ask for what you want*

> **'Whether walking on fire, or climbing a mountain, you have to know where you're going to end up and know what tools to take to get you there.'**
>
> Simon Treselyan, motivational trainer

While reading this book you may have noticed changes in your perceptions of how you think and feel about your ability to become highly motivated. The more you become aware of the power of the new learning tools and techniques you have acquired, the more you may wonder, 'How may I begin to use them?', 'How can I take this knowledge and use it to increase my skills and hasten my progress in the areas in which I want to excel?'

Borrow other people's strategies

Insight

The simplest way to increase your skills is to pick an area in which you would like to improve, say how to be a better home improvements person, computer user, parent, cook, lover, or

(Contd)

how to develop better reasoning skills. Then find someone
who has those skills and ask them 'How do you do that?'

HOW TO INCREASE YOUR REASONING SKILLS

Ask yourself lots of questions related to what you already know
about the subject, and the things you would like to know. Write
a list of your answers and, as you picture yourself using all your
tools and techniques fluently, the images you picture will contain
all the clues you need for acquiring skills patterns.

Self-questioning	Answers?
How do I reason now? What are the thinking through steps I take?	
How do I know when I have reached a conclusion? What are the signs that tell me? The feelings? The mind pictures? What do I say to myself that lets me know?	
How effective is my method of reasoning? Am I ever wrong?	
Do I sometimes have blindspots? If so, list what they are.	
Who do you know who excels at the skill you want to perfect?	
Could you watch them performing the skill in order to acquire it?	
Is there a simpler basic outline of the strategy that you could start with?	

Collect strategies to improve your situation

The trick is to keep a list of all the new strategies you have come across. You have so many tools to help you develop wider and more flexible reasoning skills. Which one will you pick?

Will you start with a very simple structure, such as AEIOU, first mentioned in Chapter 16: Assumption, Evidence, Illustration, Opinion, Unique? Would this model be useful to you?

USING THE STRATEGY

The next time you are in a meeting or situation where you want more insight, write the words down the left-hand side of the page and note whether each of the points are covered by participants in discussion. First, seek clarification of which facts are missing. Then form your questions according to the type of information to which you require answers.

RETRIEVING UNDISCLOSED INFORMATION

Useful questions to ask are, 'How do you know that?', 'What are you assuming to come to that conclusion?', 'Do you have any evidence for what you are suggesting?' Reflect on whether the information you have been given adds up, and whether the opinion is justified or not? Ask yourself, 'What has come from the discussion that is new, different or moves the situation forwards?'

A FRAME FOR YOUR QUESTIONS

ASSUMPTION?	Listen to the people present and note what assumptions are being made.
EVIDENCE?	Are the points they are making facts or opinions? If points are put across as fact, what is the evidence for it?

(Contd)

ILLUSTRATIONS?	If a person gives examples of the points they are putting forward, are the illustrations consistent? If not, ask for a better example.
OPINION?	Based on the information they have put forward, is the opinion of the person making the statement justified?
UNIQUE?	Has any new information emerged? Are there any new key points? If so, separate out what is essential from what is padding.

Always build good rapport with the people involved before asking these type of questions. Asking someone, 'Is that fact or opinion you're stating?' may come across as rude. So carry out your questioning tactfully or you may lose friends. Phrase your question in a less pointed way, perhaps saying, 'That's an interesting point you're making. Can you tell me a little about what it is based on?'

You can employ the AEIOU reasoning strategy in:

- ▶ *meetings, to gain clarity on a situation;*
- ▶ *if you are anxious about how a decision is being made;*
- ▶ *when you want to make changes;*
- ▶ *if you are dissatisfied with a decision and don't know why;*
- ▶ *if you are faced with a threat or challenge;*
- ▶ *when you want to disagree.*

Once this basic reasoning skill becomes a habit you will begin to use it every day. It will help you understand the most important points in what is going on. And, if you run your own ideas through the AEIOU questions before presenting them to others, you will understand the real objectives in a situation, be able to select an appropriate option and present your own findings logically.

Change your behaviour to enhance your results

Once you are clear about your future vision, you will know the ideal results you would like to achieve. This will make it easier for you to know the types of actions, skills and behaviours you would like to model.

Insight

Your aim is to become a 'change master', to embrace change. One of the ways you will do this is by recognizing the habitual patterns of behaviour and strategy that people around you employ to get the excellent results they want.

All tasks you undertake will become easier, as you begin to use the techniques you have acquired to identify people's winning strategies and adapt them for your own purposes. As you acquire the habitual thinking patterns and behaviours of people who excel at what they do, you will effortlessly deepen your knowledge and increase your skills. You will begin to make the changes that quickly build momentum and propel you towards your bigger goals.

If you have read this far, you will already have all the tools and resources necessary to find out how people connect with their natural brilliance. You know how to spot the beliefs, behaviours and capabilities that the most accomplished people around you are demonstrating. Let's say you want to build on your reasoning skills and go one step further. You want to model someone's thinking style to find out their strategy for how they make good decisions?

You have the tools, you have the techniques, you could use your knowledge to model a more effective decision-making strategy?

Recipe for modelling a good decision-maker

Insight

Modelling a thinking style is like making a pizza. First you look in your techniques store and assemble the ingredients you will require to model the thinking style of a good decision-maker. A good decision-maker will always have:

▶ *a framework for their questioning process, AEIOU questioning, will do to start;*
▶ *flexible thinking, so that they can employ several different ways of retrieving information about a situation;*
▶ *chunking up and down skills, that is big picture/small detail thinking.*

MODEL THE STYLE OF A GOOD DECISION-MAKER

You can start to model good decision-making skills by watching television programmes that feature personalities who display the qualities you admire and wish to acquire. Television shows are excellent starting points for acquiring skills, as they stick to a regular format that lets you see the person perform the same process many times over.

MODEL HOW TO DEVELOP GOOD DECISION-MAKING SKILLS

The first time you watch a programme, refrain from getting drawn into the content of the discussion. Instead, take a pen and paper and look for the framework and patterns of behaviour that come across in the show. Note the questioning style the presenter uses to separate fact from irrelevancy. Discover how they tease out the most important information.

CHOOSE A PERSON WHO EXHIBITS THE SKILL

Insight

Shows featuring police procedure are good to watch for picking up thinking styles, provided you can ignore the story and stick with the procedure. Remember, you are watching to obtain a decision-making strategy. List what the subject is doing and noticing and paying attention to. You may already do this subconsciously, but writing a procedure down makes it explicit and lets you uncover strategies and recognize whether any parts are missing.

There is an American television judge who tries civil litigation cases in front of a television audience, and is incredibly good at sizing up a situation and then making a ruling based on her questioning process. This is what her framework, thinking style and process looks like when written down.

Eye accessing cues

She pays attention to eye accessing cues, and where defendants look to access information. You will hear her say, 'Look at me when you answer questions, don't look away.' She holds the belief that people who do not look her in the eye when giving information are probably lying.

Shifts in people's descriptive language

The judge notices shifts in people's language and viewpoint. Someone who is being questioned about what they were doing on the day the house was burgled, may happily answer all questions: 'I went here'; 'I went there at this time'; 'I did this'; 'I did that.'

However, when asked a direct question, such as, 'Did you steal the motorbike?', they may reply with: 'I would not do a thing

(Contd)

like that.' This reply alerts her to the fact that they are probably lying. The person has shifted their viewpoint of the situation and is talking as if they are discussing someone else, from a distance.

Notice how people shift viewpoint as they speak

▶ **Position 1** *is our own point of view. We discuss a situation as seen through our own eyes. We describe what we are feeling and describe our thoughts.*
▶ **Position 2** *is from the other person's position. We put ourselves in their shoes and describe how they feel, we speak as if we were them. (Often when people tell lies, they feel uncomfortable doing it from position 1, their own viewpoint. So they may switch to position 2, distancing themselves from the act and becoming an onlooker, giving a character reference for the behaviour being described.)*
▶ **Position 3** *is neutral. The situation is seen through the eyes of an impartial third-party observer looking on a situation in which the others are engaged. By changing our thinking to that of an onlooker, particularly in areas of conflict, we can gather vital information from a distance that people who stay engaged in the other two close-up thinking positions will miss.*

Recipe for developing a good decision-making strategy

▶ *Framework: always has a structure in which the questioning takes place.*
▶ *Questioning: to gather information.*
▶ *Chunks questions up and down: to gain different types of information.*
▶ *Models each litigant's thinking and behaviour: by asking each to run through what they did and noticed from before to after the incident.*
▶ *Notices eye accessing cues.*
▶ *Notices perceptual positions.*
▶ *Metaphors: makes comparisons of situations with similar circumstances which highlights anomalies in people's thinking and behaviour.*

The above ingredients, and the judge's exquisite flexibility to move effortlessly through the different types of thinking and viewing situations, form the structure for how the judge's questioning works.

Her most noticeable beliefs are:

▶ *People who do not make eye contact are probably lying. So probe more.*
▶ *People who change viewpoints, for example instead of saying, 'I did not steal the ring', say, 'I would not do a thing like that', are lying. So probe more. She notices the person has changed their perceptual position of the situation and moved from first person to second person. So instead of thinking and talking and seeing the situation through their own eyes, they have suddenly shifted position and are talking as if they are discussing another person and are removed from the situation.*
▶ *She believes she is thorough and fair, and this belief radiates from her. The result is that most people being tried on her show, even if they lose the case, tend to believe she gave a fair ruling.*
▶ *She believes she is not just there to dispense justice, she wants to help people understand what are their mistakes in beliefs, behaviour or calculations and how to change them.*
▶ *She offers insights and good advice that she believes will help people to move on with their lives. This involves first describing repetitive thinking or behaviour patterns that people display, then offering an alternative strategy for thinking or behaving that offers better results. In its simplest form the strategy may be, 'What you are doing is harmful to yourself and others? Put a full stop behind it and move on with your life.'*

Insight

Good decision-makers develop analysis and problem-solving skills as well as good judgemental abilities. They take a step-by-step approach when sifting through evidence and are not distracted by emotional comments offered as if they are facts.

A DECISION-MAKING FRAMEWORK

Start by obtaining the big picture

The judge uses flexible thinking steps as she tries a case. She puts the situation in a framework: 'Person A says this, Person B says this. Here is my understanding of the situation.' She asks both plaintiff and defendant: 'How much of my understanding is correct?' Each question she asks follows a format, that guides the person's attention in a certain direction. What she is left with is two pictures, side by side, with some details the same and some which are different.

1 **The judge uses chunking up** *by asking each person to describe a big picture view of the whole event.*

Asks what happened and gets PLAINTIFF'S version of events. Asks, 'How much is correct?'	Asks what happened and gets DEFENDANT'S version of events. Asks, 'How much is correct?'
Looks for inconsistencies and what is different from defendant's version.	Looks for inconsistencies and what is different from plaintiff's version.

2 **The judge then chunks down,** *saying 'Here are the sticking points' and moves to small detail specific questioning. She asks* **'Who?', 'What?', 'When?', 'Where?', 'Why?'** *and* **'How?'** *questions to uncover inconsistencies.*

Defendant:	They were in the car.
Judge:	Who's 'they'? Who else was there?
Defendant:	The guys in the car, who stole the video.
Judge:	How do you know they stole the video?

The Judge models each litigant's thinking and behaviour, as they run through what they did and noticed from before to after the incident. The questioning allows her to look for inconsistencies and relevant facts to back them up.

3 **The judge then changes to position 3, impartial thinking.**
At this point she has the facts and moves to position 3, an impartial observer. From an impartial position she separates litigants' feelings from facts.

Feelings	Facts
'I know you are feeling bad sir, and looking for someone to blame.'	'But the fact is, your daughter ran off with this man. No one forced her. She went willingly.'

Often in heated situations people are illogical in what they are saying and thinking. It is always helpful to take a deep breath and separate what is fact from what is feelings to help reach an accurate conclusion.

4 **The judge summarizes the case and her conclusions** *about participants' motives and the logic of their actions and offers her own reflections, such as, 'You weren't smart, to leave your key in the ignition and walk off', or, 'I'm curious to know what occurred within two days to make you give up your morals and take the money?'*
5 **Take action.** *Finally she makes a ruling and awards compensation to the injured party, or says, 'You both behaved badly. Pay for your own expenses.' And the case is over.*

WHAT A QUESTIONING FRAMEWORK DOES

If you use a questioning framework for your own decision making it will allow you to:

▶ *ask questions to clarify your motives;*
▶ *give understanding on whether your objectives are clear;*
▶ *explore whether all options have been identified;*
▶ *quickly identify any areas in which you have been blinkered;*
▶ *show steps left out from the thinking-through process;*
▶ *know whether you have enough information to support your analysis.*

Reflection

Human beings are seldom able to scrutinize each other's thinking patterns in as much detail as you see laid out above. If you practise your modelling skills and refine your sensory awareness, you can develop this phenomenal ability.

You now know many of the decision-making tools and techniques the judge displays, and the order in which she uses them. Will you use her strategy as a springboard to enable you to unlock and understand other people's thinking styles?

▶ *Imagine actively practising these flexible thinking habits every day for a month.*
▶ *What difference will it make in the way you conduct yourself in negotiations with other people?*
▶ *What will you be saying, doing, thinking differently?*
▶ *What will other people be noticing about you that is different?*
▶ *Will you be more relaxed in negotiation and decision-making situations?*

Strategies people have modelled and why

BORROW MY BELIEF, BORROW MY TALENT

Adrian Hutchinson, a performance development consultant, chose his first modelling project because he had access to some people with outstanding abilities. He says: 'I wanted to understand, and to experience what their successes felt like in action. I wanted to identify a really effective way of creatively visualizing and to feel and see myself being successful in future projects. Interestingly, all three models used very similar techniques and confirmed that if you really believe what you want is congruent then you will behave in a more positive way that achieves it. So I've learned how to feel successful.'

WHAT MODELLING SOMEONE ELSE'S EFFECTIVE STRATEGY GIVES YOU

▶ *The chance to see up close what makes someone excel at something they do well.*
▶ *The opportunity to acquire that ability in a fraction of the time it would normally take and make it your own.*
▶ *The chance to try on the beliefs, capabilities and behaviours that combine to make that person's strategy so powerful for them.*
▶ *The opportunity to try on a strategy immediately and identify what works and what does not work.*

Become aware of your behaviour patterns

Even when modelling very practical skills you can gain new insights into how differently from us other people think. Modelling can often help you see how differently from other people you think. It can also pinpoint whether you carry unhelpful behaviours into other areas of your life.

Case study – Maria Furtek

Maria Furtek, freelance trainer and development coach, says, 'What on the surface, seemed a fairly straightforward and practical skill to model, turned out to be quite revealing in terms of my thinking styles.'

'I hadn't realized that I am very much an **options** person and have found it difficult to be governed in a step-by-step,

(Contd)

follow-the-rules way. From modelling the skill I found out that, when you assemble flat-pack furniture you have to follow the rules.'

Maria's thinking style

Procedures ....X....Options thinker

Small details ....X...Big chunk thinker

'In the past I'd thought, "This looks very easy, I don't need to follow the rules", and hence I'd always have bits left over and I'd never managed to get any furniture to stay together. I'm a **big chunk** person, real big picture stuff, and I'm not really very good at being able to manage very small detail. I find it overwhelming.

'I find it difficult to manage this in several areas of my life, one is in my professional life as a trainer – I have lots of original courses I'd like to write. I do all the big chunk stuff, the desire and passion to write is there, I have all my ideas brainstormed and then I get stuck. It was really painful to sit down and take that really small detail a bit at a time. But it's impacted on other things. I've now been able to write courses within a week with fine detail, which has been brilliant.

'Something the modelling helped me understand that I hadn't realized before, was just how much of a big chunk thinker I was. The first draft of my project was written in general terms and I hadn't put in any detail at all. When I did the modelling and had to rewrite the steps, I thought "Oh, this is really irritating, people are going to find it really boring". And of course the people that are small chunk thinkers didn't find it boring.

'I realize I am also a big picture person in real-life situations. When I have challenges, I want to get to the solution immediately, and I've found it very hard in the past to just live in the present and take things one little bit at a time.

'I used to look into the future and try and take a massive leap without any of those little steps that it's so necessary to have in between. Modelling and being able to do small chunk thinking has helped me reduce things like anxiety and worry and fear. Now I think "right I've got my vision, I know where I'm going, what do I need to do?"

'Of course, people who've already grasped this and can switch from big picture to small chunk thinking automatically may be thinking it should have happened naturally. But the fact is, it didn't. I'm great at the big things, but the small things have flummoxed me, until now.

'In terms of flat-pack furniture, I can do it now. I'm not saying I enjoy it, but I can do it so long as I stick to following the rules.'

BE AWARE OF YOUR BEHAVIOUR PATTERNS

Do you recognize a pattern in situations that keep showing up in your life. It could be that you have worked for lots of bosses who were critical of you. No matter which company you work for the same results occur. It may be that you almost get success, but it is snatched away. A common theme may be that the money is on the table but then it disappears. The cast of characters appearing in these scenarios may change but the situation remains the same.

Case study – Janet Borman

Janet Borman, a self-employed illustrator, came for coaching because she found it difficult to negotiate for payment. Janet said, 'I know my attitude to money was

(Contd)

formed in early childhood. My father spent his money as soon as he earned it. My mother saved her money. The messages I received were that money was always scarce and difficult to get hold of.

'Not surprisingly, I have difficulties negotiating fees with clients. I go into a meeting with a price in my head and the buyer beats me down. I accept the price they offer meekly, and them come away feeling angry, hurt and aggrieved.'

Negotiating money in exchange for work generates a lot of emotion. We think we are talking about money, but tied in with that are our feelings of vulnerability and self-worth. Many people are prepared to stay in a poorly paid job, and never make the leap to discover their full potential, simply to avoid negotiating money and maybe being told their labour or goods are not worth the asking price.

Ask for what you want
Question: What is the largest sum of money you think you could possibly earn in a day? Write down the amount and then say it aloud.

▶ *What are the criteria you would have to fulfil in order to earn £1,500 a day?*
▶ *What stops you from doing it?*

When asked the question in a workshop, 'How many of you can imagine earning £1,500 a day?' one woman answered, 'I already do, and I worry more about how I am going to keep it, than how I am going to make even more.'

Most people set limitations on their earning power. This ensures that if a job comes up requiring skills they possess, but offering more money than they feel they are worth, they think, 'That couldn't possibly apply to me', and so they will not even consider applying.

Make sure you think you are worth a lot of money

All money comes to us as some form of exchange. If you think you are not valuable, you may sell your services for less than you are worth. Before you ask your boss, or anyone else, for more money, some inner marketing is necessary. First, you must sell the idea to yourself that you are worth more money.

Underlying most behaviour patterns is a belief system which impacts on your self-esteem. If you do not believe that you are capable of earning more than a certain amount of money, you may go from one position to the next and will earn only as much as your expectations will allow. It is vital that, when you model the skills of someone who is good at negotiating for money, you must also take on the beliefs that support their ability.

A modelling challenge – how to ask for more money

Model a successful strategy

You have the tools and techniques so now is your chance to see what really works.

Model several different people who are good at asking for more money in order to see a range of strategies in action. Seek out people who have consistently negotiated money increases well, rather than had one-off experiences.

▶ *How are the beliefs about money held by these people different from your own?*
▶ *Are there any benefits for you in adopting the strategies of successful money negotiators and incorporating them into your own negotiating habits?*
▶ *Is there anything you would lose by adopting the beliefs of successful money negotiators?*

Model several different people who have the talent, in order to see a range of strategies in action. It may be that only one of these people have beliefs about their ability to negotiate that press your motivation buttons. You will find that the beliefs about money they hold that resonate with you and the skill in which they excel, will in some way be different from the other people you modelled.

People who inspire you and give you beliefs in your potential to do things well act like belief catalysts. Think back through your life; who were the people who acted as belief catalysts for you? What did you achieve that you might not have attained? Whoever you choose to model now, make sure your beliefs are aligned with theirs and you will achieve the result you want.

Start changing old habits and learning new strategies that work better for you. If you want to create wealth then realize that it is not an impossible dream. Making money is a skill that you can acquire, like learning to be calm, distilling the essence of a book, developing a reasoning or decision-making skill, writing with both hands, or assembling flat-pack furniture.

THINGS TO REMEMBER

▶ *Collect simple strategies that improve your situation.*

▶ *Use simple techniques to increase your reasoning skills.*

▶ *Borrow someone's beliefs, and you borrow their talents.*

▶ *Have a framework for questioning and decision making.*

▶ *Change your behaviour to enhance your results.*

▶ *Learn an effective strategy for asking for more money.*

▶ *Ask for what you want.*

20

Pulling it all together

In this chapter you will learn:
- *how committed you are to succeed*
- *the syntax for success*
- *your action plan for success*

> '**You are your own Devil, you are your own God. You fashioned the paths your footsteps have trod.**'
>
> Tieme Ranapiri, a Maori poet

You have reached the part of the book where you may start to wonder, 'Well what did I get out of that?' This book is designed to motivate you if you want to move from just thinking about the things you would like to achieve, to actually doing them.

How committed are you to being successful?

Answer each question rating yourself on a scale of 1–10.

Are you committed to being successful at whatever you do and are you prepared to raise your standards in order to get it?	
Do you have an unshakeable belief that you can get whatever you set out to achieve in life?	

Are you mentally equipped with the tools and problem-solving techniques that you need to deal with any challenges?	
Are you flexible enough to tailor your strategies to get the results you desire?	
In short, do you know what to do, the order you need to do it in, and how to apply your whole focus to achieving your goals?	

Are you on your way to designing your personal action plan for creating the future you want, aided by the tools, tips and techniques you have acquired to help you become more motivated?

Tools you will use for your future success

There are many ideas contained in this book to get you thinking about and planning your own strategies for achieving your purpose. Look at all the ideas and ask yourself, 'How could I adapt that for my uses?' Take the modelling projects illustrated in Chapters 13, 14 and 19 and brainstorm 20 ways you could adapt some of them to further your aims.

Insight

Modelling makes the transfer of knowledge in great detail available to you. You might want to:

▶ *develop greater leadership qualities;*
▶ *model high-flyers to see what makes them the best;*
▶ *support or coach others to improve their results;*
▶ *improve your working relationships;*
▶ *keep meetings focused and moving forward;*
▶ *notice and resolve problems at an early stage.*

(Contd)

You can speed up your development by identifying the key skills of the people who are good at these things. Modelling requires that you identify the behaviours, skills and capabilities, and beliefs they hold that make them so good at what they do. Then you incorporate those types of behaviours into your own.

Two of the most powerful tools you have in your personal armoury are your 'goal setting' and your 'modelling skills' abilities. You cannot control the future or decide what you will be doing five years from now when success knocks on your door, but you can decide on the next small steps you will take today and tomorrow to make the success you want a reality. Get motivated – start increasing your skills and taking the actions that make successes happen more quickly.

▶ *Get into the habit of trying on other people's strategies for achieving successful outcomes.*
▶ *Know your purpose and design a plan of action to acquire the talents and abilities you require.*
▶ *Notice good models of success strategies and stretch your thinking about how you might adapt them to achieve your own goals.*

RECAP

If you filled in your motivational skills wheel in Chapter 2, you already have an insight into how you fare in relation to many of the skills that highly motivated people possess. You may have analyzed your weak points and have been pleasantly surprised by some of your strengths.

Many of the skills we have been looking at are also those found in leaders and senior managers. In addition, leaders are often noted for their ability to live with ambiguity, they can make plans and move forwards without having every part of the jigsaw present. The leader has a clear idea of what they want to do and the strength to persist in the face of setbacks and failures. They tend to be passionate for their vocation or profession and be able to inspire others with their words. They have good listening skills (Chapter 16), which enable them to absorb a great deal of information quickly and pick out the significant key points from what people are saying.

Use the CRAFTY listening technique to increase your listening abilities. And use the AEIOU listening and questioning technique to challenge existing assumptions people are making and draw out explicit information.

Hold your vision steadfastly in your mind

To be passionately engaged in the life and work of your dreams, you need to hold your vision steadfastly in your mind, and see yourself being successful at everything you do. You also need to increase your level of achievement and observable successes in your everyday life.

Insight

Three things will help you here:

▶ *Modelling successful role models. Get into the habit of asking, 'How do you/they do that?' Find out and then assess that person's strategy, and its effectiveness and limitations.*
▶ *Understanding thinking styles, your own and other people's.*
▶ *Assessing the feedback you get from the things you do. If something you are doing is unsuccessful, change your pattern of behaviour until you get the results you want.*

Align your beliefs and values

When the actions and behaviour we follow support our deepest needs and we are free from internal conflict, we produce our most magical results. Once you know what excites and motivates you and you are prepared to take the actions to make your dreams a reality, then you will magically move towards your purpose.

Now you need a procedure for standing back and scrutinizing your ideas to know whether the goals you seek are attainable and the period of time in which they can be achieved (Chapters 2, 4 and 8).

Success means different things to different people. Someone else might see success as having the energy, fitness and body of an athlete, another person might see success as creating something unique, having a millionaire lifestyle or a loving relationship. Another person might see their success as helping others and making a difference to people's lives. However you define your success, you then need to make a plan and put an order to it.

Your goals should be SMART

- *Define your goals within the context of your values (Chapters 3 and 6).*
- *There will always be some things that you might want if there is little effort involved, but when the going gets tough you drop them in favour of goals that are more meaningful to you.*
- *Always produce a well-formed outcome on every project you intend to start. Rank your goals by level of importance to you. Make sure that you are not deflecting your energy by focusing on too many goals. Some will be distractions that will never come to fruition, but they will divert some of your attention from the things you really do want to achieve (Chapters 4 and 6).*
- *Listening skills – ultimately your goals will be achieved with the help of other people, so develop good communication, persuasion and listening skills (Chapters 11 and 16).*

Follow your passions

What do you feel passionate about? What do you burn to do? What would you do if money were no object and you could do anything in the world you wanted to do?

When creating ideas

▶ *First, comes the* **dreamer** *– you ask yourself questions such as, 'What would I do if I had no restrictions?'*

▶ *Then, the* **realist** *– 'How can I make it work?'*

▶ *Finally, the* **pragmatist** *– 'Is this a good idea?', 'Who would want it?', 'Who's done it before?', 'How can I test it?'*

Where are you now on the motivational skills wheel?

Below are some of the main skills that successful people either have or work hard towards achieving.

1 *Motivating yourself and others to do things.*
2 *Visualization – imagination and rehearsing your dreams of the future, and how it will look, feel and taste when you achieve it. Harnessing the power of emotions.*
3 *Feeling purposeful – do you know enough about your beliefs and values, and how to anchor them securely to your purpose?*
4 *Goal setting – do you know how to create well-formed outcomes? Have you learned the 21-day habit to regularly achieving your goals?*
5 *Getting rid of limiting beliefs that hold you back from being truly successful.*
6 *Training – do you know the areas in which you need to acquire more skills? Are you constantly developing new skills?*
7 *Communication – how good are you at understanding your own and other people's thinking styles when there is a need for motivation?*
8 *Modelling – do you know how to model other people's skills in order to get the results you want?*
9 *Time management. How good are you at working within timeframes. Are you 'in time', 'through time' or 'behind time?'*
10 *Pulling it all together – have you used your newly acquired skills in real-life situations, adjusting and smoothly pulling strategies together so that they can work at peak efficiency for you?*

Figure 20.1 The motivational skills wheel – building your skills and abilities.

Imagine again that each spoke of the wheel represents a skill or ability that you value and at which you want to become even more accomplished. How do you rate your level of competency under each of the headings on a scale of 1 to 10 now? Number one represents the middle of the wheel and 10 the outer rim. Again draw a dot on each of the spokes at your present competency level in each of the ten skills. Don't think about it, just do it quickly.

When you compare it with the original motivational skills wheel you completed in Chapter 2, have you scored higher at any of the competencies? Have you learned anything new or surprising about yourself and your particular strengths? Has your confidence or competency grown in any of the areas we've covered? This is really what motivation is about – building competencies, knowing yourself and what you really want, and having the confidence to act upon your dreams.

What is the next action you intend to take?

Are there any areas in your motivational skills wheel chart that you need to improve? If so, you could concentrate for a week on one area at a time, say increasing your goal setting abilities, or banishing limiting beliefs, or finding and modelling other people's strategies that work. Could you devote your efforts for a week to simply becoming more purposeful and increasing your motivational drives, or enhancing your performance?

Do you believe that you could raise your standards and become 10 per cent or even 20 per cent better at any of the topics covered? Of course you could! We can all become better in any areas on which we focus our attention.

The motivational skills wheel gives you an 'at a glance' overview of your perceived competencies – it is your blueprint for success. The trick is to know the order in which to do things so that you can become systematically more powerful in your thinking, action planning and completion drives.

Gathering your resources

Capture a feeling

Remember when you did something really well, something that made you feel really proud?

▶ *What were the beliefs you held then about your abilities to achieve your aim?*
▶ *What sort of things did you say to yourself about the thing you were achieving?*
▶ *Was your motivation drive high?*

> Recall that feeling every morning, and harness it and take it with you for the day.

Remember, in everything that's really important to us – love, life, friendship, success – feelings come first. We may spend our school life learning about logic, but all the really big decisions we make in life, such as whom we marry, where we live, what we want from life, are made with our emotions.

Martin Goodyer, motivational trainer of Reach International Associates, says, 'The feelings come before the actions. Therefore you need to be finely attuned to your feelings. When your feelings and whole attention are focused on your goal, you can attain it, providing you know the syntax for success – which is the order of how you do things.'

Your action plan for success

1 **Raise your standards.** *Whatever your standard is now, whether it's good or bad, is not relevant, it just is. Whatever you have in life, you have got everything you deserve because the actions you have taken to date have produced it. These are the standards that you have set for yourself up until now, and until you do something different you will not get a different result. Only when you raise that standard yourself can you expect to raise your expectations.*

2 **Have an unshakeable belief.** *Raising your standards is not enough. You need to have an absolutely unshakeable belief that says, 'I know I can do it'. If you do not have that you get a little voice in your head that says, 'Who are you kidding? You've never done it before. Why are you going to do it now? What makes you think you're going to do it now?'*

3 **Banish your devil.** *The voice in your head is like a little devil that follows you around. You have to banish your little devil, or at least dumbfound him so that he has got nothing to say.*

4 **Know what to do and apply it.** *Remember a time when you were able to do things that you didn't think you were able to do before? Where did you find references for doing these things successfully? Look around you now and when you see people with skills you'd like to acquire, ask them, 'How did you do that?'*

Insight

When you find simple strategies that will work, collect them and use them. There is a way of doing most things and you need to have a simple strategy that gives you the order for the process to work. While there is nothing new in this world, when we do things in a very specific order, we can create magical results.

Your purpose and destiny are intertwined. As your thoughts, plans and actions flow together, your energy grows because you are doing what you love doing. Now you are focused on creating the outcomes you want. You have the tools, you have the motivation, you feel powerful – take the next steps and journey towards your biggest ever goals.

'Don't be afraid to take big steps. You can't cross a chasm in two small jumps.'

David Lloyd George

Taking it further

Motivational trainers

The following motivational trainers offer a wide range of services including delivering courses, writing, speaking, coaching, and so on. Check their websites or phone for information.

Michael Breen, MBNLP, www.mbnlp.com
Shelle Rose Charvet, info@frankdanielsassociates.co.uk
Pete Cohen, info@petecohentv and www.petecohen.tv
Frances Coombes, www.francescoombes.com, and
francescoombes@yahoo.com
Ann Fuller-Good, FOCUS, telephone 020 8543 2288
Martin Goodyer, Reach International Associates,
www.reach4reach.com
Paul Jacobs and De Shipman, The Rainbow Journey,
www.new-oceans.co.uk
Cricket Kemp, nlpnortheast@patterning.demon.co.uk
Greg Levoy, www.heartatwork.net
Alex McMillan, Club Entrepreneur, www.clubentrepreneur.co.uk
PPD Personal Development, www.ppdlearning.co.uk
Wendy Sullivan, Discovery, www.discovery-works.co.uk
Peter Thomson, www.peterthomson.com
Simon Treselyan, Startfire, www.empowermentinstitute.com
Nick Williams, Heart at Work Project, www.nick-williams.com

Helpful books

Andreas, Steve and Connirae Andreas, *Change Your Mind – and Keep the Change*, Real People Press, 1987

Bandler, Richard, *Using Your Brain for a Change*, Real People Press, 1981

Bandler, Richard and John Grinder, *The Structure of Magic*, Vol. 1, Science and Behaviour Books, 1975

Bandler, Richard and John Grinder, *Frogs into Princes*, Eden Grove Editions, 1990

Bavister, Steve and Amanda Vickers, *Teach Yourself Coaching*, Hodder Education, 2005

Bavister, Steve and Amanda Vickers, *Essential NLP* (Teach Yourself), Hodder Education, 2010

Cameron-Bandler, Leslie, David Gordon and Michael Lebeau, *The Emprint Method*, Future Pace, 1985

Covey, Stephen, *The Seven Habits of Highly Effective People*, Simon & Schuster, 1998

Holden, Robert, *Happiness Now*, Hodder Mobius, 1999

Jenner, Paul, *How to be Happier* (Teach Yourself Happiness), Hodder Education, 2010

Kline, Nancy, *Time to Think*, Cassell Illustrated, 1999

Laborde, Genie Z., *Influencing with Integrity*, Syntony Publishing, 1987

McMillan, Alex, *Be A Great Entrepreneur* (Teach Yourself), Hodder Education, 2010

Robbins, Anthony, *Unlimited Power*, Simon & Schuster, 1986

Robbins, Anthony, *Awaken the Giant Within*, Simon & Schuster, 1992

Rose, Colin, *Master it Faster*, Industrial Society, 2000

Seymour, John and Joseph O'Connor, *Introducing Neuro-Linguistic Programming*, HarperCollins, 1993

Shapiro, Mo, *Instant Manager: Neuro Linguistic Programming*, Hodder Education with Chartered Management Institute, 2007

Williams, Nick, *Unconditional Success*, Bantam Press.

Index

achievable goals, *12, 128, 140*
achievements, celebrating, *32*
acting 'as if', *29–31*
action
    following ideas/goals, *17, 85*
    and strategic planning, *125*
    taking, habit of, *55, 56*
action plan for success, *351–2*
AEIOU technique, *288–9, 325–6, 328, 345*
affirmations, *318*
'all or nothing' thinking, *150, 162–3*
anchoring
    feelings, *48–9, 162, 302, 303*
    positive states, *59–60*
Angart, Leo (case study), *97–8*
Apollinaire, Guillaume (quote), *153*
Archimedes, *67–8*
'arrow to the throat' ritual, *171, 173*
association, ideas from, *76–7*
assumptions
    in habitual thinking, *156*
    for peak performance, *45–6*
attentiveness (CRAFTY listening), *283*
audiences, connecting with, *194–6*
auditory construct (Ac), *243, 244*
auditory dialogue (Ad), *244*
auditory recall (Ar), *243, 244*
auditory (words) sensory style, *184, 193, 250, 274*

Bandler, Richard, *102*
Bannister, Roger, *68*

Bareson, Gregory, *306*
Beardwell, Phil (case study), *179*
Beddoes-Jones, Fiona, *184–5*
behaviour
    awareness of patterns, *335–9*
    changing to enhance results, *327*
    and logical levels of thinking, *305–8, 310–11*
    and low self-confidence, *297*
    and time management, *261*
beliefs
    aligning with values, *345–6*
    for building success, *33*
    changing, *25–33, 211, 212–14*
    feeling good about, *51–2*
    and logical levels of thinking, *305, 307–10*
    and negotiation skills, *340*
    and presuppositions, *29*
    and purpose, *104*
    seemingly impossible, *69*
    and skills modelling, *239*
    staying in touch with yourself, *316–17*
    and time management, *261*
    unshakeable, *351*
    see also limiting/negative beliefs; positive beliefs
big chunk/picture thinkers, *128–9, 184, 186, 189, 192, 204, 209, 210*
biographies, reading, *168*
blueprint
    of habitual thinking, *209–10*
    for success, *36*
blueprinting technique, *221–2*

body language
    and listening skills, *274–5*
    and skills modelling, *239*
Borman, Janet (case study), *337–8*
Boulanger, Nadia (quote), *92*
boundaries, stepping to the edge of, *2, 152–66*
brainstorming, *82*
    and goal setting, *119, 141*
breathing mantra, *321*
Breen, Michael, *169, 176–7, 178*
    case study, *248*
British Airways Brainwaves scheme (case study), *73*
'buddy' systems, *315*
Burns, Paul, *277*

calm, strategy for staying, *226*
'can do' attitudes, *6*
capabilities
    and logical levels of thinking, *305–6, 308, 310–11*
    questioning, *30–1*
    and time management, *261*
career goal-setting, *138–40*
celebrating achievements, *32*
change
    modelling success to master, *323–41*
    and self-limiting talk, *24*
changing states, *158–60*
Charvet, Shelle Rose, *199–201, 205*
'Chicken Soup for the Soul' books, *167–8*
Child, Lydia, *319–20*
chunking, *129–32*
    big chunk thinkers, *128–9, 184, 186, 204*
    breaking workloads into small chunks, *268–9*
    in goal-setting, *146, 149*

    small chunk thinkers, *204, 209, 210*
    up/down, *130–2, 332*
clarifying your purpose, *50*
Club Entrepreneur, *173–6*
Cohen, Pete (case study), *93–5*
combination, ideas from, *76–7*
commitment to success, *342–3*
communication
    with audiences/others, *194–6*
    as skill, *34, 116, 145*
competency, and motivational skills wheel, *34–6, 350*
completion drive, *263–7*
confidence-building, *33, 52*
congratulating yourself, *317–18*
constructive feedback, *57–8*
control over outcomes, *11, 12*
Coombes, Frances (case study), *235–6*
'core competents', *115*
core values, *41*
cost analysis (setting outcomes), *143*
CRAFTY listening, *281–4, 345*
creative process, *81–2*
creativity
    boosting, *82–5*
    Walt Disney's strategy, *86–8*
critic role, *74–5*
critical thinking, *82*
Crosby, Bing (quote), *273*
Cross, Joan (case study), *57–8*
curiosity (CRAFTY listening), *283*

deadlines, *255, 256, 268*
decision-making, *138*
    modelling, *328–35*
    planned and unplanned, *6*
    need for fast-paced, *113*
    and thinking styles, *205–6*
    and time management, *256*

deletions (habitual thinking), *156*
desired states, metaphors for, *66*
detail-conscious thinkers, *186, 204*
devils, banishing, *352*
diary-keeping, *146, 148*
difficulties, metaphors for, *66*
Dilts, Robert, *306*
Disney, Walt, *72, 86*
distortions (habitual thinking), *156*
'do it now fever', *226–7*
doing something different, *77*
dreamer role, *87, 347*
dreamers, *287*
dreams
    achieving impossible, *69–70*
    biographies of those with, *168*
    building shared, *61–2*
    and goal-setting, *137–8*
    imagination as key to achieving, *97–9*
    unfulfilled, *18*
drug-taking, *161*

early morning writing, *317*
effective strategies, modelling, *335–7*
emotions in the workplace, *39–40*
environment
    and logical levels of thinking, *305–6, 310–11*
    and time management, *261*
Erickson, Milton H., *155*
Eurostar, *221*
excellence, habitual state of, *55*
experts, consulting your, *78–81*
extending yourself, *153*
externally referenced thinking, *187*
eye accessing cues, *240–4, 329*

failure, fear of, *13–14, 23*
    overcoming, *25–6*
Farmer, Sir Thomas (quote), *183*
fearlessness (CRAFTY listening), *284*
feedback
    and flexible behaviour, *55, 56*
    and problem solving, *177–8*
    using constructive, *57–8*
feelings
    anchoring, *48–9, 162, 302, 303*
    changing states, *158–60*
    feeling good now, *52*
    in imagining the future, *101*
    importance of, *160–1*
    and low self-confidence, *297*
    switching states, *161*
    and thinking styles, *193*
filters for sameness/difference thinkers, *186, 192, 203*
'finding things fast' skill, *225*
Finino, Marsilio (quote), *91*
firewalking, *169–73*
flashpoints, *311–12*
flexible behaviour, *55, 56, 57*
flexible thinking, *82, 128–9, 164, 185, 189–90*
flow mode of listening, *279*
focusing, *256, 270, 316–17*
Ford, Henry (quote), *23*
forethought, lack of, *126*
Forster, E.M., *317*
Foster, Dela (case study), *138–9*
Frogs into Princes (Bandler and Grinder), **102**
Fuller-Good, Ann, *221–2*
Furtek, Maria (case study), *335–7*
future, imagining your, *100–2*

generalizations (habitual thinking), *156*
Gilbert, Dr Rob (quote), *162*

goals
  aligning, *140, 141–2*
  career, *138–40*
  choosing a promising, *142*
  defining, *141, 142–3*
  and feeling good, *51–2*
  framing your plan, *144*
  how often to set, *135–6*
  if you could not fail, *13–14*
  and leverage, *119–20*
  reviewing, *148*
  and self-coaching
    questions, *8–10*
  SMART, *12, 128*
  stating positively, *12*
  timeframe for achieving,
    12, 128, 140, 144, 253
  unfulfilled, *18*
  visualizing, *58–9*
  and what you really want,
    4–8
  weeding out half-hearted, *13*
goal-setting, *127–8, 134–51*
  effectiveness at, *121–2*
  means, motive and
    opportunity for, *136–7, 154*
  and outcomes, *10–13, 346,
    348*
  power of, *135*
  as skill, *34, 116*
  in 21 days, *148–50, 348*
  and time, *262–7*
  tips for, *146–8*
Goethe (quote), *1*
Goodyer, Martin, *217, 351*
gratitude, *319–20*
Grinder, John, *102*

habitual thinking
  challenging, *155–6*
  creating a blueprint of,
    209–10
  identifying, *191–2, 207–8*

Hansen, Mark Victor (case
  study), *167–8*
happiness, *316, 321*
  how we defer/reduce, *46*
  as a way of travelling, *14*
Harding, Steve (case study), *180*
Harris, Ian (case study), *179–80*
Harris, Sydney J. (quote), *254*
Heinlein, Robert (quote), *167*
Heligan, Lost Gardens of, *152–3*
Humberston, John, *170*
Hurles, Janette (case study),
  238
Hutchinson, Adrian, *334–5*

'I can't' as limiting belief, *154–5*
ideas/idea generation, *60–8*
  from association/
    combination, *76–7*
  framing your, *80–1*
  incentives for, *72–90*
  strategy for capturing, *86*
  turning into reality, *88*
identity
  and logical levels of
    thinking, *305, 307–9, 311*
  and time management, *261*
imagination, *67*
  in achieving your dreams,
    97–9
  and beliefs, *68–70*
  and capabilities, *31*
  and creative process, *81–2*
  leaps of, *67–8*
imagining
  your outcome, *142–3*
  your future, *100–2*
imaging and shared dreams,
  61–2
incentive awards, *74–5*
incremental skills, acquiring,
  227
information chunking, *130–2*

inner team, coaching your,
294–313
> **cheerleaders,** *301–3*
> **examining your beliefs,** *296*
> **flashpoints,** *311–12*
> **and logical levels of thinking,** *304–12*
> **and self-confidence,** *295–7*
> **sorting out members,** *297–8*
> **members' intentions,** *298–301*

internally (self) referenced thinking, *187, 191, 203*

interrupting people, *276–7, 281*

intuitive thinking, *185, 277*

job interviews, *39–40, 212–13*

Judge (TV series) questioning process, *329–33, 334*

Kekule, *68*

Keller, Helen (quote), *99*

Kemp, Cricket, *249–51*
> **case studies,** *103–4, 241–2*

kinaesthetic sensory style, *250, 274–5*
> **eye accessing cues,** *244*

knowledge
> **lack of,** *126*
> **and purpose,** *104–5*

language
> **artfully vague,** *155*
> **describes inner world,** *302–3*
> **metaphors in,** *63*
> **sensory,** *274–5*
> **shifts in people's descriptive,** *329*

Lao Tzu (quote), *275*

Leach, Reggie (quote), *3*

leadership, managing state of, *197*

Levoy, Greg, *157–8*

Lewin, Peter (quote), *257*

life
> **creating one you want,** *21–37*
> **metaphor for,** *64–6*

life changes, reasons for, *16*

limiting/negative beliefs, *4–5, 21–33, 348*
> **challenging,** *34, 116, 288, 349*
> **changing,** *25–33, 117*
> **confronting,** *157–8*
> **downward progression of,** *208*
> **'I can't' as,** *154–5*
> **and inner team,** *301–2*
> **recognizing,** *23–4*
> **reframing,** *211, 212*

listening skills, *273–84*
> **AEIOU framework,** *288–9, 345*
> **body language,** *274–5*
> **CRAFTY listening,** *281–4, 345*
> **interrupting,** *276–7, 281*
> **and Psychology of Mind,** *277–8*
> **quantum listening,** *280–1*
> **and types of listening,** *279–9*
> **voice tone,** *274–5*

lists ('to do'), *121, 225–6*

living in the present, *320*

Lloyd George, David, *352*

logical levels of thinking, *304–12*

logical procedural thinking, *82*

Lombardi, Vince (quote), *17*

lookback exercises, *148*

Lost Gardens of Heligan, *152–3*

McMillan, Alex, *173–6*

Magic Spelling *see* **spelling strategy**

Mallows, Michael, *280–1*

Marcus, Stanley (quote), *77*

Maslow's hierarchy of needs, *3*

matchers, *185, 186*
means, motive and opportunity (goal-setting), *136–7, 154*
measurable goals, *12, 128, 140*
meditation (pink bubble), *320–1*
mental maps of the world, *47*
mental pictures and modelling, *248–9*
mental rehearsal, *47–9*
mentoring, *316*
metaphors, *63*
    for life, *64–6*
    of success, *63–4*
    for work, *107–8, 109–11*
mismatchers, *184, 185, 186, 189*
mission statements, *315–16*
mistakes, learning from, *269*
modelling, *345*
    choosing a skill to model, *231–1, 234–7*
    decision-making skills, *328–35*
    eliciting a strategy, *237–8*
    eye accessing cues, *240–4*
    and mental pictures, *248–9*
    observable skills, *223–4*
    as skill, *30, 116*
    strategies, *334–5*
    and textbook learning, *224*
    useful skills, *229–30*
    what to look for, *239–40*
money, negotiating for, *338–40*
motivational skills wheel, *33–4, 35, 51, 116–17, 334, 348–9*
motivation scale, *3*
motive for goal-setting, *136*
moving away from/towards thinking styles, *187, 191, 200–1, 202–3, 209*

natural rhythm cycles, *269*
necessary conditions for success, *124–5*

necessity-driven thinking styles, *191, 203, 209*
needs, Maslow's hierarchy of, *3*
negative beliefs *see* limiting/ negative beliefs
negative thinking and success, *123*
negotiation strategies
    and behaviour patterns, *238–96*
    in business, *176–7*
    modelling, *339–40*
neuro-linguistic programming (NLP)
    logical levels of change model, *305–12*
    and modelling of excellence, *102, 176–7, 250*
    principles for success, *55–6*
Newton, Sir Isaac, *68*
NLP *see* neuro-linguistic programming (NLP)

observable skills, *223–4*
obstacles to achieving goals, *144, 147*
Olivier, Sir Laurence, *228*
Onassis, Aristotle, *97, 174*
opportunity for goal-setting, *136*
option thinkers, *186*
outcome orientation, *55, 56*
outcomes
    feeling good before achieving, *51–2*
    keeping in mind, *163*
    meeting outcome tips, *275*
    setting, *127–8, 142–6*
    and strategic planning, *126*
    well-formed, *10–11, 12–13, 346, 348, 349*
outcome thinking, *7–8, 178–9*
over-competitiveness, *287*

passions
  following your, *347*
  and purpose, *92, 96*
pattern recognition skills, *126-7*
Pavlov, I., *48, 303*
peak performance, *45, 49*
people
  being fully present with, *317*
  borrowing other's
    strategies, *323-4*
  'buddy' systems, *315*
  recognizing thinking
    styles, *102-4, 183-98*
  on the same journey, *318*
  staying connected with,
    314-15
perfectionists, *268, 270*
performance
  and Club Entrepreneur,
    173-6
  peak performance, *45, 49*
personal aptitudes and
  purpose, *96*
personal mastery, *49-51*
personal stocktaking, *145*
perspective, keeping things in,
  319
physicalities as limiting belief, *23*
  overcoming, *26-7*
pink bubble meditation, *320-1*
planning (strategic), *125-6*
POM *see* Psychology of Mind
positive beliefs
  and inner team, *301-2*
  and success strategies,
    220-1
  upward progression of, *211*
positive outcome thinking, *7-8*
positive questioning and
  success, *123*
positive states, anchoring, *59-60*
positive thinking (firewalking),
  172

possibility-driven thinking
  styles, *191, 203*
Powell, Colin (quote), *21*
power to change thinking, *51-2*
pragmatism, *347*
presentations *see* audiences
presuppositions and beliefs, *29*
prioritizing tasks, *121, 269*
proactive thinking, *187*
problem solving, *177, 178-9*
  'away' and 'towards', *206-7*
procedural thinkers, *186, 192*
process for 'self'/'others'
  thinkers, *186, 191-2, 203, 209*
process thinking, *279*
procrastination, *24, 29, 34, 116,
  267-8, 271*
Proust, Marcel (quote), *152*
Psychology of Mind (POM) method
  of listening, *277-8*
purpose, *91-114*
  asking questions with a,
    284-6
  'being on', *95-9*
  and beliefs, *104*
  feeling purposeful, *34, 116,
    348, 349*
  finding a, *112-13*
  and knowledge, *104-5*
  and mission statements,
    315-16
  and values, *104*

quantum listening, *280-1*
questioning skills, *284-92*
  AEIOU framework, *288-9*
  asking with a purpose, *284-6*
  challenging assumptions,
    287-8
  and decision-making, *332-4*
  self-questioning, *286*
  and T-GROW coaching, *290-2*
  see also Judge (TV series)

random thinking, *279*
rapport-building, *55, 56*
reactive thinking, *187*
realist role, *87*
realistic goals, *12, 128, 140, 211, 347*
reasoning skills, increasing, *324–6*
resources
    gathering, *350–1*
    lack of, *126*
    and outcomes, *13, 144*
respect (CRAFTY listening), *283*
responsibility for making things happen, *49–51*
rewards, *150*
Richer, Julian (case study), *74*
risk taking, *23, 34, 116*
    overcoming fear of, *28*
Rowling, J.K., *134*

sales people (Club Entrepreneur), *173–6*
scarcity mentalities, *47*
self-actualization, *3*
self-coaching questions, *8–10, 15*
self-confidence
    and inner team, *295, 299–301*
    signs of low, *296–7*
self-discovery question strategy, *15*
self-esteem and purpose, *92*
self-fulfilment, achieving, *5*
self-knowledge and purpose, *95*
self-limiting talk, *24*
self-questioning, *286*
self-sabotage, *287*
sense of humour, *319*
sensory acuity/awareness, *55, 56*
    for imagining your future, *100–2*
sensory language, *274–5*
sensory thinking styles, *192–3, 208*

sensory-specific goals, *12*
Shaw, George Bernard, *54, 95, 185*
Shaw, Gill, *210*
Sher, Barbara (quote), *38*
Siemens (staff motivation), *75*
skills
    communication, *34, 116, 145*
    easy-to-acquire, *225–8*
    finding things fast', *225*
    flexible thinking, *82, 128–9*
    increasing reasoning, *324–6*
    incremental, *227*
    lack of, *126*
    learning new, *115–17, 348*
    observable, *223–4*
    pattern recognition, *126–7*
    see also listening skills; modelling; motivational skills wheel; negotiation strategies; questioning skills
small chunk thinkers, *204, 209, 210*
SMART goals, *12, 128*
smell in imagining the future, *101*
Smit, Tim, *153*
    case study, *152*
solution generating technique, *80–1*
sound in imagining the future, *101*
specific goals, *12, 128, 140*
spelling strategy, *103–4, 241–2*
spider diagrams, *79–80*
standards, raising, *351*
staying calm strategy, *226*
strategic planning, *125–6*
strategic thinking, *7*
strategies
    borrowing other people's, *323–4*
    collecting, *325–6*
    modelling, *334–5, 339–40*
    for capturing ideas, *86*

strategies *(Contd)*
    for negotiation, *176–7, 338–40*
    people have modelled, *334–5*
    for spelling, *103–4, 241–2*
    for staying calm, *226*
    for tidiness, *225, 245, 247–8*
    understanding other people's, *103–4*
    Walt Disney's creative, *86–8*
    see also success strategies
stress
    and habitual thinking, *208*
    in the workplace, *105*
success
    action plan for, *351–2*
    choosing patterns for, *161–2*
    creating circumstances for, *167–82*
    creating blueprint for, *36*
    criteria for, *122–5*
    metaphors for, *63–4*
    modelling to master change, *323–41*
    rating commitment to, *342–3*
    six habits that lead to, *55–6*
    strengthening mental patterns of, *47–8*
    tools for future, *343–5*
success strategies, *217–33*
    blueprinting technique, *221–2*
    noticing, *217–19*
    and positive beliefs, *220–1*
    scores as high achiever, *219–20*
    staying calm, *226*
    tidiness, *225, 245, 247–8*
    see also modelling
Sullivan, Wendy, *106, 107, 109, 254–5, 270–1*
switching states, *161*

talents, developing, *118*
taste in imagining the future, *101*
team building (firewalking), *169–71*
Temple, Shirley, *24*
T-GROW coaching, *290–2*
thinking
    'all or nothing', *150, 162–3*
    chunking, *129–32*
    flexible, *82, 128–9, 164, 185, 189–90*
    habitual, *155–6, 191–2, 207–10*
    and listening, *279*
    logical levels of, *304–12*
    and low self-confidence, *296*
    outcome thinking, *7–8, 178–9*
    pitfalls to avoid, *162–3*
    taking control own, *207–8*
thinking styles, *102–4, 183–98*
    auditory (words), *184, 193, 250, 274*
    big chunk/picture thinkers, *184, 186, 192, 204, 209, 210*
    checklist of, *202–4*
    communicating in other's, *195–6*
    and decision-making, *205–6*
    detail-conscious thinkers, *186, 204*
    externally (others) referenced, *187*
    filters for sameness/ difference, *186, 192, 203*
    as information-filter systems, *188, 189*
    internally (self) referenced, *187, 191, 203*
    matchers, *185, 186*
    mismatchers, *184, 185, 186, 189*
    modelling style of decision-maker, *328*

moving away from/towards, *187, 191, 200-1, 202-3, 209*
necessity-driven, *191, 203, 209*
option thinkers, *186*
proactive, *187*
possibility-driven, *191, 203*
and problem solving, *206-7*
procedural thinkers, *186, 192*
process for 'self'/'others' thinkers, *186, 191-2, 203, 209*
reactive, *187*
recognizing people's, *102-4*
tips, *200*
unconscious, *190-2*
visual (pictures), *185, 193, 250, 274*
Thomson, Peter, *121, 138*
case study, *119-20*
thoughtfulness (CRAFTY listening), *284*
tidiness strategies, *225, 245, 247-8*
Tieme Ra napiri (quote), *342*
time
questioning assumptions, *262*
relating to, *255-8*
sensing movement of, *269-70*
time management, *253-71*
behind-timers, *257*
beliefs, values and identity, *261*
breaking workloads into small chunks, *268-9*
and goal-setting, *262-7*
living in the future, *257*
and perfectionists, *268, 270*
prioritizing tasks, *121, 269*
as skill, *34, 116, 348*
and space management, *258-60*
through-timers, *258, 260*
in-timers, *258, 260*
see also procrastination

timeframe for achieving goals, *12, 128, 140, 144, 253*
time-specific goals, *147*
'to do' lists, *121, 225-6*
tools for future success, *343-4*
Tracey, Brian (quote), *234*
Treasure, Mike, *262-3*
Treselyan, Simon, *169-73, 323*

Unconditional Success (Williams), *108*
unconscious thinking styles, *190-2*
unhelpful pictures, *214-15*
United Kingdom Association of Suggestion Schemes, *73*
unplanned decision-making, *6*

vague language, *155*
values
aligning with beliefs, *345-6*
identifying important, *42-5*
and logical levels of thinking, *305, 307-9, 311*
and personal stocktaking, *145*
and purpose, *104*
and time management, *261*
and workplace motivation, *41-5, 106-12*
viewpoints, changing, *163*
vision
holding steadfastly, *345*
in imagining the future, *100*
visual construct (Vc), *243, 244*
visual (pictures) sensory style, *185, 193, 250, 274*
visual recall (Vr), *243*
visualization, *58-9*
as skill, *34, 116, 348*
voice tone and listening, *274-5*

wealth as a purpose, *97*
Webb, Mary (quote), *134*
well-formed outcomes, *10–11, 12–13, 348*
Williams, Nick, *108*
Witmore, Sir John, *290*
Wolff, Jurgen (case study), *77*
women and firewalking, *171*
Wood, Andrew, *72, 75, 85*
Words that Change Minds (Charvet), *199*
work
    metaphors for, *107–8, 109–11*
    modelling success at, *221–2*

workplace motivation, *38–53*
    job interviews, *39–40*
    matching own motivation, *39–40*
    and mental rehearsal, *47–9*
    and peak performance, *45, 49*
    and stress, *105*
    and thinking styles, *183–98*
    and values, *41–5, 106–12*
Wriston, Walter, *269*
writing, early morning, *317*

'yes!' (CRAFTY listening), *284*